The European Union and the Asia-Pacific

Within the European Union (EU), the question of 'identity' has emerged as a core issue for debate. The external manifestation of this – the EU's international identity – has only recently been recognized as of equal importance, in terms of its construction and representation globally.

To address this issue, this book identifies measures and compares public awareness and perceptions of the EU within the Asia-Pacific region. It deals with the under-researched issue of the public perception of the EU outside the Union and the role of the media in shaping such perceptions. It builds on what has been described as the EU's 'communication deficit', a phenomenon which has typically been explored as an internal EU dynamic but has yet to be applied to the EU's external relations.

The volume presents findings from a systematic research project designed to measure the EU's external 'communication deficit' and to raise the level of its awareness in other regions through three perception levels:

- the study of EU images in news media production
- a survey of general public perceptions and attitudes on the EU
- a survey of the elite perceptions of the EU

Drawing on research from New Zealand, Australia, South Korea and Thailand, this book will be of interest to students and researchers of politics, communication studies, European studies and Asian studies.

Natalia Chaban is a Senior Lecturer in European Studies at the National Centre for Research on Europe (NCRE) at the University of Canterbury, New Zealand.

Martin Holland is Director of the National Centre for Research on Europe (NCRE) and Jean Monnet Chair *ad personam* at the University of Canterbury, New Zealand.

The primary objective of the new Contemporary European Studies series is to provide a research outlet for scholars of European Studies from all disciplines. The series publishes important scholarly works and aims to forge for itself an international reputation.

The European Union and the Asia-Pacific

Media, public and elite perceptions of the EU

**Edited by Natalia Chaban
and Martin Holland**

LONDON AND NEW YORK

First published 2008
by Routledge
2 Park Square, Milton Park, Abingdon, Oxon OX14 4RN

Simultaneously published in the USA and Canada
by Routledge
270 Madison Ave, New York, NY 10016

Routledge is an imprint of the Taylor & Francis Group, an informa business

First issued in paperback 2011

Typeset in Times New Roman by
HWA Text and Data Management, Tunbridge Wells

British Library Cataloguing in Publication Data
A catalogue record for this book is available from the British Library

Library of Congress Cataloging-in-Publication Data
The European Union and the Asia-Pacific : media, public, and elite
perceptions of the EU / edited by Natalia Chaban and Martin Holland.
    p. cm. – (UACES contemporary European studies series)
    Includes bibliographical references and index.
    1. European Union – Public opinion. 2. European Union – Press
coverage – Asia. 3. European Union – Press coverage – Pacific Area.
4. Public opinion – Asia. 5. Public opinion – Pacific Area. 6. Elite
(Social sciences) – Asia – Attitudes. 7. Elite (Social sciences) – Pacific
Area – Attitudes.1 I. Chaban, Natalia, 1971– II. Holland, Martin, 1954–
JN30.E94128 2008
341.242′2–dc22   2007046126

ISBN10: 0–415–42138–1 (hbk)
ISBN10: 0–415–66397–0 (pbk)
ISBN10: 0–203–92745–1 (ebk)

ISBN13: 978–0–415–42138–6 (hbk)
ISBN13: 978–0–415–66397–7 (pbk)
ISBN13: 978–0–203–92745–8 (ebk)

Contents

Figures

Tables

Contributors

Jessica Bain is a recent PhD graduate of the National Centre for Research on Europe (NCRE) at the University of Canterbury, New Zealand.

Michael Bruter is a Senior Lecturer in European Politics in the Department of Government at the London School of Economics, UK.

Natalia Chaban is a Senior Lecturer in European Studies at the National Centre for Research on Europe (NCRE) at the University of Canterbury, New Zealand. She was coordinator of the Asia-Pacific Perceptions Project.

Kenneth Ka-Lok Chan is Associate Professor at the Department of Government and International Studies of Hong Kong Baptist University and Visiting Professor at the Institute of European Studies of Macau.

Yoon Ah Choi is a PhD candidate at the National Centre for Research on Europe (NCRE) at the University of Canterbury, New Zealand.

Martin Holland is Director of the National Centre for Research on Europe at the University of Canterbury, New Zealand. He was supervisor of the Asia-Pacific Perceptions Project.

Bradford S. Jones is Associate Professor of Political Science in the Department of Political Science, University of California, Davis, USA.

Heungchong Kim is Head of European Studies at the Korea Institute for International Economic Policy in South Korea.

Philomena Murray is Director of the Contemporary Europe Research Centre (CERC) at the University of Melbourne, Australia.

Sung-Hoon Park is Professor of Economics and European Studies at the Graduate School of International Studies, Korea Univesrity, South Korea.

Katrina Stats is a PhD candidate in the School of History and Politics, University of Adelaide, Australia.

Paveena Sutthisripok is a Policy Analyst at the Royal Thai Embassy/Mission of Thailand to the European Communities in Brussels, Belgium.

Acknowledgements

This publication is the result of a collaborative two-year research project involving experienced academics and young researchers drawn primarily from countries in the Asia-Pacific region – Australia, New Zealand, Hong Kong SAR, South Korea and Thailand – as well as from Europe and the USA. This geographical diversity was complemented by the multidisciplinarity of the team, involving expertise in cognitive linguistics, media studies, communications, European integration and political science. Assembling such a team, as well as securing funding of the research, was also an example of international cooperation without which this project would not have been possible.

The research team would like to acknowledge the generous support given by the European Commission's Directorate-General for Education and Culture who provided financial resources amounting to €142,000 under the auspices of the Jean Monnet Programme for the 24-month period commencing in January 2004 (Grant Agreement No. 2003-2292/001-001). This grant facilitated the successful execution of an innovative transnational comparative research project: 'Public, Elite and Media Perceptions of the EU in Asia-Pacific Region', managed by the National Centre for Research on Europe (NCRE), University of Canterbury, New Zealand. Yet, without the firm support of Professor Apirat Petchsiri (the Multidisciplinary Department of European Studies, Chulalongkorn University, Bangkok, Thailand), Associate Professor Philomena Murray (Contemporary Europe Research Centre University of Melbourne, Melbourne, Australia) and Professor Sung-Hoon Park (Graduate School of International Studies, Korea University, Seoul, South Korea), this project would never have been realized – the various EU studies research centres and associations under their supervision committed resources and human capital to the project, and without such dedication the project and this volume would have been impossible. The project was initiated through the four EU Studies Associations in the region (EU Studies Association–New Zealand, EU Studies Association–Thailand, the Contemporary European Studies Association of Australia and the EU Studies Association–Korea), all of which are members of the world European Community Studies Association body.

A specific focus of the Grant Agreement was to promote the training and expertise of young researchers in the region. Our greatest appreciation goes to a group of young talented scholars who worked under the supervision and mentoring of their more experienced colleagues and who collected the media and elite empirical data for this project, conducted detailed content analysis and elaborated comparative cases. This new vibrant research network included Katrina Stats and Fiona Machin from Australia, Jessica Bain and Yoon Ah Choi from New Zealand, Paveena Sutthisripok from Thailand and Kim Se Na from South Korea. Our special thanks go to Jessica Bain, a recent PhD graduate from the NCRE, University of Canterbury, New Zealand, who assumed responsibility for the editorial technicalities (while simultaneously trying to complete her PhD!).

We would like to express our sincere gratitude to our excellent multilingual, multinational and multitalented research team – one of the greatest achievements of the project was establishing a wider research network beyond the Asia-Pacific region, involving scholars from other countries and continents. We are grateful for the intellectual richness and varied perspectives introduced into the project and this book by Dr Michael Bruter, London School of Economics and Political Science, London, UK; Associate Professor Kenneth Chan, Department of Government and International Studies, Hong Kong Baptist University, Hong Kong; Professor Ole Elgström, Political Science, Lund University, Sweden; Associate Professor Dr Bradford Jones, Political Science Department, University of California, Davis, USA and Dr Heungchong Kim, Korea University, Seoul, South Korea.

The editors would like to acknowledge the remarkable intellectual environment of the National Centre for Research on Europe which has supported and promoted a philosophy of research excellence that has allowed the NCRE to flourish and establish a respected international reputation. Academic collegiality, the interaction of staff and graduate students and a vibrant research culture have been essential aspects behind the success of this project. That three further 'EU external perceptions' projects have subsequently been launched expanding the geographical spread of the analysis is testimony to the vitality as well as the relevance of the world's most distantly located southern hemisphere 'EU research centre'.

Finally, our joint thanks go to our respective spouses, Ann Marie and Paul, for their support and understanding when editorial deadlines interrupted normal family life.

Professor Martin Holland and Dr Natalia Chaban
National Centre for Research on Europe
Unversity of Canterbury, New Zealand

Introduction

Research rationale, theoretical underpinnings and methodological considerations

Natalia Chaban and Martin Holland

The question of the EU's external identity

In 2007, the European Union (EU), an unprecedented project of international peaceful integration, celebrated its 50th anniversary. The unstable yet distinctive manner of the EU's development, where it moves 'from crisis to crisis',[1] has brought critical attention and raised fundamental questions about the Union during most of those years, both from within and outside the polity. With 50 years under its belt, has this perpetual 'objet politique non-identifié'[2] discovered what makes it so unique for Europe and for the rest of the world? Does the EU have its own geo-political and socio-economic identity? Is a more coherent identity crucial to advance European integration? Does the process of European integration affect how the EU is seen among major global players? Is the Union satisfied with this vision, compared to its self-perceptions? Where has all the talk about identity come from? Why now?

Since its inception in 1957, this community of European states and nations has delivered to the world half a century of stability, peace and prosperity on a continent previously torn by wars and conflicts. It has helped to raise the living standards of ordinary Europeans, built a single Europe-wide market and strengthened Europe's voice in the world. The success of the Union's economic stability and growth attracted new members and, in the 1980s and 1990s, the European Community outgrew its initial economic focus and began new initiatives. Among these were internal political collaboration, which made possible such projects as the single currency, ongoing enlargement and a borderless Europe. In terms of its more externally focused actions, the then Community took steps towards a common foreign and security policy and its own military corps. Continuous change indeed seems to be one of the trademark accessories of the EU's image. Predictably, then, identifying what the Union is and stands for has been challenging both for its own citizens and the international public.

The difficulties of self-identification and in the presentation of a coherent image to the outside world also stem from the indefinite nature of the EU integration model, one which oscillates between a centralized federal supra-state to a kind of loose intergovernmental coalition. Yet, despite the challenges posed by its ongoing transformation and ever-present ambiguity, the EU has never been without international attention. The pros and cons of its peaceful process of regional integration are increasingly considered not only by such well-established organizations as Mercoursor, the African Union, ASEAN and the Pacific Islands Forum, but also by nascent regional groupings inspired by the EU's integrationist example such as the South Asian Association for Regional Cooperation,[3] or even by Australia and New Zealand who are revisiting the Australia–New Zealand Closer Economic Relations Agreement with the possibility of a common currency.

The most recent outside interest in Europe's integration model was provoked by a series of crises inside the Union. Among these were the record low turn-out for the June 2004 elections to the European Parliament; the emergence of anti-EU parties; a lack of popular support for an EU Constitution in France and the Netherlands (two founding Member States); the cautious reaction by the general public to further EU enlargement to the east; and an ongoing debate between and within European publics and elites about the membership prospects of Turkey. The relevant literature partially attributes these crises to three shortcomings in the EU's effective democratic functioning – namely, deficits in democracy, legitimacy and communication. Still intensely debated in the scholarly community,[4] this triad of interconnected deficits has increasingly been acknowledged by EU policy-makers as the primary impediment to the EU's integration process.[5]

The democratic deficit is evidenced by the indifference and disengagement of ordinary EU citizens in and with the EU.[6] The EU's institutional architecture with its unelected Commission, limited European parliamentary power in policy-making and the dominance of national issues on the European agenda does not seem to provide individual citizens with a voice on EU issues.[7] Moreover, the EU institutions are considered to be failing to create the necessary conditions for democratic engagement and public support within the Union. In addition, and connected to many of these democratic failings, the EU is argued to exhibit the features of a communication deficit.[8] This particular deficiency is conceptualized as a failure by the various EU institutions to effectively use the media to facilitate the links connecting EU decision-making mechanisms to the needs, thoughts and hearts of ordinary Europeans.[9] This leads to a failure to communicate the positive aspects of the EU to its citizens, and to the public's apparent disillusion with the European integration project.

The communication deficit is also understood as a deficit of attention paid to the EU by national, regional and local media in Europe. Its low media visibility, but also the noticeable negativity, indifference and scepticism in many media portrayals of the EU are considered to be highly detrimental to the Union's image.[10] It has been suggested that the EU's democratic deficit, aggravated and perpetuated by the communication deficit, ultimately contributes to the Union's lack of legitimation by its citizens, the phenomenon known as the EU's legitimacy deficit.[11] This triple set of deficits in the democratic functioning of the EU has recently become a matter of serious concern and subsequent action on the part of the European Commission.[12] The Commission Vice President Margot Wallström claimed that 'the real problem in Europe is that there is no agreement or understanding about what Europe is for and where it is going'.[13] Predictably, a principled emphasis on communicating the EU to its own citizens has resulted in the recognition of a need for a new, shared perception of what Europe is about.[14]

This search for the so-called 'European identity' in the EU context is not entirely new. Francis Bacon referred to 'we Europeans' as early as 1623.[15] A modern notion of 'European identity', according to Stråth, entered official EU rhetoric much later at the Copenhagen summit of 1973,[16] and since then the notion has been heavily ideologized and its more exact content and meaning intensely debated.[17] The 'politics of identity' were claimed by Manners and Whitman to be the 'central problem for the EU to resolve'.[18] Without this contemporary common narrative on the idea of Europe, the EU risks encountering a dearth of trust and understanding among EU citizens.

One of the ways to identify the EU's otherwise problematic Self is to construct it in relation to the external presence of the Other. Demarcation from others (or an awareness of the differences between the Self and Other) is a necessary component of identity building.[19] As one identity scholar put it, quite simply, 'Europe does not exist without non-Europe and can only be realized in the mirror of Others.'[20] Or as Manners and Whitman comment, the process of constructing a 'reflective identity' for the EU is twofold. First, it involves the search for an 'external definition of identity',[21] and second, it highlights 'expectation[s] of … external actors or others'.[22]

The first channel of 'Othering', that is, the search for an external definition of the European identity, suggests an initial exploration of how the 'idea of Europe' (and of the EU in this context) is constructed and represented globally. What are the factors which socially construct the EU's identity outside the Union's borders? How is the EU understood around the world? What are the EU's strategies to profile itself to the international community? Both the construction and representation of the EU's identity externally suggest an insight into the complex cognitive constructs of international information processing and international political knowledge on the EU. In this context, the three key elements of the EU's reflective identification are: a highly systematic and rigorous account of the content of the EU images existing in various discourses outside the Union's borders; an account of the strategies and policies used by the EU to represent itself to these external parties; and, finally, the identification of the dominant cognitive patterns and accompanying attitudes towards the EU in the minds of international public. According to Samur:

> This constructivist approach to international relations is especially appropriate in the case of the EU, because the EU aspires to be more than an international society: a supranational one. This means that the EU needs to create its own norms, values and practices to a greater extent than any international society.[23]

The second channel of 'Othering' is identifying the expectations of the external Others. The EU's external functions in this aspect are often characterized, using Hill's argument, as displaying a particular limitation, described as a 'capability-expectations gap'; in its foreign policy.[24] According to Hill, a gap exists between the excessive expectations on the EU from both inside and outside its borders, and an insufficient capability by the EU to match these expectations. However, some EU scholars have noted a 'reverse' gap which appears when the expectations for the EU in the international arena remain low despite its growing weight and influence as an international actor.[25] This gap was named an 'expectations deficit',[26] and several factors have been canvassed as the source of the deficiency. Among them are mutual indifference, lack of understanding of complex EU policy-making, the absence of a single EU 'voice', preferences for bilateral relations with major EU countries, the failure of the Common Foreign and Security Policy (CFSP), as well as different values and interests.

Arguably, introducing the communication deficit argument into the study of a capability–expectations gap could provide additional support to the notion of an expectations deficit. Indeed, the previously discussed concern with the EU's internal shortcomings in democracy, legitimacy and communication has yet to be explored in the EU's external relations. Currently, EU institutions give somewhat limited attention to the role of external political communication in legitimating EU governance. An underdeveloped EU public diplomacy worldwide,[27] the absence of a focused strategy to account for the existing EU imagery in various international discourses, dissonant actions by EU institutions to raise the international profile and awareness of the new Europe, as well as weak links between the EU institutions and the international systems of political communication, ultimately result in an invisible profile of the EU as a global actor.

An imbalance between the growing capability of the EU as an international actor and low expectations from the EU's global partners is potentially detrimental and could resonate in a further 'cognitive gap'[28] between the EU's intentions to be recognized as an international political authority and the actual simplified international public perceptions of the EU (e.g. only as an economic power). Since one of the components for evaluating EU actor capacity in international affairs is outsiders' recognition and the acceptance of EU competence,[29] such an imbalance could result in the EU's self-reflection as an 'invisible giant' in the international arena – a vision that could potentially imperil any incentive to develop a proactive EU foreign policy. Similarly, this lack of external recognition might also negatively influence internal integration. The perception of Europe 'failing' in foreign affairs – be it in Iraq or in responding to the Asian tsunami – threatens to undermine the very legitimacy of the integration process for EU citizens.[30] In light of these potential risks then, a thorough and sober account of the existing external imagery of the EU becomes an urgent necessity.

Objectives and context of the research project

To address the external dimension of the EU's communication deficit, the transnational research project, 'Public, Elite and Media Perceptions of the EU in the Asia-Pacific Region', was launched at the National Centre for Research on Europe, University of Canterbury, New Zealand.[31] From 2002 onwards, the Centre initiated a series of research projects which aimed to identify, measure and compare public awareness and perceptions of the EU within the Asia-

Pacific region. Four studies have been executed. First, a pilot study in one Asia-Pacific country, New Zealand; which was followed by a pioneering comparative study involving two Asian and two Pacific countries (South Korea and Thailand, and Australia and New Zealand); the third study involved nine Asian locations (Japan, Mainland China, SAR Hong Kong, South Korea, Thailand, Vietnam, Indonesia, the Philippines and Singapore); and, most recently, a comparative study of three global regions (the Pacific, South-East Asia and Southern Africa) has commenced.[32] The leading research questions guiding all of these projects have been, 'What are the dominant images and the leading perceptions of the EU in the external public discourses internationally?' and 'What is the impact of these images and perceptions on the policy-making?'

This volume will focus on reporting and analysing the findings of the second research project – the transnational investigation, 'Public, Elite and Media Perceptions of the EU in Asia-Pacific Region: Australia, New Zealand, South Korea and Thailand: A Comparative Study'. The selection of those four countries for the project was conditioned by the ability of the participating research institutions to meet the co-sponsoring responsibilities required under the two-year research grant administered by the European Commission.[33] A multidisciplinary research design integrated approaches drawn from political science, EU studies, media studies, discourse analysis, cognitive linguistics and image studies. To secure comparability, rigid control over the systematic data collection and processing was ensured – researchers from each country participated in extensive training to enable consistency in the data gathering and analysing techniques.

While all are powerful voices in Asia-Pacific politics, the four countries in the study are different in terms of their politico-economic status and cultural backgrounds. Among the four there is a federal-state system in Australia, a unitary presidential republic in South Korea, a constitutional monarchy in Thailand[34] and a parliamentary democracy in New Zealand. Although all four countries operate market economies with democratic media practices, three of them (Australia, New Zealand and South Korea) are members of the Organisation for Economic Cooperation and Development (OECD), while Thailand is a developing economy. In a cursory summary, the two 'Pacific' countries in the sample, New Zealand and Australia, have had significant cultural connections to Europe – both are former colonial outposts of the British Empire with significant European immigration. In the 'Asian' case, there were also extensive European cultural influences in the process of the modernization in Thailand and in South Korea during the nineteenth and early twentieth centuries, yet neither was ever colonized by European powers. Despite their obvious differences, the four countries have one particular feature in common; namely, the EU is a significant, if not vital, economic partner for each of them. The EU is Australia's largest trading partner, and for New Zealand its significance in terms of trade is second only to New Zealand's closest neighbour, Australia. The Union is South Korea's third largest trading partner, and it accounts for more than 15 per cent of Thai international trade. Additionally, the EU is a leading investor and a major source of tourists for all four Asia-Pacific countries.

Yet the EU is not only a key economic counterpart, but is also growing in importance as a political partner for the four states. The EU's contribution to stability in South East Asia is best exemplified through its involvement in the Asia Europe Meetings (ASEM) framework since 1997 and by a dialogue with the Association of South East Asian Nations (ASEAN) that was first established in 1967. The EU's aid relief and reconstruction after the Asian tsunami in 2004, its negotiating efforts on the Korean peninsula and its peacekeeping mission in the Indonesian province of Aceh have further raised its political profile in the region. In the Pacific, the EU is the second largest donor of development aid – behind only Australia – and is an important partner to the Pacific Forum process which aims to create a lasting stability in the region. The negotiations toward an Economic Partnership Agreement between the EU and the Pacific ACP (African Caribbean Pacific) states are further testament to the EU's regional involvement and imprint. Lastly, for both Asian and Pacific regions, the EU, as a *sui generis* organization, also provides a powerful reference point for the ongoing debate on regional integration processes.

Confined by the selection of countries, the project attempted to both identify and compare the EU's perceptions across four different social systems in the Asia-Pacific region. Another line of comparison was drawn between the two geo-political centres of Asia and the Pacific. The comparative approach is claimed by Lazarsfeld to 'open up new and rather exciting subjects for investigation',[35] and following suggestions by de Vreese,[36] the parameters of comparison were clearly outlined. For example, the 'Pacific' pair (New Zealand and Australia), and the 'Asian' pair (Thailand and South Korea) were assumed to be relatively similar in geo-political and cultural terms within their pairings. Thus, comparing Australian *vs* New Zealand and Thai *vs* South Korean perceptions was viewed as comparison between *similar* entities. The comparison between 'Pacific' and 'Asian' perceptions, on the other hand, were considered to be comparisons between *dissimilar* entities. Both comparative parameters are relevant and may produce insightful and vivid findings, and thus both are pursued in this volume.

Theoretical background

The leading hypothesis underlining the external perceptions project and all contributions to this book is that the EU's deficiencies in external communication add to the gap between the EU's growing international capabilities on the one hand and low expectations of the EU by its global partners on the other. The investigation's major concern with political communication brings into focus relationships between mass media, the public and policy-makers, following Soroka's recommendation of 'delving into the media's role in the formation of public opinion and public role, and the degree to which public policy follows or leads public opinion'.[37]

The study follows an assumption that:

> [The] international reality is not merely the product of physical forces and material power, whether military and economic, but is a phenomenon socially constructed through discursive power (the power of knowledge, ideas, culture, ideology, and language).[38]

Recognizing a multiplicity of discourses available for assessing the images projected of and by the EU, this volume presents a systematic analysis of the EU images existing in the public discourses of four countries in the Asia-Pacific. More specifically, it focuses on the EU's representations in the media discourses, the perceptions of the EU among the general public, and the EU's images held by influential national elites. Correspondingly, this volume features a tripartite structure. The first two chapters identify and compare EU images existing in the news media across the four Asia-Pacific countries and query the local media strategies underlying these EU media representations. The second part of the volume presents three chapters which explore public opinion on the EU in the region, while the final part introduces two chapters presenting analyses of the opinions and attitudes held by the respective national policy- and decision-makers. To ensure the validity and reliability of an internationally comparative communication research project, the research design of the study and of this book followed by Chan and colleagues' prioritized theory, ensured meticulous and consistent sampling procedures, clearly identified lines of comparison and recognized the dual nature of international communication (a process and a product).[39]

One theoretical approach underlying the chapters in this volume (as well as the study more broadly) is grounded in the 'common knowledge' paradigm of political communication studies elaborated by Neuman *et al.*[40] This theoretical paradigm focuses on how political information is organized and structured in the public discourses of different media, and how that information *compares* with public and elite perceptions. This paradigm advocates investigating a 'three-way interaction of individual, medium, and issue',[41] emphasizing a 'more balanced inquiry into the interaction of media, media message, and public understanding',[42] and calling for 'the systematic integration of multiple methodologies'[43] (in our case, content analysis of media texts, public surveys and semi-structured in-depth elite interviews). To account for the methodological challenges in bringing together the media, public and elite agendas noted by Martin and Shaw,[44] this study followed the suggestion of Semetko and Mandelli and integrated two approaches used widely in communication studies,[45] namely, *cognitive* and *agenda-setting* approaches. The two paradigms provided a set of interconnected foundational concepts which were employed in the research project.

The approach of *agenda-setting*[46] provided a set of contingent conditions required in order to produce an effect. Among those conditions summarized by Hügel *et al.*[47] and incorporated into this study are the audiences' need for orientation on political issues, which they seek to meet through their use of the media; interpersonal communication and the personal experience of audience members as an alternative to media use; audience members' issue sensitivity expressed in seeking out and attending to information which is considered to be relevant; and, finally, issue quality (visible *vs* unobtrusive issues). An agenda-setting framework for this research provides, in the worlds of Soroka, a chance to 'accommodat[e] both media-public dynamics and the relationships between these actors and the policy process'.[48]

The leading assumption of the *cognitive* approach is that information and its patterning, processing and communication are central to culture, cognition and social behaviour.[49] More specifically, this analysis employed the key cognitive notion of schema, defined by Graber as simplifying maps of how political facts and figures can be organized into a meaningful whole.[50] The incorporation of a cognitive approach in analysing media discourses in particular was advocated by Fairclough and Wodak.[51]

The integration of agenda-setting and cognitive approaches in this study brought forward the key notions of *priming, framing* and *stereotyping.* Priming is identified here as the 'activation of concepts in human memory due to the media exposure resulting in the heightened accessibility to the concept'.[52] The key research questions of this study which used this notion were as follows:

- Is the concept of the EU primed in public opinion in the Asia-Pacific?
- What conditions can potentially prime the concept of the EU for the Asia-Pacific public?

Framing is defined in this study following Entman's ideas as the 'selection of some aspects of perceived reality to make them more salient in a communication text, in such a way as to promote a particular problem definition, caused interpretation, moral evaluation and/or treatment recommendations'.[53] Similar to Scheufele's work, this study recognizes two types of frames;[54] namely, media frames (or, as van Dijk put it, the emphasized aspects of a represented reality)[55] and audience frames (the emphasized aspects of perceived reality).[56] Respectively, the research questions that utilized these notions asked:

- What are the leading media frames of the EU produced by the regional news media?
- What are the dominant audience frames of the EU existing in the public and elite opinions?
- How do the leading media frames compare to the dominant audience frames?

Stereotyping was understood in this approach as a cognitive necessity arising in response to humans' limited capacities for information processing – a simplified categorization of the world that exists in the long-term memory and is resistant to sudden environmental pressures.[57] Stereotypes are often viewed as a concept held by one social group about another and which are used frequently to validate certain biased and prejudiced behaviours. The project's research questions reflecting this notion inquired:

- What images of the EU have become stereotypical in the minds of the Asia-Pacific public?
- What are the mechanisms involved in the construction of these stereotypes?
- What are the pragmatic consequences of these stereotypes to the relations between the EU and the Asia-Pacific region?

In its quest for answers, this study's multidisciplinary analysis was led by another assumption, namely, that a disjuncture exists between the required level of international knowledge necessary to function in an ever-globalizing world and the low level of public knowledge about foreign countries, peoples and events. With its focus on distant places and happenings, international information may seem to be largely irrelevant to the domestic public. These foreign information flows frequently introduce unknown and often complex concepts, a complete understanding of which requires a multifaceted cognitive background and regular follow-up information. In the case of the EU, a geographically remote counterpart for the Asia-Pacific, understanding its decision-making from outside its immediate borders is particularly challenging: according to Ginsberg, it requires an understanding of the interplay between national actors (as influenced by subnational, regional and international stimuli) and European actors, and 'Europeanized' institutional norms and practices.[58]

EU representations in media discourses

Relevant research has shown that the relationship between the media, public and policy-makers can vary in direction, each one sometimes leading or following.[59] This study argues that the news media possesses a heavier influence on the formation of public perceptions on the EU in the Asia-Pacific since most people in that region have limited first-hand access to international affairs. Media representations of foreign events are therefore argued to contribute significantly to informing and educating the citizenship on foreign policy issues,[60] and the EU in particular. In addition to its information transfer function, the media also form particular evaluations, enabling the audience members to judge other nations. A special role in this process belongs to the *news* media. International news is claimed to impact foreign policy through the so-called 'CNN-effect',[61] which suggests that policy-makers react in response to the reality created by the news media, rather than to reality itself.

Insights into the particulars of the EU's media framing have emerged from numerous studies of the EU imagery in European media discourses.[62] In contrast, there is a lack of research assessing EU imagery in media discourses *external* to the EU – at best such research has been infrequent, invisible and unsystematic. In the Asia-Pacific, few relevant studies existed or were suitable as a point of reference, and of those available, the focus was on elite perceptions only and excluded media influence and public opinion.[63] To address this scholarly deficit, this volume opens with 'Images and Portrayals of the EU in the Asia-Pacific Media' featuring two chapters which are co-authored by the members of the research team – Natalia Chaban, Jessica Bain, Katrina Stats, Paveena Sutthisripok and Yoon Ah Choi. These chapters – 'Mirror Reflections? The EU in Print and Broadcast Media in the Asia-Pacific' and 'The EU in Metaphors: Images of the EU Enlargement in the Asia-Pacific News' – demonstrate the various media framing strategies particular to the individual countries and media in the study.

To avoid a 'blame-the-media' attitude, the volume and content of EU news flows are assessed in this book from a twofold perspective; namely, both as a *process* and as a *product*. Seen as a *product*, international news (and EU news in particular) is shaped by the forces of supply and demand and is treated as a commodity[64] that is increasingly difficult to sell unless it involves warfare and conflict, natural catastrophe or financial crisis.[65] Its production faces constraints and pressures such as high costs, a reduced involvement of domestic reporters and a higher reliance on a very limited group of major international news agencies. These limitations exist against a background of decreasing attention on behalf of the news consumers toward 'hard' news in general, and towards foreign news in particular.[66] This is of paramount importance to the study of the EU's presence in international news as EU coverage often falls victim to the very integrationist and peacemaking nature of the project.

In light of these constraints, the two media chapters presented in this book adopt a content analysis approach that targeted the daily routine coverage of the EU in the four Asia-Pacific countries in 2004 – in total, 3,811 newspaper items from 20 leading regional newspapers and 186 items from eight national primetime television newscasts. The particular year of analysis was a special year for the EU as it featured a number of significant milestones in the process of integration – the largest and most controversial EU enlargement from 15 to 25 members; European Parliament elections; the appointment of a new European Commission; the conclusion of the Constitutional Convention; and, the decision to agree to accession negotiations with Turkey. 2004 was also marked by some extraordinary events in the life of the EU: the tragic event of the Madrid bombings; the unusual event of the Ukrainian 'Orange Revolution' in which the EU played a mediating role; and the controversial event of the failed referendum in Cyprus on the eve of enlargement. It was assumed that these highly newsworthy events of global significance would raise the EU's media visibility in the Asia-Pacific.

The two chapters dealing with EU media representations are presented through two cases illustrating how the 'commodification' of the news in an environment of media 'hyper-competition'[67] influences the production of EU meanings in media discourses external to, and independent of, the Union. Chapter 1 explores the similarities and differences in the print and broadcast media frames of the EU across and within four countries. Chapter 1 also addresses EU news as a *process*, accounting for a complex web of domestic 'newsroom' practices by discussing the opinions and practices held by the regional newsmakers. Such themes as the organization of EU coverage, the predominant editorial approaches towards reporting the EU, strategies to make EU news more 'attractive' to the largest number of news consumers, as well as the leading EU news selection criteria, were all considered. The newsmakers' perceptions of their audience's preferences in foreign news generally, and EU news specifically, were also addressed.

Chapter 2 analyses the Asia-Pacific reportage of the 2004 EU enlargement in a 'peak' period of coverage (April–June 2004). The chapter presents a detailed content analysis of the most covered EU topic that year – EU enlargement – and reconstructs the conceptual structures underlying the   media representations. This chapter employs a discursive intertextual approach by locating metaphors in the relevant news texts and identifying the deep meanings underlying these linguistic expressions. Conceptually, Chapter 2 explores another strategy of meaning production employed under circumstances of severe media competition. By illuminating some features of the presented concepts (the enlarging EU in our case) and overlooking others, metaphorical categorizations allow the introduction of new and complex political concepts to an average reader or viewer in familiar and simplified terms. Moreover, being emotively charged cognitive mechanisms, metaphors are even more attractive to audience members – audience interest seems to be drawn to compelling narratives which 'tickle' the emotions and incorporate drama and conflict. In order to win the audiences' attention over national and local domestic news, as well as over other international news, the makers of foreign news are compelled to create vivid and dramatic imagery to sell their stories, thus explaining the proliferation of metaphorical categorizations.

Chapter 2 compares framings of the EU in terms of the most visible metaphorical categorizations appearing in two different angles of news reporting – EU enlargement reported either outside of the local contexts or within them. Such visions are argued not only to contribute to the priming of the concept 'the EU', but also to be rather effective in supporting stereotypes of the EU. Indeed, metaphors are ideological in the sense that they 'can contribute to a situation where they privilege one understanding of reality over others'.[68] As Postman notes:

> [w]hether we are experiencing the world through the lens of speech or the printed word or the television camera, our media-metaphors classify the world for us, sequence it, frame it, enlarge it, reduce it, color it, argue a case for what the world is like.[69]

Public opinion and perceptions of the EU

Since foreign policy-making is the prerogative of a rather limited, highly selective and specifically trained group of national elites, the input of public opinion is often underestimated at best and overlooked at worst in both research and policy practice. Regrettably, most existing studies which investigate the EU's foreign policy actions and discourses overlook international public opinion. Moreover, most of the EU's foreign policy-makers appear unaware of the international public's views on the project of European integration and the role of the EU as a global actor. Addressing this scholarly and practical deficit, the second part of this book – 'The EU in the Views of the General Public in the Asia-Pacific' – features three chapters which scrutinize different cases in the EU's perceptions among the general public of the Asia-Pacific. These cases examine the results of national surveys of public opinion and attitudes towards the EU undertaken in 2004 in the four countries. The chosen methodology involved a randomly sampled structured telephone survey lasting on average 15 minutes. Computer-Assisted Telephone Interview (CATI) technology was employed, and the services of a professional social research group were used to guarantee reliability. Each selected national sample (400 adults in each country aged 18 years and over) was stratified according to national census figures on region, age, gender, ethnicity and education. The $n = 400$ sample provided a margin of error of ± 4.9 per cent.

A comparative perspective was adopted in all three public opinion chapters. Chapter 3 'Exposure, Accessibility, and Difference: How Australians and New Zealanders Perceive Europe and the European Union' by Bradford Jones compares the two 'Pacific' cases. Chapter 4 'Bringing Public Opinion Back In: Perceptions of the EU in Thailand and South Korea' by Kenneth Ka-Lok Chan, contrasts the two 'Asian' cases. Finally, Chapter 5 'Europe from Within, Europe from Without: Understanding Spontaneous Perceptions of the European Union in the Asia-Pacific' by Michael Bruter brings together the 'Asian' and 'Pacific' visions of the EU and compares them across the four countries in the study, as well as with the images of Europe that exist among European general public.

Public opinion on foreign affairs, nations and people is recognized in these analyses to be a system with multiple effects, influencing both the process and the outcome, with the news media seen as a leading factor in opinion formation on foreign counterparts. Conceptually, the leading audience frames of the EU were compared with the dominant media frames, and the overarching project was designed to facilitate such a comparison. Specifically, the identified primed media frames were incorporated into the survey questionnaires in each country, and the public perceptions were subsequently measured and compared across the countries and the cases. Chapter 3 and 4 discuss these primed frames through the lists of issues which were perceived to exert an impact on the local–EU relationship, and were rated in terms of their importance. The dominant frames provided by the Asia-Pacific news media were found to be readily adopted by news audiences into their mental schemata of the EU, and to significantly influence the public's view of the EU and its role in the region.

However, the high costs of foreign news production and the pervasive presumption by newsmakers that their audiences are uninterested in foreign news in general[70] has led to a subsequent decrease in volume of 'hard' international news worldwide and an increase in 'light' news (sports, entertainment, etc.) from close to home.[71] Arguably, the less exposure the Asia-Pacific public has to 'serious' international news (EU news included), the more impaired the public's knowledge of a nation's important foreign partners will be. In parallel with this diminishing influence of foreign news, McLeod *et al.* noted that a number of conditional effects may intervene before, during and after media exposure.[72] The list of those effects includes the extraneous factors of 'real-world conditions',[73] as well as the internal factors of human 'cognitive autonomy'.[74] Among the former, there are national economic concerns, media competition in a particular country and the characteristics of a state's political system, for example;[75] among the latter, the influence of general education, personal experience and interpersonal communication. These internal factors are claimed by many researchers to significantly and potentially influence public attitudes, cognition and behaviours in relation to foreign counterparts.[76] If people have access to at least one of the abovementioned internal inputs, their mental representations of foreign counterparts will develop in volume and complexity. But if people have access to more than one of the inputs they may, in the words of Beaudoin, 'reap differential gains in international knowledge [due to] ... opportunities for double-checking, clarifying, or elaborating on information'.[77]

Chapter 3 discusses a comprehensive list of variables which are hypothesized to condition public opinion in Australasia. The scrutinized factors include the channels of information acquisition, the importance assigned to the EU, connectivity with the EU/Europe and the demographic characteristics of the general public in each location (gender, age and socio-economic status). The effects of these variables on public opinion formation were contextualized in several ways: through respondents' orientation towards EU political issues, the issue's sensitivity and quality use of the media.

Public opinion is assumed by Brewer *et al.* to incorporate a 'range of perceptions from the nature of personal interactions among people of differing nations to mass attitudes about foreign policy to the practice of public diplomacy'.[78] Building on this, Chapter 4 presents a comprehensive overview of the meanings assigned to the EU by the general public in the two Asian countries, focusing extensively on the patterns of connectivity and contextualizing the findings within a more general paradigm of Asia's foreign relations; that is, within the triangle of Asia–USA–Europe/EU interactions.

Lastly, Chapter 5 pays special attention to the responses to a key open-ended question in the survey questionnaire — the identification of three spontaneous images of the EU by each respondent. A detailed and highly systematic content analysis of these texts was used to reconstruct the leading schemata of public perceptions for the concept 'EU' with comparisons across the four Asia-Pacific public discourses, as well as with the parallel perspective *within* the EU.

Elite opinion and perceptions of the EU

The third section of this book – 'The EU through the Eyes of Asia-Pacific National Elites' – features two chapters that investigate a more traditional line of inquiry in foreign policy studies; perceptions of the national elite. If compared with public opinion, there is a fine-grained distinction between the patterns of meanings assigned to foreign counterparts by the public and by elites.[79] This is unsurprising, given that in foreign affairs the national elite of any country is reported to be 'more participant, more informed, [and] more mobile'[80] than the general public. Due to this higher level of personal involvement with international events and personalities, the study of the elite images of foreign counterparts becomes crucial. According to Brecher, elite perceptions and attitudes in this case become one of the key inputs into a foreign policy system: 'decision makers act in accordance with their perception of reality, not in response to reality itself'.[81] Correspondingly, the identification of the patterns of foreign actors' perceptions at the 'elite' level was assumed in this project to enhance the understanding of the conduct of foreign policy towards the EU in the four countries of Asia-Pacific.

An elite-driven project from its inception, the EU could arguably discover additional perspectives of its own image if it examined itself through the eyes of international elites. A growing body of literature in the field of the EU's foreign policy studies recognizes this claim and increasingly focuses on the EU's images and perceptions held by national elites outside the Union's borders.[82] In line with these studies, the third stage of this analysis focused on the perceptions of the EU held by the Asia-Pacific policy- and decision-makers and opinion-formers. The sampling strategies, data collection approaches and data analysis techniques were chosen to guarantee an output of 'rigorous and reliable data [which could be] used in providing evidence-based policy recommendations'.[83]

The sampling strategy involved the random selection of key informants and comparison of their perceptions across three sectors – *business, political* and *media elites*. The interviews took place in the political and economic centres of each country between May and September 2005 (in Australia, New Zealand, and Thailand) and in 2006 (in South Korea). In total, data from 90 elite representatives were collected through face-to-face 45-minute interviews. *Political elites* were identified as the current members of national parliaments representing different parties, *business elites* were the leaders of national business communities and leading traders of key commodities, while *media elites* were identified as the editors, directors of news, and lead reporters of the media outlets monitored during the first phase of the project. Including media professionals in the interview sample enhanced the understanding of the EU news production. *Academic elites* (included in the South Korean study only) were identified as the leading academic experts in South Korea on foreign policy in general and the EU in particular. The size and profile of the sample and the kind of data contemplated reinforced the choice of data collection strategy, namely, individual, semi-structured and on-record interviews.

To ensure comparability across the three stages of the research, the elites' questionnaire design included a number of questions that paralleled those asked in the public opinion questionnaire. Matching methodological designs provided further grounds for the comparative analysis of media, elite and public images and perceptions of the EU in the Asia-Pacific. The two 'elite' chapters provide insights into the patterns of elite views on the EU in the region, using contrasting yet complementary approaches. The first case, argued by Philomena Murray in Chapter 6, 'What Australians Think about the EU: National Interests in an International Setting', presents a unique longitudinal perspective on the images of and attitudes towards the EU in one particular case – Australia. A comparative principle was again at play – the dynamics of Australian elite in views on the EU were traced over time, with a subsequent focus on the most recent 2005 survey. In this context, this case study's major finding of negative and invisible perceptions of the EU among the Australian elites will be a matter of concern for both sides.

In contrast, Chapter 7 by Jessica Bain, Katrina Stats, Sung-Hoon Park and Heungchong Kim, 'The Asia-Pacific Power Elite and the Soft Superpower: Elite Perceptions of the EU in the Asia—Pacific', provides a cross-sectional analysis of the elites' dominant views on the EU in the four Asia-Pacific countries. This chapter focuses on the EU's perceived current and future importance for each of the four countries and perceptions of its international leadership. Spontaneous associations of the EU held by the regional elites were also assessed and compared.

Finally, the pragmatic implications of these perceptions were assessed and some recommendations for both improving perceptions of and relations with the EU were suggested.

Concluding remarks

This book aims to contribute to the study of the EU's external images and perceptions – an overlooked (even neglected) theme in the field the EU's foreign policy, identity and public policy studies. Featuring a multidisciplinary approach and a four-country case study, this volume offers unique and original insights into the systematic analysis of the EU's images and public predispositions resulting from the processing of those images in one particular region. The leading rationale behind this volume is twofold. First, this original multilevel investigation attempts to raise the EU's profile in the Asia-Pacific, one of the world's global centres. By informing regional policy-makers on the leading meanings assigned by public discourses to the EU, the book aims to reduce the communication deficits between the Asia-Pacific and the EU, one of the region's vital counterparts. Secondly, our research aims to alert EU stakeholders to the leading representations of the EU outside its borders. The growing global interconnectedness unavoidably exposes more aspects of the domestic existence to foreign peoples and events, and extensive international knowledge, global interest and understanding are becoming a modern necessity. Hence, the pragmatic consequences from the EU's external imagery are argued to be of paramount importance to the EU, both as an ongoing integration project, and as an aspiring global power.

To conclude this introduction, the academic team involved in this research was drawn from the Asia-Pacific (Korea, Thailand, New Zealand and Australia), the USA and from the EU. Such an ambitious project requires significant funding and this study has only been made possible through a Commission DG-EAC grant of €142,000. While funded largely by the Commission, the analysis, results and conclusions drawn in this volume remain the sole responsibility of the academics involved and are fully independent from any EU input. And, as the findings suggest, the EU has much to learn and to address if it wishes to enhance what is largely an under-valued EU presence in the Asia-Pacific world.

Notes

1 A. Duff, 'Plan B: How to Rescue the European Constitution', *Etudes and Recherchers* 52, p. 30, Available <http://www.andrewduffmep.org.uk/resources/sites/217.160.173.25-406d96d1812cb6.84417533/EU%20Constitution%20Briefing/Plan%20B%20for%20the%20Constitution.pdf> (Accessed 10 August 2007).
2 Jacques Delors as cited in P. Schmitter, 'Examining the Present Euro-Polity with the Help of Past Theories', in G. Marks, F. Scharf, P. Schmitter and W. Streeck, *Governance in the European Union*, London, Sage, 1996, p. 1.
3 The South Asian Association for Regional Cooperation was established when its Charter was formally adopted on 8 Dec. 1985 by the Heads of State or Government of Bangladesh, Bhutan, India, Maldives, Nepal, Pakistan and Sri Lanka.

4   See e.g. G. Majone, 'Europe's 'Democratic Deficit': The Question of Standards', *European Law Journal* 4 (1998), 5–28; A. Moravcsik, 'In Defence of the "Democratic Deficit"': Reassessing Legitimacy in the European Union', *Journal of Common Market Studies* 40 (2002), 603–24; T. Zweifel, '… Who is without Sin Cast the First Stone: the EU's Democratic Deficit in Comparison', *Journal of European Public Policy* 9 (2002), 812–40. The two main 'debaters' against a democratic deficit are Majone and Moravcsik. Majone argues essentially that the EU is not intended (or desired) to move towards political integration, and therefore it is little more than a regulatory body and should be treated as such, in which case there is not a democratic deficit. Similarly, Moravcsik argues that the standards used to assess the EU's democratic legitimacy are too idealistic, and that most national democracies would not hold up against them. Another anti-democratic deficit proponent is Zweifel, who compared the EU's democratic standards to those in the USA and Switzerland, and found in fact that the EU was not lacking (at least not compared to two of the world's most revered federal democracies).

5   M. Wallström (June 2005) 'Communicating a Europe in Stormy Waters: Plan D', *SPEECH/05/396*, available <http://europa.eu/rapid/pressReleasesAction.do?reference=SPEECH/05/396&format=HTML&aged=1&language=EN&gui Language=en> (Accessed 10 August 2007); M. Wallström (April 2005) 'Slow Progress on Communication Strategy due to Commission's Internal Problem', *Euractiv*, available <http://www.euractiv.com/en/opinion/slow-progress-communication-strategy-due-commission-internal-problems/article-137580> (Accessed 10 August 2007).

6   R. Eichenberg and R. Dalton, 'Europeans and the European Community: The Dynamics of Public Support for European Integration', *International Organization* 47 (1993), 507–34, as cited in C. De Vreese, S. Banducci, H. Semetko and H. Boomgarden, 'The News Coverage of the 2004 European Parliamentary Elections Campaign in 25 Countries', *European Union Politics* 7 (2006), 478.

7   J. Coultrap, 'From Parliamentarism to Pluralism: Models of Democracy and the European Union's "Democratic Deficit"', *Journal of Theoretical Politics* 11 (1999), 108; R. Kuper, 'The Many Democratic Deficits of the European Union', in A. Weale and M. Nentwich (eds), *Political Theory and the European Union*, London, Routledge, 1998, pp. 144–57; F. Scharpf, *Governing in Europe: Effective and Democratic*, New York, Oxford University Press, 1999, as cited in C. de Vreese *et al.*, 'News Coverage', p. 478.

8   C. Meyer, 'Political Legitimacy and the Invisibility of Politics: Exploring the European Union's Communication Deficit', *Journal of Common Market Studies* 37 (1999), 617–39; C. de Vreese, 'Communicating Europe', Foreign Policy Centre, British Council and Weber Shandwick Public Affairs, 2003, available <http://fpc.org.uk/publications/73> (Accessed 10 August 2007); P. Anderson and A. McLeod, 'The Great Non-Communicator? The Mass Communication Deficit of the European Parliament and its Press Directorate', *Journal of Common Market Studies* 42 (2004), 897–917.

9   P. Anderson and A. Weymouth, *Insulting the Public: The British Press and the European Union*, New York, Longman, 1999, p. 31; P. Anderson, 'A Flag for Convenience? Discourse and Motivations of the London-based Eurosceptic Press', *European Studies* 20 (2004), 151–70 as cited in de Vreese *et al.*, 'News Coverage', p. 478.

10 De Vreese *et al.*, 'New Coverage', p. 478; Anderson and McLeod, 'The Great Non-Communicator?'; C. de Vreese, *Framing Europe: Television News and European Integration*, Amsterdam, Aksant, 2002; D. Kevin, *Europe in the Media: A Comparison of Reporting, Representation and Rhetoric in National Media Systems in Europe*, London and Mahwah, NJ, Lawrence Erlbaum Associates, 2003.

11 Meyer, 'Political Legitimacy and the Invisibility of Politics'.

12 Wallström, 'Slow Progress on Communication Strategy'. Moreover, in 2006, the European Commission opened a 'Debate Europe' website, created a network of more 400 local Europe Direct information centres, and established the free telephone helpline of the Europe Direct contact centre from anywhere in the EU.
13 Wallström, 'Communicating a Europe in Stormy Waters'.
14 *Ibid.*
15 Cited in J. Hale, *Civilization of Europe in the Renaissance*, London, Harper Collins, 1993, p. 4.
16 B. Stråth, 'A European Identity: To the Historical Limits of a Concept', *European Journal of Social Theory* 5 (2002), 388–9.
17 See, for example, GARNET-JERP 5.2.1, Final Conference 'The Europeans: The European Union in Search of Political Identity and Legitimacy'. Florence, 25 and 26 May 2007.
18 I. Manners and R. Whitman, 'Towards Identifying the International Identity of the European Union: A Framework for Analysis of the EU's Network of Relations', *Journal of European Integration* 21 (1998), 235.
19 See for example: I. Neumann, 'Self and Other in International Relations', *European Journal of International Relations* 2 (1996), 139–74; S. Hall, 'The Spectacle of the "Other"', in S. Hall (ed.), *Representation: Cultural Representations and Signifying Practices*, London, Sage in association with the Open University, 1997, pp. 229–37; A. Smith, 'National Identity and the Idea of European Unity', *International Affairs* 68 (1992), 75.
20 Stråth, 'A European Identity', p. 397.
21 I. Manners and R. Whitman, 'The "Difference Engine": Constructing and Representing the International Identity of the European Union', *Journal of European Public Policy* 10 (2003), 380–404.
22 *Ibid.*, p. 381.
23 H. Samur, 'The Power of Discourse in the EU Playground', *Journal of European Affairs*, EU Policy Network 31 (2004), p. 31, available <http://www.europeananalysis.com/jea/JEA2-2.pdf> (Accessed 26 October 2007).
24 C. Hill, 'The Capability–Expectations Gap, or Conceptualizing Europe's International Role', *Journal of Common Market Studies* 31 (1993), 305–28.
25 See e.g. M. Tsuruoka, 'Why EU–Japan Partnership Cannot Flourish: Expectations Deficit in EU–Japan Relations', paper presented at the British International Studies Association (BISA) Conference, University of Warwick, 20–22 Dec. 2004.
26 G. Lundestad, *'Empire' by Integration: The United States and European Integration, 1945–1997*. Oxford, Oxford University Press, Oxford, 1998; W. Cromwell, *The United States and the European Pillar: The Strained Alliance*, Basingstoke, Macmillan, 1992; K. Featherstone and R. Ginsberg, *The United States and the European Union in the 1990s: Partners in Transition*, Basingstoke, Macmillan, 1995; R. Kagan, *Of Paradise and Power: America and Europe in the New World Order*, New York, Alfred A. Knopf, 2003; W. Mead, 'Goodbye to Berlin? Germany Looks Askance at Red State America', *National Interest* 75 (2004), 19–28; T. Forsberg, 'The EU–Russia Security Partnership: Why the Opportunity was Missed', *European Foreign Affairs Review* 9 (2004), 247–67; all cited in Tsuruoka, 'Why EU–Japan Partnership Cannot Flourish'.
27 P. Fiske De Gouveia and H. Plumridge, *European Infopolitik: Developing EU Public Strategy*, London, Foreign Policy Centre, 2005.
28 K. Reif, 'Cultural Convergence and Cultural Diversity as Factors in European Identity', in S. Garcia (ed.), *European Identity and the Search for Legitimacy*, London, Pinter, 1993, pp. 131–53.
29 J. Caporaso and J. Jupille, 'States, Agency and Rules: The EU in Global Environmental Policy', in C. Rhodes (ed.), *The European Union in the World Community*, Boulder, CO, Lynne Rienner, 1998, pp. 213–29.

30 M. Holland, 'The Common Foreign and Security Policy', in L. Cram, D. Dinan and N. Nugent (eds), *Developments in the European Union*, London, Macmillan, 1999, p. 243.

31 The project was made possible by the generous support of the European Commission Directorate General for Education and Culture (Grant agreement 2003-2292/001-001).

32 For more information on those projects please check the websites <http://www.europe.canterbury.ac.nz/appp/> and <http://esia.asef.org/>.

33 The scope of the research addressed perspectives of the 'EU and Dialogue between Peoples and Cultures' funding priority of the Directorate-General on Education and Culture, Jean Monnet Programme, of the European Commission. The project was co-sponsored by four EU studies associations in the region – EUSANZ, EUSA-Thai, CESAA and EUSA-Korea – all of which are members of the world ECSA body. The powerful multiplier effect of the projects' outcomes was ensured through the unprecedented mobilization and consolidated multidisciplinary expertise and cross-border academic cooperation of four academic institutions: the National Centre for Research on Europe, University of Canterbury, New Zealand, Jean Monnet Chair (leading organization); the European Studies Program Chulalongkorn University, Bangkok, Thailand; the Contemporary Europe Research Centre, University of Melbourne, Australia, Jean Monnet Chair; and the Graduate School of International Studies, South Korea, Jean Monnet Chair.

34 The data for Thailand predates the 2006 military coup and does not therefore distort this feature.

35 P. Lazarsfeld, 'The Prognosis for International Communications Research', in H.-D. Fischer and J. Merrill (eds), *International and Intercultural Communication*, New York, Hastings House, 1976, p. 487.

36 De Vreese, *Framing Europe*, p. 14.

37 S. Soroka, 'Issues Attributes and Agenda-Setting by Media, the Public, and Policymakers in Canada', *International Journal of Public Opinion Research* 14 (2002), 264.

38 E. Adler, 'Seizing the Middle Ground: Constructivism in World Politics', *European Journal of International Relations* 3 (1997), 319–63; T. Hopf, 'The Promise of Constructivism in International Relations Theory', *International Security* 23 (1998), 171–200, as cited in Samur, 'Power of Discourse'.

39 T.-K. Chang, P. Berg, A. Ying-Him Fung, K. Kedl, C. Luther and J. Szuba, 'Comparing Nations in Mass Communication Research, 1970–97: A Critical Assessment of How we Know What we Know', *Gazette* 63 (2001), 415–34.

40 R. Neuman, M. Just and A. Cligler, *Common Knowledge: News and Construction of Political Meaning*, Chicago, IL and London, University of Chicago Press, 1992. The authors deliberately refrained from using the term 'theory', using instead 'paradigm'.

41 *Ibid.*, p. 16.

42 *Ibid.*

43 *Ibid.*, p. 19.

44 D. Shaw and S. Martin, 'The Function of Mass Media Agenda Setting', *Journalism Quarterly* 69 (1992), 902–20.

45 H. Semetko and A. Mandelli, 'Setting the Agenda for Cross-National Research: Bringing Values into the Concept', in M. McCombs, D. Shaw and D. Weaver (eds), *Communication and Democracy*, Mahwah, NJ, Lawrence Erlbaum, 1997, p. 206.

46 M. McCombs and D. Shaw, 'The Agenda-Setting Function of the Mass Media', *Public Opinion Quarterly* 36 (1972),176–87.

47 R. Hügel, W. Degenhardt and H.-J. Weiß, 'Structural Equation Models for the Analysis of the Agenda Setting Process', *European Journal of Communication* 4 (1989), 191–210.

48 Soroka, 'Issues Attributes and Agenda-Setting', p. 265.
49 J. Beniger, 'Communication: Embrace the Subject, Not the Field', *Journal of Communication* 43 (1993), 18–25.
50 D. Graber, *Mass Media and American Politics*, 2nd edn, Washington, DC, Congressional Quarterly Press, 1984.
51 N. Fairclough and R. Wodak, 'Critical Discourse Analysis', in Teun van Dijk (ed.), *Discourse as Social Interaction*, London, Sage, 1997, p. 266.
52 P. Brewer, J. Graf and L. Willnat, 'Priming or Framing: Media Influence on Attitudes toward Foreign Countries', *Gazette* 65 (2003), 494.
53 R. Entman, 'Framing: Toward Clarification of a Fractured Paradigm', *Journal of Communication* 43 (1993), 52.
54 D. Scheufele, 'Framing as a Theory of Media Effects', *Journal of Communication* 49 (1999), 103–22.
55 T. van Dijk, 'Critical Discourse Analysis', in D. Tannen, D. Schiffrin and H. Hamilton (eds), *Handbook of Discourse Analysis*, Oxford, Blackwell, 2001, pp. 352–71.
56 *Ibid.*
57 See B. Berelson and G. Steiner, *Human Behavior: An Inventory of Scientific Findings*, Oxford, Harcourt, Brace & World, 1964; J. Aldrich, J. Sullivan and E. Borgida, 'Foreign Affairs and Issue Voting: Do Presidential Candidates "Waltz Before a Blind Audience"?' *American Political Science Review* 83 (1989), 123–42; T. Higgins and G. King, 'Accessibility of Social Constructs: Information-Processing Consequences of Individual and Contextual Variability', in N. Cantor and J. Kihlstrom (eds), *Cognition, Social Interaction and Personality*, Hillsdale, NJ, Erlbaum, 1981, pp. 129–62; S. Fiske and S. Taylor, *Social Cognition*, Reading, MA, Addison Wesley, 1984; J. Hurwitz and M. Peffley, 'Public Perceptions of Race and Crime: The Role of Racial Stereotypes', *American Political Science Review* 41 (1997), 374–401.
58 R. Ginsberg, 'Conceptualizing the European Union as an International Actor: Narrowing the Theoretical Capability–Expectations Gap', *Journal of Common Market Studies* 37 (1999), 435.
59 Soroka, 'Issues Attributes and Agenda-Setting', pp. 269, 281.
60 D. Perry, 'News Reading, Knowledge about, and Attitudes toward Foreign Countries', *Journalism Quarterly* 67 (1990), 353–8; M. Salwen and F. Matera, 'Public Salience of Foreign Nations', *Journalism Quarterly* 69 (1992), 623–32.
61 S. Livingston, *Clarifying the CNN Effect: An Examination of Media Effects According to Type of Military Intervention*, Harvard University Kennedy School of Government Joan Shorenstein Center for Press and Politics, 1997, available <http://www.ksg.harvard.edu/presspol/research_publications/papers/research_papers/R18.pdf> (Accessed 14 August 2006); M. Belknap, 'The CNN Effect: Strategic Enabler or Operational Risk?', U.S. Army War College Strategy Research Project, 2001. available <www.iwar.org.uk/psyops/resources/cnn-effect/Belknap_M_H_01.pdf> (Accessed 10 August 2007); C. Naveh, 'The Role of the Media in Foreign Policy Decision-Making: A Theoretical Framework', *Conflict and Communication Online* 1 (2002), available <www.cco.regener-online.de> (accessed 15 June 2006); M. Peña, 'News Media and the Foreign Policy Decision-Making Process, CNN or Washington', *Razón y Palabra* 32 (2003), available <http://www.cem.itesm.mx/dacs/publicaciones/logos/anteriores/n32/mpena.htm> (Accessed 21 June 2006).
62 Research by Amsterdam School of Communication Research (among its many studies there are De Vreese *et al.*, 'News Coverage'; De Vreese, *Framing Europe*; J. Peter, H. Semetko and C. de Vreese, 'EU Politics on Television News', *European Union Politics* 4 (2003), 305–27; H. Semetko and P. Valkenburg, 'Framing European Politics: A Content Analysis of Press and Television News', *Journal of Communication* 50 (2000), 93–109. Other researchers that have contributed to the field are M. Van de Steeg, 'Rethinking the Conditions for a Public Sphere in the European Union', *European Journal of Social Theory* 5 (2002), 499–519; C. Meyer, 'The Europeanization of Media

Discourse: A Study of Quality Press Coverage of Economic Policy Co-ordination since Amsterdam', *Journal of Common Market Studies* 43 (2005), 121–48; H.-J. Trenz, 'Media Coverage of European Governance: Exploring the European Public Sphere in National Quality Newspapers', *European Journal of Communication* 19 (2004), 291–319; Kevin, *Europe in the Media*; N. Gavin, 'Imagining Europe: Political Identity and British Television Coverage of the European Economy', *British Journal of Politics and International Relations* 2 (2000), 352–73; Anderson and Weymouth, *Insulting the Public*; P. Norris, 'Blaming the Messenger? Political Communications and Turnout in EU Elections', in *Citizen Participation in European Politics*, Demokratiutredningens skrift, 32, Stockholm, Statens Offentliga Utredningar, 2000; P. Norris, *A Virtuous Circle: Political Communications in Post-industrial Societies*, Cambridge, Cambridge University Press, 2000.

63 P. Murray, 'Australian Voices: Some Elite Reflections on the European Union', *CESSA Review*, 29 (2002). Final Report 'Survey Analysis of EU Perceptions of South East Asia', January 2003. Framework Contract AMS/451-Lot. A.R.S. Progetti S.r.l. Ambiente, Risorse e Sviluppo; Final Repoprts 'Perceptions of the EU's Role in South East Asia', Framework Contract Commission 2007, EuropeAid/123314/C/SERmulti, Lot no. 4. 2007/144031, Gruppo Soges.

64 J. Hamilton, *All the News that's Fit to Sell*, Princeton, NJ, Princeton University Press, 2004, p. 7.

65 P. Arnett, 'Goodbye, World: International News Reporting in U.S. Papers', *American Journalism Review* 20 (1998), 50–68.

66 C. Moisy, 'Myths of the Global Information Village', *Foreign Policy*, 107 (1997), 78–87.

67 J. Blumler and D. Kavanagh, 'The Third Age of Political Communication: Influences and Features', *Political Communication* 16 (1999), 218.

68 P. Chilton, *Security Metaphors: Cold War Discourse from Containment to Common House* (Conflict and Consciousness), New York, Peter Lang, 1996, p. 74.

69 N. Postman, *Amusing Ourselves to Death*, New York, Viking, 1985, p. 1.

70 J. Hoge, 'Media Pervasiveness', *Foreign Affairs* 73 (1994), 143; J. Hamilton and E. Jenner, 'The New Foreign Correspondence', *Foreign Affairs* 82 (2003), 131; W. Soderlund, M. Lee and P. Gecelovsky, 'Trends in Canadian Newspaper Coverage of International News, 1988–2000, Editor's Assessments', *Canadian Journal of Communication* 27 (2002), 75.

71 D. Wu and J. Hamilton, 'US Foreign Correspondents Changes and Continuity at the Turn of the Century', *Gazette* 66 (2004), 518.

72 J. McLeod, G. Kosicki and Z. Pan, 'On Understanding and Misunderstanding Media Effects', in J. Curran and M. Gurevitch (eds), *Mass Media and Society*, London, Arnold, 1991, p. 254.

73 L. Erbring, E. Goldenberg and A. Miller, 'Front-Page News and Real-World Cues: A New Look at Agenda-Setting by the Media', *American Journal of Political Science* 24 (1980), 18.

74 K. Krippendorf, 'The Past of Communication's Hoped-for Future', *Journal of Communication* 43 (1993), 41.

75 For reviews, see J. Blumer (ed.), *Communication to Voters: Television in the First European Parliamentary Elections*, London, Sage, 1983; H. Semetko, J. Blumer, M. Gurevitch and D. Weaver, *The Formation of Campaign Agendas: A Comparative Analysis of Party and Media Roles in Recent American and British Elections*, Hillsdale, NJ, Lawrence Erlbaum Associates, 1991; D. Domke, K. McCoy and M. Torres, 'News Media, Racial Perceptions, and Political Cognition', *Communication Research* 26 (1999), 570–607.

76 For reviews see S. Fiske and S. Taylor, *Social Cognition*, Reading, MA, Addison Wesley, 1984; S. Ball-Rokeach, 'The Origins of Individual Media-System Dependency: A Sociological Framework', *Communication Research* 12 (1985), 485–510; D.

Lasorsa and W. Wanta, 'The Effects of Personal, Interpersonal and Media Experiences on Issue Salience', *Journalism Quarterly* 67 (1990), 804–13; W. Wanta and Y.-C. Wu, 'Interpersonal Communication and the Agenda Setting Process', *Journalism Quarterly* 69 (1992), 847–55; D. Weaver, J.-H. Zhu and L. Willnat, 'The Bridging Function of Interpersonal Communication in Agenda–Setting', *Journalism Quarterly* 69 (1992), 856–67; R. Wicks, 'Schema Theory and Measurement in Mass Communication Research Theoretical and Methodological Issues in News Information Processing', in S. Deetz (ed.), *Communication Yearbook* 15, Beverly Hills, CA, Sage, 1992, pp. 115–45; J.-H. Zhu, J. Watt, L. Snyder, J. Yan and Y. Jiang, 'Public Issue Priority Formation: Media Agenda Setting and Social Interaction', *Journal of Communication* 43 (1993), 8–29; S. Livingstone, 'The Rise and Fall of Audience Research: An Old Story with a New Ending', *Journal of Communication* 43 (1993), 5–12; P. Rossler, 'The Individual Agenda-Designing Process: How Interpersonal Communication, Egocentric Networks, and Mass Media Shape the Perception of Political Issues by Individuals', *Communication Research* 26 (1999), 666–700.

77 C. Beaudoin, 'Antecedents of International Knowledge', *Gazette* 66 (2004), 463.
78 P. Brewer *et al.* 'Priming or Framing: Media Influence on Attitudes Towards Foreign Countries', p. 493 citing L. Bartels, 'The American Public's Defense Spending Preferences in the Post-Cold War Era', *Public Opinion Quarterly* 58 (1995), 479–508; J. Manheim, *All of the People, All the Time: Strategic Communication and American Politics*, New York, M. E. Sharp, 1991; J. Manheim, 'Strategic Public Diplomacy: Managing Kuwait's Image during the Gulf Conflict', in W. Lance Bennett and David Paletz (eds), *Taken by Storm: The Media, Public Opinion, and Foreign Policy in the Gulf War*, Chicago, IL, University of Chicago Press, 1994, pp. 131–48; M. Peffley and J. Hurwitz, 'International Events and Foreign Policy Beliefs: Public Response to Changing Soviet–US Relations', *American Journal of Political Science* 36 (1992), 431–61.
79 L. Hooghe, 'Europe Divided?: Elites vs. Public Opinion on European Integration', *European Union Politics* 4 (2003), 282.
80 H. McClosky, 'Personality and Attitude Correlates of Foreign Policy Orientation', in James N. Rosenau (ed.), *Domestic Sources of Foreign Policy*, New York, Free Press, 1965, p. 60.
81 M. Brecher, *India and World Politics: Krishna Menon's View of the World*, New York and Washington, DC, Frederick A. Praeger Publishers, 1968, p. 298.
82 N. Chaban, O. Elgström and M. Holland, 'The European Union as Others See it', *European Foreign Affairs Review* 11 (2006), 245–62; N. Chaban '"Constellation" or a "Giant Star"? Perceptions of the European Union by New Zealand National Elites', in W. Gellner and M. Reichinger (eds), *Deutschland nach der Bundestagswahl 2005: Fit für die globalen Aufgaben der erweiterten EU?*, Baden-Baden, Nomos Verlag, 2006, pp. 211–18. O. Elgström and M. Smith (eds), *The European Union's Role in International Politics: Concpets and Analysis. O. Elgström, Leader or Foot Dragger? Perception of the European Union in Multilateral International Negotiations*, Report 1, 2006. Available <http://www.sieps.se/pulb/rapporter/2006/2006_1.html> (Access 27 February 2008).
83 G. Enticott, 'Multiple Voices of Modernization: Some Methodological Implications', *Public Administration* 82 (2004), 743–56, 743.

1 Mirror reflections?

The EU in print and broadcast media in the Asia-Pacific

Natalia Chaban, Jessica Bain, Katrina Stats and Paveena Sutthisripok

Introduction

The ability of the news media to 'both reflect and construct relationships'[1] is widely acknowledged.[2] Despite continued debate over the potency and predictability of media effects, in the context of increased urbanization and globalization the news media provide what is for many their only source of information about events outside their immediate experience but with the potential to impact their lives.[3] The more distant, exotic or unfamiliar the subject, the more people rely on the news media for information, explanation and analysis. As a result, when it comes to international affairs, news consumers are aptly described by Gavin as 'dependent "observers" rather than active "participants"',[4] while the news media are acknowledged to be 'a first-rate competitor for the number-one position as international image-former'.[5]

The media's power to construct both domestic and international relationships derives from the control they wield over *which* events become news and *how* they are reported. In news production, the term 'framing' refers to the decisions, taken at each stage of the news production process, that determine the manner in which the various events, issues and actors that constitute the news are presented to news consumers and, indeed, *which* events, issues and actors constitute the news. Even the most cursory reflection would reveal that framing, whether inadvertent or deliberate, is inevitable in order to make sense of the infinite number of potentially newsworthy events. However, this process is not benign since it results in the production and repetition of particular narratives so that 'apparently scattered and diverse events [can be] understood within regular patterns'.[6] Such narratives, or media 'frames' inform and guide public perceptions by providing a 'central organizing idea for news content that supplies a context and suggests what the issue is through the use of selection, emphasis, exclusion and elaboration'.[7]

The effects of media frames are particularly potent in the case of international news, where audiences typically lack alternative narratives against which to contrast those found in the news media. The construction and maintenance of such narratives demands attention since, as Siamak Movahedi argues:

> images and perceptions of other nations provide the basic framework within
> which the conduct of international relations and conflict resolution takes

place ... [a]ny foreign policy decision or strategy of conflict resolution is anchored in a system of cultural presuppositions and ideology. This system helps to delineate national interests, define international conflicts, determine international events, and structure international perceptions.[8]

It is his conviction that the mass media play a crucial role in the formation of public perceptions by providing the public 'with a new vocabulary of motives for the purpose of accounting for or rationalising the policies and actions of the government'.[9]

However, little attention to date has been devoted to systematically examining the way the European Union (EU) is framed in the media discourses of its international partners. The Asia-Pacific Perceptions (APP) project was designed to remedy this academic blind spot. This chapter investigates media images of the EU created in, and disseminated through, the news media discourses of four Asia-Pacific countries. Employing data generated by twelve months of comprehensive quantitative and qualitative media analysis of twenty leading daily newspapers and eight television news bulletins across the region, this chapter explores the similarities and differences in the print and broadcast media across and within Australia, New Zealand, South Korea and Thailand. Interesting differences were found to exist not only between the four countries and two subregions; that is, between Asia (South Korea and Thailand) and the Pacific (Australia and New Zealand); but also between the two analysed news mediums (print and broadcast).

The chapter begins with a discussion of the importance of newspapers and primetime television news bulletins as leading sources of news for the general public and national elites. The findings of the study then are discussed from a twofold comparative perspective; comparing, first, EU representations in the print and broadcast media and, secondly, comparing the media framings of the EU between two cases, namely the two Asian countries and the two Pacific countries. Further, the detected representations of the EU are contextualized within the peculiarities of the media chosen for analysis. The Asia-Pacific newsroom practices influencing the organization and production of EU coverage are subsequently surveyed and discussed.

Design of study (media analysis)

The media component of the APP project was influenced by 1979 UNESCO study *Foreign News in the Media*, which 'explicitly placed information issues in the wider context of international relations and changing constellations of global forces'.[10] Based on the UNESCO model, the APP project called for the identification and analysis of all EU news items in a representative sample of the national print and broadcast media in the four Asia-Pacific countries for a twelve-month period between 1 January and 31 December 2004, in order to generate a baseline from which images and perceptions of the EU in the Asia-Pacific region could be evaluated in greater detail.[11]

The design of this large-scale comparative study was challenged by two contradictory requirements. Although the legitimacy of findings increases with the size and range of the sample, it was necessary to keep the media sample relatively narrow 'in nature and scope in order to facilitate realistic execution' of the study.[12] Thus, despite the documented authority of radio as a source of news and current affairs,[13] and the ever-increasing popularity of online news media, the study was limited to television and newspaper coverage of the EU in order to keep the scope within manageable bounds. Both media are 'typical daily sources'[14] that audiences in the Asia-Pacific rely on for the majority of their everyday news. Moreover, each targets slightly different audiences. While in a media environment of 'hyper-competition'[15] newspapers remain a key source of political information to more educated, cosmopolitan, and older audiences,[16] including national elites,[17] television is the most popular source of news around the world,[18] thus targeting a broader demographic. This choice of media for the analysis of EU media images was supported by the findings of the public survey conducted as part of the APP project in each of the four countries (discussed in Chapters 3 and 4). Television news programmes and newspapers were named by 78.5 and 59 per cent of respondents respectively as their most important sources of EU news, exceeding other sources of news including radio (23.5 per cent) and the internet (31 per cent). Table 1.1 presents newspapers and television outlets chosen for the monitoring during the APP media stage (for more information on the four countries' media environments and media outlets selected for analysis, please see Appendix I).

Research questions

As the leading sources of information about the EU for the general public and elites in the four Asia-Pacific countries, our subsequent analysis concentrates on the framing of the EU in the selected newspapers and television news programmes. Since, as noted, newspapers and television news broadcasts cater for and target different types audiences, differences in their framing of the EU were expected. Hence, the following research questions for this chapter were formulated and examined:

RQ1: What differences in the EU media framing were observed between the two leading news media in the region – newspapers and television?

RQ2: What differences in the EU media imagery were observed between the two case studies, namely an 'Asian' media framing of the EU (EU images in South Korean and Thai news) and a 'Pacific' media framing (EU images in Australian and New Zealand news)?

RQ3: What are the leading considerations motivating the identified framings of the EU produced by regional newsmakers?

The answers to these questions are discussed in the light of the possible pragmatic implications of the EU media imagery for EU relations with the Asia-Pacific.

Table 1.1 Newspapers and television broadcasts selected for monitoring in the four Asia-Pacific countries

	Newspapers	*Television newscasts*
Australia	*Herald-Sun*	*ABC News* at 7 pm
	Sydney Morning Herald	*Channel Nine News* at 6pm
	The Australian	
	Australian Financial Review	
	Canberra Times	
New Zealand	*New Zealand Herald*	*TV 1 News* at 6 pm
	Waikato Times	*TV 3 News* at 6 pm
	Dominion Post	
	ThePress	
	Otago Daily Times	
South Korea	*Donga Ilbo*	*KBS News* at 9 pm
	Joongang Daily	*MBC News* at 9 pm
	The Chosun Ilbo	
	Korea Times	
	Metro	
Thailand	*Thai Rath*	*Channel 7 News* from 6 to 6.30 pm
	Matichon	and from 7.30 to 8.30 pm
	The Manager	*ITV News* at 6.00 pm
	Bangkok Post	
	The Nation	

Methodology

All news items that included even an incidental reference to either of the two search terms, 'European Union' or its abbreviated form 'EU', were collected and analysed. All sections of the newspapers and television news bulletins were included in the search to ensure an accurate and full representation of how the EU is portrayed in the Asia-Pacific media.[19] Data collection techniques included compiling a library of news texts reporting the EU related events (texts were located in electronic databases of the selected media outlets). Adapting the research design of several relevant media studies,[20] all EU news items were coded according to both the formal and content characteristics of the items. The *formal* details examined in this chapter included 'surface' characteristics such as the volume and dynamics of the news and the sources of the news (local writers, foreign correspondents, news syndicates or international wire services).[21] These formal characteristics provide information about the visibility of the EU and the origin of EU news reaching Asia-Pacific audiences. The visibility accorded to an actor is significant since it serves as an indicator for news consumers of the perceived salience and significance of a reported foreign counterpart (both for the country of reportage and the international community).

However, visibility is only half of the picture. As Neuman *et al.* note, 'learning is not a simple function of exposure'.[22] Thus, as well as assessing the dynamics, volume and sources of coverage, the *substance* of the news items was examined more closely. To begin, two 'in-depth' characteristics were considered. The first was the centrality of the EU to the news item – whether it was the main, secondary or minor focus of the news item.[23] The second characteristic was the focus of domesticity – that is, whether the news was located in the home country (Australia, New Zealand, South Korea or Thailand), the EU or a third country.[24] In addition, the news was divided into three main thematic frames – economics, politics and social affairs – and subframes based on the topic of the article portraying the actions of the EU and its actors.[25] For example, the *political* frame included such subframes as internal and external policy-making; the *economic* frame was constructed by such subframes as the state of economy in general, trade, industry, agriculture, business and finance; and the *social* frame incorporated such subframes as social legislation and welfare, migration, multiculturalism and multilingualism, research and education, culture and entertainment, sports and health care. Any EU actors mentioned in the article were recorded including EU Member States and EU candidate countries, as well as their respective leaders, institutions, officials and citizens. The content features highlight peculiarities of the EU news information flow reaching Asia-Pacific audiences on a daily basis. The unit of analysis in this chapter was a news item as a complete message.

Results: formal characteristics

Key events

Given that the EU is a large and powerful global actor, and actively engaged with each of our Asia-Pacific countries, fairly similar levels of coverage in the four countries and across the various outlets were expected. Somewhat surprisingly then, it was found that the volume of coverage differed not only between the countries, but also between the media outlets. One of the first observations of the media analysis was the relatively high quantity of print news per month and per outlet when compared with television, although even this comparatively heightened level was still far lower than the volume of news involving other major international actors such as the United States.[26] The newspapers chosen for monitoring in the four countries demonstrated a similar dynamic trend in the EU news reporting (Figure 1.1), while the dynamic patterns of EU appearances on television newscasts were extremely sporadic and unique in each country (Figure 1.2).

In their coverage of the EU, both media in the four countries were observed to first focus on key *EU* events and then key events for the *local polity*. Many of the peaks common to all four countries corresponded to significant EU events such as the Madrid train bombings in March, the fifth enlargement in May, the controversial European Parliament elections and the conclusion of the Constitutional Convention in June, and the appointment of a new Commission

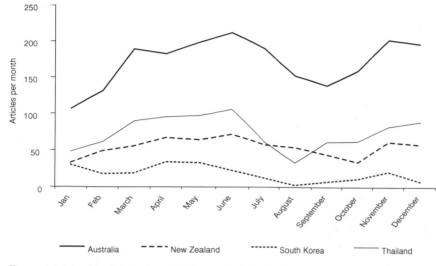

Figure 1.1 Monthly distribution of EU news in Asia-Pacific newspapers

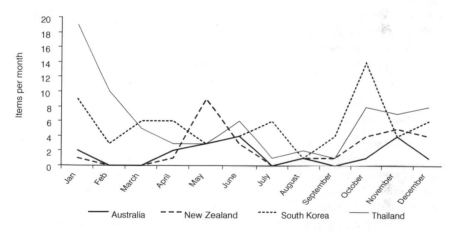

Figure 1.2 Monthly distribution of EU news on Asia-Pacific television

in October. The peak in the November coverage represented reporting on the EU's heightened external involvement with various partners such as Ukraine (in particular, the EU's participation as an observer and mediator in the contentious Ukrainian presidential elections which led to the 'Orange Revolution'), the Middle East (more specifically, during November, the EU had entered into negotiations with Iran about its uranium enrichment programme) and the USA (shown in the EU reaction to the US presidential elections).

Variance between the four countries' coverage dynamics is explained by country-specific events in which the EU played a role. For example, the EU attracted even greater coverage in June in Australian newspapers because of its controversial decision to support Russia's WTO bid in exchange for Russian support of the Kyoto Protocol – a treaty which Australia's Howard government prominently declined to ratify. In New Zealand, the heightened EU visibility in April and May was due not only to reports on the enlargement, but also to the coverage of a number of high-profile visits to the EU by New Zealand officials as well as traditional coverage of First and Second World War commemorations. Thai television showed a significant peak in January to coincide with the bird flu crisis (it is worth noting that, although the Thai print coverage of the EU did not peak that month, bird-flu related reportage constituted the vast proportion of the coverage in January). All four countries and both media demonstrated a steady decline in the middle of the year – a drop that is partially attributable to the fact that the June–August period is a traditional European vacation time – before increasing again in the last three months of the year when there were several prominent events connecting the Asia-Pacific countries to the EU. South Korean newspapers devoted a lot of attention to the visit of the Korean President to the EU in September–October. In Thailand, the November peak included abundant coverage of the EU reaction to the threat of the avian flu pandemic in Asia and fears of it spreading to Europe, as well as an EU–Thai dispute concerning the General System of Preferences (GSP) scheme.[27] For both Thailand and South Korea, the end-of-year-peak in the EU coverage includes themes of the EU's role in the Asia Europe Meeting (ASEM) process, and its dealings with the Association of South East Asian Nations (ASEAN). These topics were not observed to be given significant attention in the newspapers or television news of the two Pacific countries.

Distribution of sources

Two patterns of sourcing were observed in newspaper coverage of the EU (Figure 1.3). In their representation of the EU, Australian, New Zealand and South Korean newspapers relied more heavily on local sources. Among those sources, there were the home agencies (e.g. NZPA in New Zealand or MATP in Australia), or outlet staffers – either writers inside the country (i.e. editors, the regular opinion columnists, feature writers, etc.), or domestic correspondents placed in foreign locations. In contrast, in their coverage of the EU, Thai newspapers preferred international sources.

In the four countries, Western news agencies were utilized as an important source of print news on the EU, though this was less so in the cases of Australia and South Korea who relied far more heavily on local sources, whether stationed in the home country or abroad. Of the Western news agencies that were used by the print news producers in the four countries, the three major wires, Reuters (based in London), Agence France Presse (AFP) (based in Paris) and Associated Press (AP) (based in New York) supplied the bulk of news on the EU when a foreign news service was utilized. The preferred sources of news were found to differ from country to country. New Zealand and Thailand, for example, demonstrated a preference for the British agency, Reuters, with 48 and 41 per cent respectively of all foreign-sourced articles relating to the EU originating from this agency. In

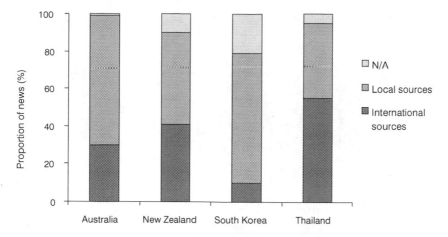

Figure 1.3 Distribution of sources of EU News in Asia-Pacific newspapers

the Thai case, however, this was closely followed by use of the French AFP wire service. While it did not form such a large component of their total coverage, Australian and South Korean print newsmakers did also use the foreign wires and, of these, AFP was the most frequently used in the Australian newspapers reporting on the EU – 51 per cent of all Australian stories using foreign material came from the French agency. In Korea, 43.75 per cent of all EU news originating from foreign agencies was purchased from AP and the same quantity from AFP.

Sometimes, the choice of sources is conditioned by historical connections and beneficial arrangements. For example, from 1947 the New Zealand Press Association (NZPA), a New Zealand domestic news agency, was both part owner and partner in Reuters.[28] Predictably then, Reuters was the leading news wire used by newspapers in New Zealand. Alternatively, the choice of sources may sometimes be grounded in a linguistic preference. Thai newsmakers, for example, explained that their preference for using AFP stemmed from the French agency writing in English as a second language – the newsmakers felt that news filtered through a non-native language was simpler and more accessible for non-English speakers around the world.[29]

In the television news analysis, the identification of sources was sometimes challenging, with 61 per cent of television news in Australia, for example, being unattributed. Local sources led the New Zealand television news and dominated Korean television news. In contrast, 51 per cent of EU news on Thai television originated from international sources (Figure 1.4). The unattributed items leave the picture of television news sources rather incomplete. However, it was noted that when a report was posted by a local journalist, it was always given a by-line and attributed to that local author. As it is in news networks' interests to promote their news as the product of independent resources and individual research, it seems fairly safe to assume that any unattributed reports were purchased from the wires.

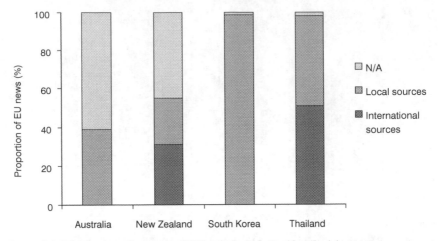

Figure 1.4 Distribution of sources of EU news in Asia-Pacific television news

Results: substantive characteristics

Distribution according to the focus of domesticity

In the print sample, a split between the trend of New Zealand on the one hand and those of the three other countries on the other was observed in distribution of the foci of domesticity. In their coverage of the EU, Australia, South Korean and Thai newspapers featured a higher share of news reports focused on events happening in, and relating to, the Union *outside* the domestic context – 73 per cent in Australia, and 75 per cent both in Thailand and in South Korea. This highlighted a difference with New Zealand – only 61 per cent of EU news was reported outside the New Zealand context (Figure 1.5).

Arguably, this trend could be explained by the traditionally more parochial orientation of the New Zealand news media, acknowledged by both country's media scholars and media practitioners.[30] In addition, three out of five monitored New Zealand newspapers belong to Rupert Murdoch's News Corp (see Appendix I) which is currently known for heavily focusing on cost-cutting and a low investment in serious foreign news,[31] and increasing editorial investment, albeit mainly in local content and stories recycled from its Australian titles.[32] Alternatively, a higher share of EU news with a domestic New Zealand anchor in the local press could also be explained by New Zealand's long-lasting historical and cultural links with Europe and strong present-day political and economic alliances with the EU. In such a context, Europe seems to be an ever-present part of the New Zealand self-narrative, prioritized among New Zealand official and public interests.

Within the news reporting the EU outside the domestic context, two more specific levels of representation were identified, namely, EU news reported in the EU context and EU news reported in the context of a third party (neither the EU nor the country of reportage). According to this more 'finely grained' analysis, when reporting the EU outside domestic context, the Australian press

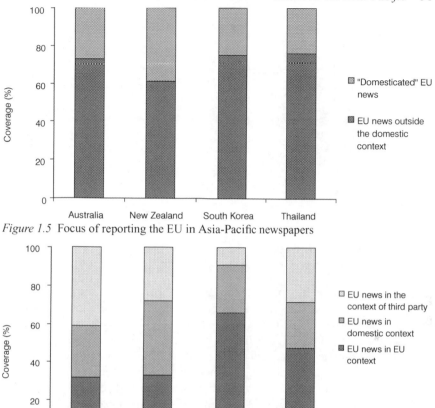

Figure 1.5 Focus of reporting the EU in Asia-Pacific newspapers

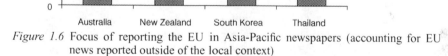

Figure 1.6 Focus of reporting the EU in Asia-Pacific newspapers (accounting for EU news reported outside of the local context)

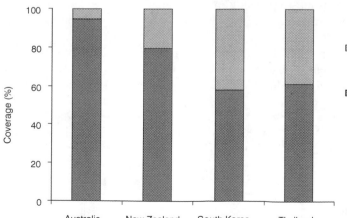

Figure 1.7 Focus of reporting the EU on Asia-Pacific television news

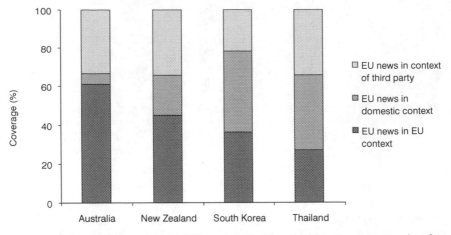

Figure 1.8 Focus of reporting the EU on Asia-Pacific television news (accounting for
EU news reported outside of the local context)

tended to report the EU in the context of the third party, while the New Zealand
press reports tended to be more balanced in their distribution of the two angles of
external domestication. The two Asian countries revealed a tendency to feature
a higher share of 'pure' EU news (or news reported in the EU context), with the
South Korean sample presenting the highest share of EU news which located the
EU primarily within EU discourses – 66 per cent (Figure 1.6).

   An Asia/Pacific split in the focus of domesticity was really only clearly evident
in the television coverage of the EU. In contrast to the newspaper case, the share
of EU broadcast news belonging to the category 'EU news in the local context'
was significantly higher in the two Asian nations' primetime television news.
The Pacific television channels by contrast featured significantly less EU news
belonging to this category with Australia presenting the lowest share of this focus
across the four countries. The representations of the EU grounded purely in the
EU context appeared most frequently in the two Pacific television discourses,
while the two Asian cases of the study featured a lower share of news in this
category (Figure 1.7).

   Again analysing the more 'finely grained' distinctions within the external focus
of domestication in television news, three countries in the sample (Australia, New
Zealand and Thailand) revealed a very similar share of news that presented the
EU in the third party context – 33, 34 and 35 per cent respectively. In the South
Korean television news bulletins, the distribution of this focus was significantly
lower – 19 per cent. A more obvious difference was in the share of news purely
presented within the EU context. Australia presented the highest share of news
with this focus – 61 per cent – followed by New Zealand and South Korea (45 and
39 per cent respectively). Thai television news accorded this particular focus the
least visibility with 25.6 per cent (Figure 1.8).

   We suggest that the prevalence of a domestic focus in EU reporting (as was
identified in the New Zealand press and in the two Asian countries' television

newscasts) could lead to a framing of the EU as an actor whose actions have immediate consequences for the local discourses, thus bringing the EU 'closer to home'. A predominant third party focus of the EU news (as was noted in the Australian press) could indicate a peculiar profiling of the EU as a global actor growing in significance and involved with many international counterparts, yet acting 'somewhere out there', distant and not touching local lives. It is worth noting that both media in South Korea revealed an especially low share of EU news with this particular focus. Focusing attention in EU news items solely on an EU/European context (as happened in South Korean and, to a degree, in the Thai press and on Australian television news) is arguably controversial in its potential effects. First, it could result in more detailed 'zoomed-in' images of the EU, which might educate news audiences about the intricacies of the EU's existence. Yet, by positioning the EU outside of the local and global contexts, this focus may also contribute to an image of the EU as a self-absorbed entity completely removed from local Asia-Pacific happenings and not extensively involved in the world.

Distribution according to the degree of centrality

The New Zealand print coverage of the EU again stood apart in terms of the centrality of EU news. The share of coverage in newspapers which reported the EU from a main perspective was relatively higher in the two Asian cases and in Australia, with Korean newspapers featuring the highest share of such EU news content (58 per cent) followed by Thailand (43 per cent) and Australia (40 per cent). New Zealand featured a relatively smaller proportion of news focusing on the EU as a 'major' focus (29 per cent) (Figure 1.9), while reporting the EU from a minor perspective, namely as a fleeting reference, was the most common in the New Zealand press. In contrast, the two Asian countries and Australia did not prioritize this particular manner of EU reporting.

This explicated preference of the New Zealand press, again, may carry a twofold explanation. On the one hand, the minor positioning of an important international partner could indicate less local attention to its developments, a practice typical for parochially oriented media reports. Alternatively, a high volume of minor representations could also indicate that local newsmakers regard the subject as being well known to their local audiences, and thus do not give it a more substantial contextualization.

Both the Australian and New Zealand primetime television news broadcasts included a high proportion of coverage which featured the EU as the primary focus. In contrast to the print media, the primetime television news in the two Asian countries featured a much higher share of news where the EU was reported from a minor perspective. In comparison, the Australian and New Zealand television newscasts featured a lower share of news belonging to the 'minor' category and, as in the case of their Asian counterparts, this share was in direct opposition to the foci distribution in print media (Figure 1.10).

It can be noted, then, that in the distribution of the foci of domesticity and degree sof centrality, the television news patterns in New Zealand and in the two Asian

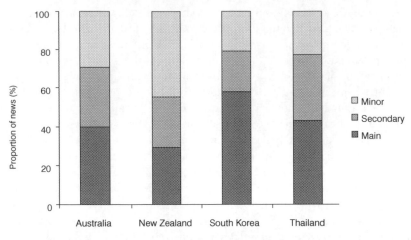

Figure 1.9 Centrality of the EU in Asia-Pacific newspapers

countries were observed to be almost directly opposite those of the print media. While the New Zealand television news displayed a tendency to report the EU as a major theme within the EU context, the New Zealand press leant more towards minor and secondary representations of the EU situated in the local context. A reverse contrast between the media was observed in the Asian case. Here, the Thai and Korean press depicted the EU predominantly with a major focus locating it in the EU context, while the Asian television news presented the EU as a minor or secondary theme in the local context. The Australian case was different – in the Australian print coverage the EU was located as a major focus in the context of a third party, and in its television reportage (similar to New Zealand) the EU was the major focus of a news item and was located in the EU context.

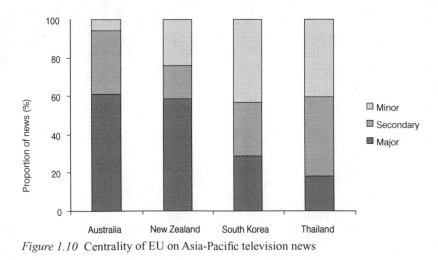

Figure 1.10 Centrality of EU on Asia-Pacific television news

Leading frames

In order to expose those facts *about*, images *of* and developments *in* the EU that are prioritized by the media discourses of the Asia-Pacific, the located EU news items were divided into three broad categories (or primary frames) according to whether they related to the EU's political, economic or social affairs and actions (reportages of the EU's actions in the developmental and environmental fields were very low in numbers across the four countries, thus they were not considered as separate frames). Additionally, and within each of the three frames' analysis, the study investigated which actors were seen to represent the EU in its various spheres of action. True global actors are expected to have recognizable leaders,[33] and this aspect of the EU's global 'performance' is frequently challenged by references to Henry Kissinger's question, 'When I want to speak to Europe, whom do I call?' Four major groups of actors were detected in the news texts referencing the EU: EU officials, EU institutions, the EU Member States (the fifteen states which constituted the Union before 2004 as well as the ten newcomers), and the EU-15 leaders. What follows is a discussion of the framing of the EU and its actors within each of these three primary frames.

The economic framing of the EU in the Asia-Pacific media

Though the EU still struggles to define and assert its role as a political actor, both domestically and internationally, the successes of European integration as an economic project are impressive. The EU is today the world's largest single market, the largest economy[34] and the largest donor of aid.[35] Its economic 'muscle' means that the EU is increasingly able to exert significant influence outside its own borders, and it is an important economic partner for all of the four countries in our sample. The EU is Australia's largest trading partner,[36] and second only to Australia in terms of its economic significance for New Zealand.[37] It accounts for more than 15 per cent of Thailand's international trade[38] and is South Korea's third largest trading partner.[39]

Given these strong trade links, it was unsurprising to observe that the EU is relatively highly visible as an economic actor in the print news media of each of the countries. News reports featuring the EU as an economic actor accounted for between 36 per cent of the total EU news articles in Australia and 47 per cent in South Korea. It was more surprising, perhaps, that economically framed EU news did not exceed the proportion of political coverage overall (see Figure 1.11) given the common public perception of the EU as primarily an economic configuration and lingering doubts about its efficacy as a political player.[40]

In the television news coverage, the framing of the EU as an economic actor received varying, and much lower, levels of media attention (Figure 1.12). Overall, economic representations formed the second most prominent primary frame in the television coverage after the political frame in each of the two subregions (Asia/Pacific), although it was less prominent than the social affairs frame in both New Zealand and South Korea. The New Zealand television news media gave

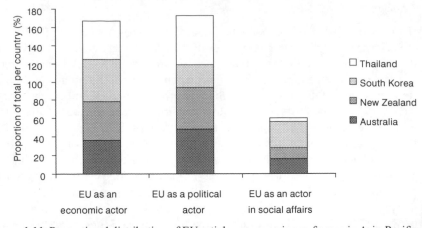

Figure 1.11 Proportional distribution of EU articles across primary frames in Asia-Pacific newspapers

economic framing of the EU the least amount of attention; only 7 per cent of all New Zealand television news reports depicted the EU in this manner. The EU's economic news did not fare much better in South Korea, where it accounted for 13 per cent of all EU-related news, while Australia and Thailand both had reasonably steady levels of economically framed EU news, 22 per cent and 38 per cent respectively. The much higher level of economic news coverage in the Thai television news discourses is primarily due to the avian influenza crisis of 2004 and the impact this outbreak had on Thai–EU trade.

In the economic print coverage, approximately forty repeatedly mentioned topics of EU action were identified and categorized, forming six subframes: economy in general, finance, business, industry, international trade and agriculture. The EU's actions in the field of *trade* formed the most popular subframe overall. It was overwhelmingly the dominant subframe in South Korea and the second most popular in Australia after *economy in general*, and in New Zealand and Thailand after *agriculture* (Figure 1.13).

Of the forty prominent topics identified in the press, only five were common to all four countries. These were the EU's protectionist policies, its actions in the context of the WTO (the two most visible topics overall), its international trade, the state of the EU economy and domestic trade with the respective Asia-Pacific economies, though all but these last two barely registered in the Korean press. In fact, the state of the EU economy and its trade with South Korea were the only two topics of significant interest in the South Korean print media. Overall, the Korean press contained the least diversity of economic topics and the least intense points of interest (measured by the number of references to each topic). The Australian press had the greatest diversity of economic themes while the Thai press featured the highest level of intensity on a single topic, namely, the avian flu crisis.

There was no discernible Asia-Pacific split in the topics of the economic coverage. Rather, Australia, New Zealand and Thailand shared an interest

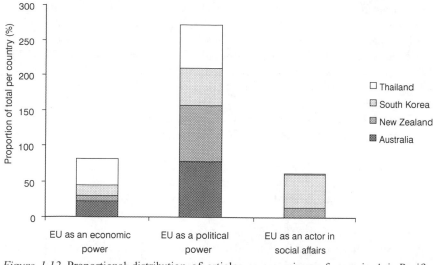

Figure 1.12 Proportional distribution of articles across primary frames in Asia-Pacific television news coverage

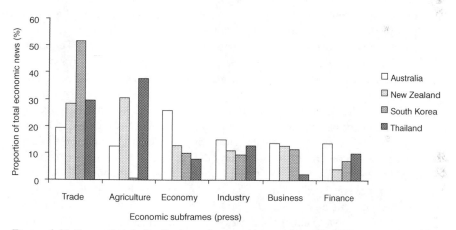

Figure 1.13 Proportional distribution of news items referencing EU economic affairs across subframes in the Asia-Pacific newspaper coverage

in the WTO negotiations and the EU's actions in this forum because of their common agricultural backgrounds. While the EU has argued strongly that the 'WTO negotiations should not be limited to the narrow agenda of agriculture and services',[41] agriculture has been the defining issue in the negotiations for these three countries, all members of the Cairns Group of agricultural exporting countries formed to counter the dominance of the EU and US in the WTO. This point of contention was also reflected in the prominence of the topic of the EU's agricultural subsidies in the Australian and New Zealand press. The Common Agricultural Policy (CAP) has been a traditional sticking point in the EU relationship for these two countries since the accession of their most important economic partner, the UK, to the Union in 1973. Both the WTO negotiations and the EU's agricultural subsidies were of less consequence for South Korea since this country does not rely on agriculture and is not in conflict with the EU in the WTO. The two Pacific countries and, to a lesser extent, South Korea shared a strong interest in the EU's actions in relation to competition regulation and anti-trust legislation.

In addition to these shared interests there were a number of topics receiving substantial coverage that were unique to one country. In Australia, the press focused heavily on the new international accounting standards scheduled for implementation in January 2005. This interest was fuelled by the fact that Australia's commitment to their implementation was being challenged by opposition to the new standards in Europe. In Thailand, EU monetary policy and, as mentioned earlier, the GSP were both of particular interest, the latter, because of its crucial importance to the Thai shrimp industry.

The subframe *industry* tended to be dominated by national interests in each country, industries such as textiles in Thailand, pharmaceuticals in Australia (a major and growing import/export product between the EU and Australia[42]), car manufacturing in Korea and various agricultural industries in New Zealand. It is worth pointing out that most of the interest in the EU's economic activities reported in the press was driven by national interest. Even in those topics not directly related to the Asia-Pacific countries, such as the state of the EU economy, for example, interest derived from the perceived potential domestic impact of the EU's financial health for each of the Asia-Pacific economies and the region as a whole.

Only five subframes were identified in the economic television news coverage, although within these, there were fourteen different topics of EU action, indicating a relative variety of national interests within this sphere of EU activity. While the five economic subframes in television news did vary slightly from those identified in the print news media, *trade* once again was the most prominent of these.

While the coverage dedicated to EU economic news in the four television news discourses was generally limited (except in the case of Thailand, as discussed above), it was almost exclusively portrayed in a manner which highlighted the direct impact of the EU's actions on the domestic news audience. In Australia, these connections were noted in the EU's involvement at the WTO and the ruling made there about EU sugar tariffs, which impinge on Australia's own sugar trade with the EU. While the economic frame received marginal television news attention in New Zealand, the domestic connection of the EU was found in the debate about CAP reform – seen to be a victory for agricultural nations like New Zealand – and the new trading opportunities post-enlargement. For Korea, trading matters were prominent also, but it was the various South Korean industries, particularly the car manufacturing industry, that were connected with events in the EU. In Thailand locally concerned EU coverage was primarily related to the avian flu crisis and the devastating impact of this outbreak on poultry exports from Thailand to the countries of the EU.

Reflecting the dominance of the trade subframe within the economically framed EU news items, it was unsurprising then to find that in the actors' analysis, the European Commission and specifically former Trade Commissioner Pascal Lamy were the most visible EU actors. Similarly, the European Central Bank (ECB) was also found to be a leading EU institution within the print news media specifically. The other visible personalities in each country's economic coverage tended to reflect the most prominent local issues for that country. For example, David Byrne, Commissioner for Health and Consumer Protection, stood out in Thailand due to the prominent role he played during the Asian bird flu crisis. In New Zealand, Franz Fischler was relatively visible, the Commissioner being responsible for New Zealand's most important industry, agriculture, whereas in Australia, interest in a number of international competition disputes meant that Mario Monti, the Commissioner for Competition, featured frequently. In Korea, with the exception of the local European Chamber of Commerce which was featured on a number of occasions, no EU institutions or officials were identified in the economic coverage, and the preference was instead for presenting the EU as a large and generally anonymous entity.

On television news in the four countries monitored there were no references to any EU officials acting in the sphere of EU economic news and the various institutions of the EU were also absent entirely, with the exception of Thailand. In the Thai television coverage of EU economic news, the Commission, the European Parliament (EP), the ECB and the Council were all mentioned on various occasions, but one other EU institution was particularly dominant. The EC Delegation to Thailand featured in six of the thirty-one television news items relating to EU economic news, making it not only the most prominent EU institution to appear in Thai television news on the EU, but also the most prominent EU actor across the Asia-Pacific EU economic coverage overall. The EU also has delegations in both Australia and South Korea, and an office headed by a *chargé d'affaires* in New Zealand, and yet none of these made even one appearance in the television news broadcasts.

The other major group of actors involved in the European integration process are, of course, those representing the various EU Member States. Of those fifteen Member States belonging to the Union prior to the May 2004 enlargement, the 'big 3' – France, the United Kingdom (UK) and Germany – were the most visible, as were their respective leaders. In both the print and television news media, France was the leader of the economic coverage in all countries, except South Korea, where the UK was the leading Member State. Despite France being slightly more visible than its two other 'big 3' counterparts, German Chancellor Gerhard Schröder was the most visible EU leader, followed by French President Jacques Chirac and UK Prime Minister Tony Blair, while Mr Schröder was the only EU leader to appear in the televised EU economic coverage.

Of the ten countries acceding to the EU in 2004, Poland was the most visible in the economically framed news, where it was seen making a rather noisy entrance because of its agricultural concerns.

The political framing of the EU in the Asia-Pacific media

While the EU is renowned for its economic prowess, it is, perhaps more infamously, regarded as relatively impotent as a political actor – the term 'political dwarf' is often bandied about. The EU has attempted to raise its political profile through various means; by establishing the positions of an EU High Representative for the Common Foreign and Security Policy (often informally referred to as the EU's 'Foreign Policy Chief') and a Counter-Terrorism Coordinator; by actively engaging with the world's 'superpowers' like the US, China and Russia; through involvement in global 'hot spots' like the Middle East; and through playing the role of human rights and democracy advocate in the international arena.

Such attempts at strengthening its political persona might finally be paying dividends for the EU. This research revealed that the coverage of the EU's political actions in the Asia-Pacific media in 2004 was not only given substantial attention, but, in fact, exceeded economic coverage in the print media of the researched countries, apart from South Korea, and led in the television news coverage in all four countries. In fact, in the television news coverage, political EU news was overwhelmingly the norm in the two Pacific countries (78 and 76 per cent for Australia and New Zealand respectively), and also in Thailand (60 per cent). South Korea had a greater level of balance between its political and social depictions of the EU (46 per cent of South Korean television coverage was political) (see Figures 1.11 and 1.12).

Although the dominant public perception of the EU in the region at present is still as an economic entity,[43] it is interesting to note that this does not appear to correspond to the information that the general public was receiving about the EU in 2004. Yet this dominance of political themes in the EU news coverage that year could be due to the fact that 2004 was an exceptional year in the EU's political life and it featured such major politically oriented events as the EU's fifth enlargement, European Parliament elections and the appointment of a new European Commission. Analysis of the EU media coverage in New Zealand in 2000–2, as well as analysis of the Asian media coverage in 2006 (both periods among the EU's so-called 'routine'[44] years) revealed a predominance of economic themes.[45]

In the print news, a variety of topics concerning all manner of the EU's political activities were identified and the most prominent of these divided into the subframes shown in Figure 1.14.

Interestingly, the four leading subframes of the political coverage in the Asia-Pacific print media were all concerned with the EU's internal political affairs (enlargement, anti-terrorist actions, constitutional debates and the EP election). In terms of its external political actions, the print media highlighted the EU's engagement with the Asian members of ASEM, particularly the debate over the participation of Myanmar in the 5th ASEM Summit Meeting, held in Vietnam in October 2004. However, it should be noted that almost 90 per cent of this news coverage was supplied by the Thai newspapers, an immediate neighbour of Myanmar, an ASEM member, and one of the brokers between the international

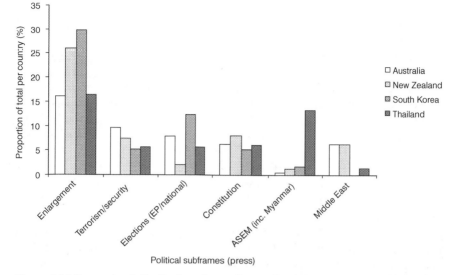

Figure 1.14 Proportional distribution of news items referencing EU political affairs across subframes in the Asia-Pacific newspaper coverage

community and the Burmese junta. The EU's role as one of the mediators in the Middle East conflict between Israel and Palestine was the second most prominent issue in the print news discourses of the four monitored countries, and it was most highly visible in the Australian press.

The relative higher visibility of the EU's internal affairs, particularly in the twenty monitored newspapers, may once again be connected to the time period in which this research was conducted. In 2004, a number of major internal EU developments took place which were aimed at both widening (the fifth enlargement and associated events such as the failed Cyprus referendum and the Turkish application) and deepening (the constitutional debate) of the integration process. The EP elections, which were held shortly after the enlargement, also received substantial attention perhaps as a 'spill-over' result of the increased media attention on the EU generated by the enlargement. In 2004, the EU also became one of the world's 'hot spots', after the Madrid train bombings, and thus it was unsurprising that the subframe *terrorism* received significant attention in both media.

Diverse topics representing the EU's political activities were detected in the television news media, and the most visible of these have been grouped into the subframes shown in Figure 1.15. Unlike the Asia-Pacific press coverage where internal political events prompted the EU coverage, in the television news coverage, it was matters relating to the EU's external political actions that were highly visible, and a relatively wide range of topics was identified. Within the prominent subframe of the *Middle East*, the specific area of EU involvement highlighted was different in each country. Australian television coverage devoted greater attention to the EU's involvement with Iraq and Iran, particularly the ongoing negotiations regarding Iran's uranium enrichment program. New Zealand, while also depicting the EU engaged with Iraq, showed interest in the EU's role in the Israel–Palestine situation, and the Korean and Thai television news bulletins portrayed the EU involved in the Middle East area generally.

One of the interesting features of the political news coverage of the EU – whether in the press or on the television news bulletins – was the general lack of a local angle in the reporting. As noted earlier, in the economic coverage, many of the EU's actions highlighted by the media included a particular connection to the domestic news audience – EU activities were often seen to have direct consequences for the home populations. In the political news coverage however, this was not generally the case. With the exception of the subframe *ASEM/ASEAN*, which did directly concern particularly the Asian countries in this study, news relating to the EU's political affairs was primarily framed in terms of its actions either within its own borders, or with another international counterpart but was rarely connected to the four countries involved in this study.

In terms of the EU actors that were identified within the politically framed news, those representing the Union's institutions were markedly limited in both the print and the television coverage. Former President of the European Commission Romano Prodi and EU 'Foreign Policy Chief' Javier Solana were the most visible in the four countries' press depicting the EU's political affairs, although in South Korea this was marginal. Perhaps reflecting the EU's attempts at raising its international political profile, Solana was the only EU official to appear in the EU television coverage of the political events in more than one country – appearing in the Australian and Thai news – while Prodi and current Commission President José Manuel Barroso were identified only once each in Australia and New Zealand respectively.

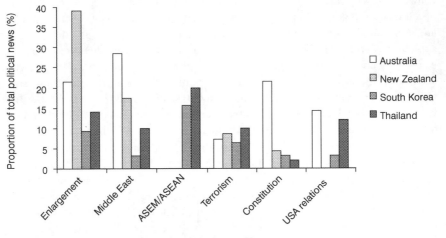

Figure 1.15 Proportional distribution of news items referencing EU political affairs across subframes on Asia-Pacific television news

It was rather striking that in the politically framed print news the EP was more visible than the Commission, the EU's executive branch, however this may be due to the time factor, as 2004 saw the EP hold elections and find itself the victim of terrorist attacks and threats, and while it also saw the introduction of a new Commission, this may have proved challenging for newsmakers to deal with. As was the case in the economic framing of the EU television news, EU institutions were marginalized in the Asia-Pacific broadcast media presenting EU political affairs. The EP was noted in Australia and New Zealand only, while the Commission and the Presidency of the Union were noted in New Zealand also.

Similarly to the economically framed news items, within the political sphere, members of the 'big 3' once again were the most visible of the EU Member States, although in this frame it was the UK and Tony Blair who featured most prominently. Germany and France, and their respective leaders, had to settle for being only as visible as Italy and Ireland. The relative political prominence of Ireland can be attributed to Ireland holding the rotating EU Presidency in the first half of 2004. The Netherlands, which held the Presidency in the latter half of the year, was not nearly as prominent as Ireland, but this may be connected to the time frame of monitoring, and not a lack of action on the part of the Netherlands. Ireland's Presidency rotation fell within the period of the EU's enlargement, and thus it had a significant role to play in those events.

In addition to having featured frequently in the economic news, Poland was also regarded as the political 'face' of the fifth enlargement in the newspapers of Australia, New Zealand and Thailand. After Poland, Cyprus was quite prominent, largely due to the high volume of news about the prospects for the reunification of the small Mediterranean island nation prior to the May enlargement. In both the print and television coverage, Turkey was also highly visible. After the 2004 enlargement, the prospect of Muslim Turkey's membership in 'the Christian club' of the EU reignited interest in the enlargement theme in the Asia-Pacific coverage in the latter half of 2004.

The social affairs framing of the in the Asia-Pacific media

One of the ruling news values underlying the media and audience's choice of news is 'human interest'.[46] Reports on EU social affairs were assumed to correspond to this value, and thus to be a popular topic in media representations of the EU was outside the EU borders. It is presumed that news audiences can more easily relate to such topics, particularly because the EU's political and economic existence is constantly changing and is extremely complex, while human interest matters are readily transferable to the daily existences of news audiences globally. However, it was observed that both newspapers and television news in the four countries did not prioritize the 'human face' of the EU. Moreover, across the four national media discourses, the media framing of the EU as an actor in the social field was the least visible (as demonstrated earlier in Figures 1.11 and 1.12). The members of the Pacific pair jointly afforded the least media attention to the EU in this field: 10.7 per cent of all monitored news stories in Australian newspapers and 16.4 per cent in New Zealand ones; and 17 per cent in New Zealand television news, while this area of EU action was completely absent from the Australian television news coverage. Where the two Pacific countries were similar in their approach to social affairs coverage, the Asian pair instead demonstrated two extremes – 25.6 per cent of the total newspapers coverage in South Korea and 3.6 per cent in Thailand; 41 per cent in South Korea in television news and 1 per cent in Thailand. If the four media discourses are compared, the South Korean news media paid the most attention, proportionally speaking, to the EU's representations as a social actor, while Thai newsmakers (both in newspapers and on television) stressed this aspect of the EU's existence the least.

The social affairs frame was extremely diverse in terms of the topics featured within it – twenty topics were located in the four countries' newspapers and nineteen different topics on the regional primetime television news (although it should be noted that the vast majority of these were identified in the South Korean case). Such diversity is hardly surprising – each of the four countries' news media prioritizes differing aspects of their own nation's social affairs, and thus incorporating the EU into the picture inevitably highlighted diverse issues. New Zealand and Australia share a common Anglo-Saxon heritage and a history of European migration. These certain similarities that exist between the EU and the two Pacific countries and their socio-cultural profiles were assumed to be absent in the case of the two 'Asian' countries. South Korea and Thailand often claim that their dominant cultural values are different from the European ones.[47] This claim is especially strong in the Thai case, with Thailand being proud to be the only one of its immediate neighbours not to have been colonized by a Western power.

Despite cultural and historical diversity among the Asia-Pacific countries and the EU, nine topics were found to feature in the print coverage in more than one of the monitored countries within this social affairs frame. Among these were EU cultural activities, health standards, sports, travel, immigration, legislation and regulations, research and science, safety and matters of the multicultural existence of the EU. Actions by the EU in its capacity as a *normative* power – namely, reportage of the EU's legislation and regulations in the field of social affairs – formed by far the most visible subframe in the four countries (Figure 1.16).

In some instances, the nine located subframes presented EU social affairs in a manner which highlighted almost identical themes. For example, the most visible topic – that of EU social affairs *regulations and legislation* – across the four countries' newspapers was comprised of reports of various EU initiatives in human rights legislation, EU regulations for the tobacco industry, labour laws and animal rights. New Zealand and Australia are both countries based on immigration where related policies are currently at the centre of public and political debate, and the EU's practices in this field are closely watched. The subframe representing the EU's *multicultural* nature (most visible in the two Pacific countries) highlighted themes of religious diversity in the EU (and related to it, problems of anti-Semitism and anti-Islamism in modern Europe), as well as the linguistic diversity of the EU. The *health* subframe featured reports on the threat of bird flu to the EU, as well

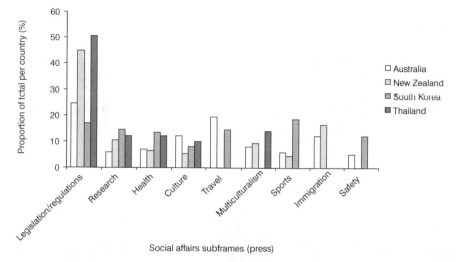

Social affairs subframes (press)

Figure 1.16 Proportional distribution of news items referencing EU social affairs across subframes in the Asia-Pacific newspaper coverage

as the safety of food consumed by EU citizens and the necessity of keeping food standards strict.

Despite the similarities in many of the social affairs subframes of the Asia-Pacific print coverage, differing representations within those nine subframes also emerged in the various national media discourses. For example, in the reports of *immigration* matters (detected only in the two Pacific countries with the New Zealand press featuring the highest share), the Australian media stressed the theme of Muslim immigration to the EU, while New Zealand newspapers highlighted the migration concerns associated with the recent EU enlargement. Notably, the topic of migration to and within the EU was not present in the monitored newspapers of the two Asian countries. Arguably, being nations of migrants, both Australia and New Zealand observed and discussed the relevant EU practices to assist in addressing their own migration concerns. In Australia, New Zealand and Thailand, the theme of the EU's efforts in the field of *research* and *science* touched on EU funding and support provided to research enterprises, while South Korean representations highlighted a rather specific angle – EU research in space.

In most of the studied representations, EU actions in the area of social affairs were seen to be directed internally, thus affecting the EU's own citizens. Yet in some less frequent examples in the print media, EU actions in the social affairs field were seen as having external effects immediately concerning the domestic populations of the four countries in the study. For example, the EU film festival in Bangkok received some press publicity; the migration of EU citizens to New Zealand was discussed; festivities and the special events of both the enlargement celebrations and D-Day commemorations in Australia involving the EU were reported; and the EU as a travel destination for South Koreans on vacation was covered. Presumably, also, the internally oriented coverage was reported to Asia-Pacific audiences because of its internationally normative implications (particularly in the case of social legislation such as cigarette labelling).

In the television coverage, differences in both subframes and accents were more prominent than similarities. While there was relative diversity in the identified subframes, none of these topics intersected across all three countries (Australia being excluded from this particular analysis because of the absence of EU social affairs news on its television news bulletins). A higher number of subframes were identified in the South Korean coverage, owing to the proportionally high levels of the social affairs frame found in South Korean television news on the EU.

On television news, smoking related issues were identified in all three countries. In the case of Thailand this was connected to research about the health risks of smoking, while in South Korea and New Zealand, emphasis was instead placed on the EU's innovations in cigarette labelling regulations, which now require cigarette manufacturers to display graphic health images on their packaging in an effort to discourage smokers. All other social affairs subframes were identified on television news in only one or two countries. *Cultural news* was found in both South Korea and New Zealand, but the specific national angle given varied. In South Korea, it was movies and the entertainment world that featured, while in New Zealand the cultural affinity between New Zealand and the countries of the EU was highlighted through coverage given to the commemorations of Second World War battles. Television news relating to the EU's *legislation and regulations* was relatively common in both South Korea and New Zealand, but while South Korean coverage was devoted more to somewhat socio-political issues, like initiatives fighting unemployment and the banning of a popular South Korean candy from being sold in Europe, the New Zealand television news media were more concerned with certain eco-chemicals that continue to be used in New Zealand, despite various EU Member States having banned them years ago. *Health* was a particularly prominent issue in the South Korean television coverage, and this subframe did appear in Thailand – with the aforementioned risks related to smoking. In Korea, news relating to this topic depicted the problems of drug abuse in the EU and the various agri-diseases and their outbreaks, including foot and mouth disease and bird flu. A number of other topics were identified in the South Korean television news, ranging from weather and Christmas celebrations in Europe, to the ever-popular football (soccer) coverage.

Despite this diversity, the images of the EU as an actor in the social sphere were almost invisible in the television news in both regional cases under consideration (they were completely absent in Australian monitored television newscasts) except in the case of South Korea where news belonging to this frame almost matched the levels of coverage accorded to EU political news.

Within the social affairs' framed news, very few EU actors were identified with any particular frequency. Notably, despite being the central EU institution for expressing the EU's *vox populi*, the EP was virtually invisible, making only intermittent appearances in Australian and New Zealand newspapers, and on South Korean television news bulletins. The Commission was the most visible institution, being particularly so in the Thai print coverage, and a range of European

Commissioners were identified, although each appeared only once or twice. President of the European Commission José Manuel Barroso was mentioned by New Zealand newspapers on one occasion, while Australian newspaper reports referenced European Parliament president Pat Cox, EU Justice Commissioner Antonio Vitorino, EU Foreign Policy Chief Javier Solana, EU External Relations Commissioner of the EU Chris Patten, the EU's Research Commissioner, and the EU's Competition Commissioner (though the latter two were not referred to by name, only their positions within the Union). Thai newspapers referred to Trade Commissioner Mario Monti, former President of the European Commission Romano Prodi, and Commissioner for Health and Consumer Protection David Byrne, while the Korean newspapers mentioned only Javier Solana and David Byrne.

In the social affairs' coverage, particularly on television news, the EU Member States were the most visible actors, and France was the most visible of these. The Gallic nation was closely followed by the UK, Germany and Italy however, and Belgium, Spain and Denmark also made one-off appearances. Perhaps surprisingly, given its historical connections with many of the EU Member States, and the UK in particular, New Zealand did not feature any mentions of the EU 'Big Three', instead depicting Italy and Denmark as representatives of the EU's social actions. In the print news coverage, the UK again was the most visible actor in the area of social affairs except in South Korea, where France was the leader.

In contrast to the economic and political frames, the EU Member State leaders were infrequently included in social affairs reports. Jacques Chirac, Tony Blair, Gerhard Schröder, Dutch Prime Minister Jan Peter Balkenende, French Prime Minister Jean-Pierre Raffarin, Irish Prime Minister Bertie Ahern, Italian Prime Minster Silvio Berlusconi, Danish Prime Minister Anders Fogh Rasmussen, Greek Prime Minister Costas Karamanlis were each sporadically mentioned in the socially framed newspaper coverage. To a certain extent, the EU 'faces' in each country corresponded to specific events of local significance – for example, visibility of the Danish Prime Minister in the Australian print media in 2004 was due to the fact that Australian citizen Mary Donaldson was engaged to marry the Danish Crown Prince Frederik, and the Danish government had granted her Danish citizenship bypassing existing Danish laws.

Once again, Poland was identified as the most represented EU newcomer in the social affairs frame. Yet it was closely followed by the Czech Republic and, in this frame, only these two Eastern European states were referenced across all four countries in this study. Poland and the Czech Republic were reported in New Zealand as a source of unwanted labour migration to the 'old' EU-15. In Australia and South Korea, the Czech Republic was popular in the social affairs frame due to its reputation as a tourist destination. In Thailand, the Czech Republic entered the news agenda with stories on the alleged appalling treatment of mental patients. Poland and the Czech Republic were also the only two accession countries to appear on the televised social affairs' news, and what was particularly interesting about the television coverage of these two states was that it was only indirectly related to their accession to the EU. In Thailand, Poland was shown as a tourist destination, while in New Zealand it was the relations between the two countries that had developed post-Second World War. The reference on Korean television news to the Czech Republic was, in fact, connected to a movie prize won by a South Korean director.

Regional case studies and country comparisons

It was expected that given the striking differences between the social, cultural, political and economic contexts in the two regions that are the focus of this study (see the Introduction to this volume), that there would be divergent pictures of the EU presented in their media also. Intriguingly and perhaps surprisingly, however, the media content analysis showed more commonalities than differences in the images of the EU formed by the news media in the two subregions – Asia and Pacific. The leading print media outlets chosen for monitoring in the two regional cases (with exception of South Korean newspapers) as well as the primetime television newscasts prioritized the representations of the EU in terms of its political, rather than economic or social, actions. Within the political frame, the EU was shown by the Asian and Pacific news media to be acting both inside and outside of its borders, but seldom in a manner which connected directly with the domestic news audiences of this study. The EU's attempts to create a cohesive foreign policy role for itself globally were visible particularly in the representations of the EU's external political actions. In 2004, the leading regional newspapers in the two Asian countries and the two Pacific countries notably featured the EU acting prominently in the crisis situation in the Middle East; in regular interactions with the USA, China, Russia and ASEAN; and, increasingly, in the ratification of the Kyoto Protocol.

Representations of the EU's internal political decision-making in the analysed media of both regional cases featured those processes and activities designed to lead to an ever-increasing state of unity. For example, there was extensive reporting of the EU enlargement, and coverage of the EP elections and the constitutional debate. In addition, anti-terrorist actions taken by the EU to secure its internal existence were depicted as actions performed across the borders of the EU Member States. Representations of the EU's external actions featured the EU as an actor establishing diplomatic ties with other global powers (such as the US, China and Russia) and acting towards other international actors that allegedly lack peace, democracy, wealth or stability. Importantly, media representations of the EU as developmental or environmental actor were sporadic and very low in visibility in both media across the four countries. Yet, while newspapers across the two Asian countries and the two Pacific nations attempted to provide some insights for their readers into the EU's political reality and the more mundane developments in the integration process of this important foreign counterpart, television primetime newscasts both in Asia and in the Pacific focused instead on the more impressive and dramatic events.

Yet these progressive steps towards wider and deeper European integration and the appreciated attempts at unified action on the international stage were juxtaposed by both Asian and Pacific newsmakers with their consistent portrayal of EU Member State actors as more prominent and involved in these political processes than their Community counterparts. In other words, when reporting on EU political affairs, Asia-Pacific commentators were more interested in the opinions and actions of the UK or Jacques Chirac than those of the European Commission or Javier Solana. The greater frequency of Member State rather than EU leaders in the political frame reflects greater fragmentation of the EU image in this field. Such depictions induced an overall political image of the EU which is somewhat amorphous – instead of a cohesive and strong political actor, the EU was represented by the Asia-Pacific news media in a manner which highlighted its many different components. While this depiction may in fact simply be a reflection of the reality of the EU's political policy – an area dominated by its intergovernmental decision-making processes – it also creates an image that becomes a 'grey' area in the minds of news audiences. It arguably results in the portrayal of the EU as a significant, but not necessarily wholly clear and comprehensible political actor, both internally and externally.

Since the public survey and elite interviews conducted as part of this project (and reported in Chapters 3–5) indicated that the public of the Asia-Pacific region primarily conceive of the EU in economic and specifically trading terms, it came as something of a surprise that the economic frame was not the leading but the second most visible frame in all of the monitored media outlets except South Korean newspapers (where it was the leading frame). Nevertheless, in the dominant representations within this economic frame, the EU was depicted in both the Asian and Pacific cases as a powerful and influential international actor whose actions did carry domestic implications for its Asia-Pacific partners.

The EU's actions in the economic frame were often portrayed by the Asian and Pacific news media as being executed from a common position ranging from trade (e.g. signing Free Trade Agreements or negotiating in the WTO) and agriculture (e.g. reducing or not agricultural subsidies, establishing GMO standards or reacting to the bird flu), to business and finance (e.g. promoting anti-trust business legislation or establishing new accounting standards) and industry (e.g. EU actions in the energy sector, fisheries, car manufacturing, IT, aviation, etc.). This common position was reflected in the fact that, across the two regional cases, the EU's supranational leaders and representatives were far more prominent than Member State officials in the framing of the EU's economic affairs (unlike the political and social frames). This fact suggests that, in contrast to the two other frames, when the EU is discussed in terms of its economic power, it is predominantly pictured by the Asia-Pacific news media as an integrated, unitary whole; a cohesive entity with its own supranational leaders. Such a representation may also echo the reality of the EU economic situation. The EU-27 (in contrast to the individual European countries) is indeed among the largest trading and investment partners for the four countries in the study, a partner who directly and perceptibly impacts the economic realities of the domestic environments.

Despite an obvious human interest at stake, representations of the Union's social affairs were the least visible of the three detected media frames and across the two regional cases. Yet, these representations were extremely diverse in terms of the topics covered. While there were less images of this frame, they were more connected to the domestic situations and thus more directly relevant for the everyday lives of the news audiences – for example, representations in the four countries included such topics as the EU's social legislation (the most visible topic), actions of the EU in the public health arena, and the EU's support of research and science. The prominence of the EU in a normative capacity perhaps reflects the EU's stated goal to become the world's most dynamic knowledge economy, and a relative prominence of the European Commission in the frame across the two cases is arguably connected to the fact that it is the designated initiator of legislation in the EU.

Two slightly differing patterns in referencing EU social-affairs actors were observed in the Pacific and Asian print news cases. In the news of EU social affairs, Thailand and Korea tended to feature big entities, such as the EU itself or the European Commission. The names of specific individuals seldom appeared – no more than a dozen individual 'names' appeared in each Asian country's coverage of the EU's social affairs. On the other hand, the Australian and New Zealand newspaper stories within this frame listed a multitude of both EU political leaders and ordinary citizens.

It is suggested that the overall commonalities in the media's framing of the EU in the Asian and Pacific cases might be explained by a commonality of ownership (observed in the Pacific case) and similar patterns of use of material from international news agencies (observed in both the Pacific and Asian cases). Three out of the five monitored newspapers in New Zealand belong to the International Newspaper Limited (INL)/Fairfax group, INL's main shareholder being Rupert Murdoch's News Corporation. Murdoch's News Corp and Fairfax are among the four media groups that account for over 80 per cent of Australian newspaper titles and 96 per cent of their readership.[48] In terms of the use of foreign news sources, both the Asian and Pacific media discourses relied heavily on EU news originating from international news sources. The three largest news agencies, namely AFP, AP and Reuters, were noted to be the leading wire services used across newspapers in the four countries. Additionally, recognized sources of international news such as the *Independent, Guardian, Bloomberg, Newsweek, New York Times, The Times* and the *BBC* were found to be used by newspapers in both cases. Television-wise, it was concluded that the sources of most of the news items (including unattributed items, presumed to have been purchased from the wires) were also of an international nature.

Predictably, each country had an exceptional feature in its coverage of the EU that could be matched in each case to the pattern of sources. The South Korean media, for example, was anomalous in several instances, the most prominent being the dominance of economic representations over political ones in the print media. This peculiar portrayal of the EU could be explained by the reliance of the press newsmakers on local, South Korean sources in print coverage, while predominantly using international sources on television. In contrast, print newsmakers in Thailand showed the highest share of international sources used in press coverage among the four countries. In a different example, the New Zealand print media profiled the EU mostly from a minor perspective grounding it in local discourses. This finding could be explained by the fact that so many of the monitored New Zealand newspapers belong to Murdoch's news 'empire' in which foreign news coverage is conspicuously deprioritized in favour of local news (as discussed earlier). Finally, the Australian print and television news media demonstrated a tendency to feature the EU as a major theme outside Australian contexts, consistent with its use of international sources in the television coverage but somewhat at odds with its high employment of local sources in the press.

It is suggested that the frequent positioning of an issue as foreign news without a national 'hook'[49] to ground the issue in the domestic discourse alienates that issue from the immediate interests of the intended news audience. Foreign news is thus rendered as information about 'worlds out of sight, out of mind and out of touch'.[50] Arguably that was the message sent to their respective audiences by the media frames dominating both Pacific television and the Australian and Asian newspapers in our study. Conversely, the newsmakers' strategy of 'localizing' the EU promotes the image of the Union as a partner whose development has a major and direct impact on domestic affairs. This meaning was arguably transmitted by the media framing of the EU in the New Zealand newspapers and on Asian television. With newspapers targeting, as they do, an older, more educated, cosmopolitan audience, as well as national elites, and with the television targeting a much broader demographic (and a greater proportion of that audience since most people watch the whole of a news bulletin but skim papers for news they are interested in), the respective splits in the media imagery potentially triggers splits in the EU imagery amongst the general public and national elites (something explored/identified in Chapters 3–7).

News room insights

This study of EU media representations has focused on two media in the Asia-Pacific, namely, print (newspapers) and broadcast (television), which some claim to be in a state of competition with each other and other media. Evidence of this fierce competition between media to attract and secure an audience is said by Postman to be found in the declining and ageing audience *reading* newspapers, a trend which has emerged as the number of younger people *watching* the news on television has grown.[51] To complicate the situation, currently, the new medium of the internet challenges the dominance of the 'old media' triad of newspapers, radio and television.[52]

Other researchers have developed the 'media war'[53] argument further, stating that despite inherent animosity and the ongoing battle for audiences, media exist in an 'ecological system'.[54] In this system, when media compete with each other, 'each medium tends to seek out its own *niches*'.[55] This search for niche markets becomes apparent when we consider the two media under investigation in this study – newspapers and television – as each 'favour[s] different cognitive skills and habits'.[56] Gozzi argues that the print media features such characteristics as being still, unmoving and silent; it is full of abstract symbols in which meaning comes from convention and it is a medium that employs the connection of logic and reason. By contrast, the electronic media (including television) is moving, active, and noisy; it is full of concrete symbols with iconic relationships to the object. The meaning of those symbols comes from associations with particular contexts. Hence television is a medium that carries connections of narrative and drama.[57]

Our study argues that the representations of the EU in two different media demonstrated the process of 'securing' informational niches in the 'ecological system' of the media environment. We found that, within the same monitored period, the framings of the EU in two different media resembled a 'connected vessel', each balancing the information on an important international actor in an almost mirrored reflection. The first example of these 'reflections' and 'balancing acts' was found in the volume of EU representations. The Asia-Pacific newspapers presented a much heavier flow of EU news than did the primetime television news broadcasts, which featured a significantly lower number of EU news items per month and per outlet. This observation is primarily explained by the very nature of newspapers – a medium with greater space and time advantages – which allows newspaper editors and staff greater capacity for producing a variety of news items, whereas television news is far more limited in time and space. According to Cohen, the press is 'an atlas of places, personages, situations, and events; … an atlas of policy possibilities, alternatives, choices', a medium that is able to convey the 'full range of the political phenomena'.[58] A medium of this nature is one suitable for informing the public about the multi-layered developments of the EU as a case of an unprecedented international reality. Since, as a medium, television focuses primarily on narrative and drama, it came as no surprise that EU news was often overlooked by television news producers because EU news often lacks a compelling story to be told, it has unknown features and diverse actors, and depicts events that are complex, non-sensational and seemingly irrelevant to the local audiences. One Thai television newsmaker interviewed during the course of the APP project summed this notion up succinctly:

> Priorities are given to issues with impact on Thailand. And since we're television people, I tell my staff to put emphasis on images. Sometimes, the content may not relate to Thailand but it can get into our news bulletin because it's interesting or has interesting images, like something eventful, cute, colorful or of human interest.[59]

Australian television news editors, while not so overt about the emphasis placed on images, corroborated the need for audience relevance: 'Well, I suppose, for us it gets back to the significance of it for the EU as an institution, the relevance for Australia and our audiences in Australia.'[60]

A second example of the two investigated news media seeking safe 'informational niches' was observed on a finer, content-related, level. According to the findings, in almost every country in the sample, the two media were 'off-beat' with each other in terms of distribution of foci of domesticity and 'complementary' to each other in terms of distribution of degrees of centrality of the EU images (with exception of Australia). In the Pacific case, while the New Zealand newspaper representations of the EU had a tendency to profile the EU in a local context mentioning it as a minor or secondary reference, the New Zealand television news bulletins framed the EU as a main theme in the EU context. The reverse was true in the Asian case, that is, Thai and South Korean newspapers preferred to portray the EU as a major topic in the EU context, while their television counterparts cast the EU as a minor theme predominantly in the domestic context. Both Australian media under observation echoed each other's representations and tended to depict the EU as a major theme in an outside context. Arguably, in this case we observe a 'resonance' effect in media interactions which may result in multiplied support for a peculiar political imagery that is disseminated via the news media.

By applying specific accents in their framing of the EU, the two different media discourses constructed images of the Union unique to their particular medium and 'tailored' for their specific consumers' cognitive habits and skills. It might be argued that the survival strategies employed by media to secure informational 'niches' provides audience members who access more than one medium with more or less balanced representations of the EU. However, should audience members tend to access just one medium as a source of news, then the peculiar framings of that medium are likely to be uncontested. As a result, an intensified 'niche' market may have 'serious implications for the kind of informed citizens that we would want'.[61] Considering a universal trend towards declining readerships and reduced circulation numbers for press, as well as the reported tendency in the Asia-Pacific region of obtaining information on the EU primarily from television newscasts,[62] it seems that the television media frames of the EU will be more pervasive for the general public in the region. However, based on the extremely low numbers of EU portrayals on primetime television news, it seems fair to suggest that the EU is a virtually invisible partner for lay people in the Asia-Pacific. Given the extent of the historic and contemporary ties between this region and the EU, such a finding is of concern, not only for the EU, but also for policy-makers in the Asia-Pacific. One of the key roles which the news media occupy is that of global 'map-maker'; drawing an effective and operational political map of the world.[63] Thus, if it suffers from a lack of representation in the news media, a foreign policy event, for all intents and purposes, effectively did not 'take place' as far as the audience is concerned, and the foreign policy actor remains unappreciated in the eyes of the general public. Indeed, as has been noted, 'if something does not appear on television, it does not exist'.[64]

The bitter fighting between media and outlets over precious and fickle audience loyalties has been triggered by what Habermas labelled the 'commodification' of news media; the dominance of a commercial orientation amongst media outlets to sell news by any means.[65] This commercial imperative pushes newsmakers to work against time and for maximum profit. As a result, several commentators have observed a decline in high-quality journalism, especially in the field of foreign news reporting.[66] In an environment of tough competition, international news is the first in line to lose editorial funding or to be eliminated altogether. A lack of foreign news resources generally, and for EU news specifically, was noted by regional newsmakers to be a factor limiting EU news output. Additionally, there had been a recent downsizing of Europe-based news bureaux, as one Australian television newsmaker lamented:

> We used to have a bureau in Brussels which covered Western Europe. That was closed a couple of years back for budget reasons which was a great shame ... we've shifted most of our ... coverage [that was] done in Brussels to the London bureau. We've put a small amount of additional resources into the London bureau to try to do that but it's obviously not anywhere near the kind of coverage we had both with the dedicated bureau in Brussels with dedicated staff looking at European affairs and also the fact of being on the ground on the continent.[67]

Such was the extent of this 'downsizing' that, across the four Asia-Pacific countries, none of media outlets monitored now had Brussels-based news quarters. As a result, even the most well-resourced outlets of the twenty-eight surveyed in this study relied on thinly spread and overstretched correspondents based operating out of the UK or France. The less well-resourced outlets relied on local authors, the international wire services, and syndicated material from other outlets with reputable and extensive international affairs coverage (including *The Times*, *Independent*, *Los Angeles Times*, *Washington Post*, *The Economist*). In many cases, the local authors were neither Europe/EU specialists, nor devoted solely to European affairs, while the foreign correspondents are expected to cover half the globe. As one Australian news producer bemoaned, '[With just three correspondents] it's impossible to cover [Europe] properly'.[68] Therefore, both local and foreign journalists become jacks of all trades, masters of none.

The challenge of quality foreign news production, generally the most expensive and time-consuming stories to produce, is met with an additional challenge – the decline in foreign news consumption.[69] Unless foreign news presents a sensational, dramatic or even tragic event and/or involves celebrities, news outlets are more inclined to include stories with a domestic twist. Recognizing this, our study expected to observe a low volume of EU news, since news relating to this unconventional international actor tends to be of the variety that is unpalatable to typical news consumers, namely peaceful, complex and concerning a very distant decision-making reality. Even in the print medium, which, as discussed, is able to devote greater detail and depth to subjects, EU representations were superseded by those of other significant foreign counterparts to the Asia-Pacific such as the US.

Asia was also considered by newsmakers in the four countries to be a more relevant 'Other' for domestic audiences than the EU and therefore was devoted more attention.[70] According to one Australian reporter, media outlets were 'far more likely to spend money and dedicate resources to an Asia-Pacific issue rather than an EU issue'.[71] In the case of Thailand, it was explained that this was because 'EU news seems to hardly relate to Thai people'.[72] This point was reiterated by an Australian television news editor who argued that:

> There's always a balance … between what the program demands back here because our programs back here for news and current affairs are almost entirely a mixture of national, domestic and international coverage so we don't have a program that's always crying out for just European coverage. And that has to be balanced on the news and current affairs agenda and requirements each day.[73]

New Zealand newsmakers also commented on this increasing Asian importance, but noted that even Asia was not their primary foreign news focus, and that Europe was definitely considered well down the priority list:

> American foreign policy … tends to be a major focus … and then yes, Trans-Tasman. Then, I think there's an increasing … sort of awareness in two areas – Pacific and Asia, particularly South East Asia, then after that … perhaps you've got Europe.[74]

This was also the case for the print media. For this reason, none of the media elites interviewed in this study believed that EU coverage was likely to increase; rather, further decline was predicted.[75]

Conclusions

While this study accepts that news audiences do not passively consume and accept meanings proposed by news discourses, certain forms of media discourse do have a stronger persuasive power than others, and foreign news is one of those forms. As foreign policy-making is a prerogative of a selected and limited group of national elites, and with foreign affairs being out of the immediate reach of the majority of populations, foreign news is often an uncontested source of information for the general public.[76] Foreign news representations in domestic discourses may therefore influence what people see as the most important information about foreign affairs and policy-making, and thus influence people's 'mental representations' of distant and foreign international partners.[77]

Despite the noted differences between the Asian and the Pacific cases in the fine-tuning of EU news content, the twenty reputable newspapers and eight national television broadcasts from the four Asia-Pacific countries presented a coherent and specific vision of the EU overall. These media discourses framed the EU predominantly as a political actor undertaking specific and targeted actions, yet the foreground of this framing was occupied by the EU's individual components (such as the Member States and their leaders and institutions), often obscuring the EU as a whole. Arguably, a push for narrative and drama (even in the print medium due to increased competition for audience attention) dictates a need to pinpoint 'leads' who are familiar to the public worldwide, who act in a dramatic and sometimes scandalous manner, and who are willing to be in the spotlight of media attention. In a mediated world which favours fame and glory, the EU officials and institutions have not yet become international political 'celebrities' to the same extent that some EU Members States and their leaders have. This representation does not necessarily indicate EU disunity though – perhaps merely evidence of the very nature of the EU decision-making processes. In politics, for example, it was observed that Member State actors are primed, but then they are the primary actors involved in that sphere of EU action because it is an intergovernmental 'pillar' of European integration. It is also possible that the prominence of Member States actually indicates a lack of understanding of the EU's complex political reality by international newsmakers, or a tendency on their part to assume that their readers and viewers will only understand Member State actors and not the Community ones. Yet, this newsroom practice may mean a vicious cycle for the international media representations of the EU. The more newsmakers portray only the Member State components, the more the public will come to view the EU only in this fragmented way and the more newsmakers will have to prioritize such images in the future in order to retain their audiences' interest.

News reports of economic actions of the EU surprisingly did not lead the coverage of the EU in 2004 in Asia-Pacific region. This trend could be an exception which has occurred due to a heavy share of political events in the EU's life in 2004 – a thought that indicates the need for consistent longitudinal analysis of the EU imagery in the region. However, the detected media imagery could also possibly indicate a changing perception of the EU as a unity becoming more visible around the world as a political actor. It is worth stressing that, in contrast to the political framing, the economic framing of the EU featured more frequent images of Community actors and not Member State ones. The EU's economic prowess stems from its Community approach and its Community competence with regard to all things trade and economy within the Union – whether it is at the WTO or negotiating trading agreements with its foreign partners, the EU acts as one in the sphere of economics and this unity appeared to spill over into the representations of this area of EU action in the Asia-Pacific media.

Finally, the representations of the EU as an actor in the social sphere (both inside and outside the EU) commanded the least attention of newsmakers despite the obvious appeal of topics related to 'human interest'. It is worth noting that the EU's actions in the developmental and environmental affairs were even less visible in the news reports across the four countries. Due to a low volume and extreme diversity in topics, the media images failed to produce a cohesive picture of the EU as an entity with a 'human face', adding to a certain cognitive confusion on behalf of the Asia-Pacific audiences.

The repercussions of such imagery for public opinion (which is heavily influenced by television) and elite opinion (partially shaped by newspapers) are of consequence to both the Asia-Pacific and the EU. The fact that the EU is framed (albeit infrequently) in the popular medium of television in a manner which creates validity for it as a political actor in the world is significant and may lead both regions – the EU and the Asia-Pacific – to a positive shift in public stereotypes and also a shift towards a shared sense of positive action by citizens within the EU. Yet the relative invisibility of the EU on primetime television in the region is potentially detrimental to the international profile and awareness of the newly reshaped Europe. Such media framing may lead Asia-Pacific actors to possibly overlook important future connections with the EU as it continues to grow in international importance.

Notes

1 P. Putnis, J. Penhallurick and M. Bourk, 'The Pattern of International News in Australia's Mainstream Media', *Australian Journalism Review* 22 (2000), 14.
2 See e.g. M. McCombs and D. Shaw, 'The Agenda-Setting Function of Mass Media', *Public Opinion Quarterly* 36 (1972), 176–85; M. McCombs and D. Shaw (eds), *The Emergence of American Political Issues: The Agenda Setting Function of the Press*, St Paul, MN, West Publishing Co., 1977, pp. 69–87; D. Shaw and S. Martin, 'The Function of Mass Media Agenda Setting', *Journalism Quarterly* 69 (1992), 902–20; J. McLeod, L. Becker and J. Byrnes, 'Another Look at the Agenda Setting Function of the Press', *Communication Research* 1 (1974), 131–66; M. McCombs, 'The Evolution of Agenda-Setting Research: Twenty-Five Years in The Market Place of Ideas', *Journal of Communication* 43 (1993), 58–67.
3 This was confirmed by the findings of the public survey conducted as part of this project (and reported in Chapters 3–5). Approximately 81 per cent of survey respondents said that they accessed news media on a weekly (or more frequent) basis for international news.
4 N. Gavin, *The Economy, Media and Public Knowledge*, Leicester, Leicester University Press, 1998, p. 357.
5 J. Galtung and M. Ruge, 'The Structure of Foreign News', *Journal of Peace Research* 2 (1965), 64.
6 P. Norris, M. Kern and M. Just, 'Framing Terrorism', in P. Norris, M. Kern and M. Just (eds), *Framing Terrorism: The News Media, the Government and the Public*, New York, Routledge, 2003, p. 11.
7 J. Tankard, L. Hendrikson, J. Silberman, K. Bliss and S. Ghanem, 'Media Frames: Approaches to Contextualization and Measurement', paper presented at the meeting of the Association for Education in Journalism and Mass Communication, Boston, 1991, p. 3.
8 M. Siamak, 'The Social Psychology of Foreign Policy and the Politics of International Images', *Human Affairs* 8 (1985), 19.
9 *Ibid.*, p. 20.
10 See A. Sreberny-Mohammadi *et al.* (eds), 'Foreign News in Media: International Reporting in 29 Countries', *Reports and Papers on Mass Communication*, 93, Paris, UNESCO, 1985.
11 N. Chaban, K. Stats, S.N. Kim and P. Sutthisripok, 'When Enough is Enough? Dynamics of the EU Representations in Asia-Pacific Print Media', *Asia-Pacific Journal of EU Studies* 2 (2004), 191.
12 Sreberny-Mohammadi, 'Foreign News', p. 10.
13 J. Brand, D. Archbold and H. Rane, *Sources of News* and *Current Affairs – Stage Two: The Audience*, Australian Broadcasting Authority, 2001, available <http://www.aba.gov.au/newspubs/radio_TV/documents_research/news_ca.pdf> (Accessed 27 April 2004).
14 M. Robinson and A. Kohut, 'Believability and the Press', *Public Opinion Quarterly* 52 (1988), 184.

15 J. Blumler and D. Kavanagh, 'The Third Age of Political Communication: Influences and Features', *Political Communication* 16 (1999), 218.
16 See e.g. G. Stempel and T. Hargrove, 'Mass Media Audiences in a Changing Media Environment', *Journalism and Mass Communication* 73 (1996), 549–58; R. Mulgan, *Politics in New Zealand*, Auckland, Auckland University Press, 2004.
17 W. Shulz, 'Foreign News in Leading Newspapers of Western and Post-Communist Countries', paper presented at the 51st Annual Conference of the International Communication Association, Washington, DC, 2001.
18 J. Bain, 'The Power of Television News: Images of the EU Asia-Pacific Broadcast Media', paper presented at the 2nd Asia-Pacific EU Studies Association Conference, University of Canterbury, Christchurch, New Zealand, 9–11 September 2004.
19 The UNESCO study (see Srebemy-Mohammadi, 'Foreign News', p. 14) limited their search for international news to the general news pages and excluded all specialized sections including finance, fashion and travel, etc. as well as any special reports which resulted in an over-representation of international news by political affairs and political actors and the under-representation of the total amount international news.
20 See Sreberny-Mohammadi, 'Foreign News'; J. Peter, H. Semetko and C. de Vreese, 'EU Politics on Television News', *European Union Politics* 4 (2003); D. Kevin, *Europe in the Media*, London, Lawrence Erlbaum Associates, 2003.
21 Placement of the news items in the paper or news bulletin and the length of the articles (characteristics used in the media content analysis disused in the research by Peter *et al.*, 'EU Politics on Television News') were accounted and presented in other publications of APP project team (see Appendix II in this volume). They are not included in the presented analysis of this chapter.
22 W. R. Neuman, M. Just and A. Crigler, *Common Knowledge: News and the Construction of Political Meaning*, Chicago, IL, University of Chicago Press, 1992, p. 3.
23 Kevin, *Europe in the Media*.
24 The *focus of domesticity* of news used in this paper is also similar to the 'concept of domesticity of EU stories' used by Peter *et al.*, 'EU Politics on Television News', and the 'domestic or European' focus used by C. de Vreese, *Framing Europe: Television News and European Integration*, Amsterdam, Aksant, 2003. See also Shulz, 'Foreign News in Leading Newspapers'. The other studies of the data within the APP project additionally focused on the character of the news or its news value as well as the journalistic attitudes (see Appendix II).
25 The characteristic of evaluation (suggested by Peter *et al.*, 'EU Politics on Television News') was excluded from the presented chapter. For the purposes of this study, evaluations were believed to be very subjective whereas the other criteria are fairly objective. Nevertheless, evaluations assigned to the EU imagery were discussed in other publications of the APP project team (see Appendix II), and additionally, evaluations are considered in Chapter 2 of this volume.
26 When the same type of search was conducted in the sampled Australian newspapers for the first three months of the period of analysis, the single search term 'United States' was detected in over 10 times as many articles. See K. Stats, 'Reading Europe: Representations of the European Union in the Australian Media', *La Trobe Forum*, 25, Political Science Society, La Trobe University, 2005, p. 22.
27 The Generalized System of Tariff Preferences (GSP) is a scheme under which the EU will grant trade preferences, in form of either duty-free access or a tariff reduction, to certain products imported from beneficiary developing countries. The GSP preference on certain products can be withdrawn, however, under certain circumstances such as an increase in market share. The withdrawal of GSP has become a source of tension between the EU and Thailand.
28 E. Taira, 'Foreign News in New Zealand's Metropolitan Press', unpublished MA thesis, University of Canterbury, 2003, p. 117.
29 Pairat Pongpanit, *Matichon* foreign editor, interviewed in Bangkok, June 2005.

30 Neal Wallace, an NZ newspaper editor, panel discussion 'EU and Dialogue Between Peoples and Cultures: Seeing the EU through the Eyes of Others', Te Papa, Wellington, New Zealand, 25 November 2005

31 D. Guttenplan, 'Britain: Dumb and Dumber? A Transatlantic Spat over the Quality of the "Quality Press"', *Columbia Journalism Review* (1997), 18–19.

32 W. Owen, 'Fairfax Man in his Comfort Zone', *Independent* (3 December 2003), 26; Fairfax Holdings Ltd, *Fairfax Annual Report 2004*, Sydney, Fairfax, 2004, p. 18.

33 I. Manners and R. Whitman, 'Towards Identifying the International Identity of the European Union: A Framework for Analysis of the EU's Network of Relationships', *Journal of European Integration* 21 (1998), 237.

34 The EU's overall GDP exceeds that of the United States, however, on a per capita basis, the US GDP still remains higher. See S. Chantry, *The European Union and World Trade: Basic Statistics on European Union Trade. Comparisons with the United States, Japan and Regional Trading Areas*, Communications and Public Affairs Section, European Commission Delegation, Washington, DC, June 2004. Available <http://www.eurunion.org/profile/EUUSStats.pdf> (Accessed 14 May 2006).

35 P. Mazzocchi, 'EU Expansion: Increased Trade or Increased Trouble', Speech at EU Business Lunch to Commemorate the Netherlands Presidency of the European Union, 7 July 2004, organized by the Consulate of the Netherlands and the EC Delegation, Melbourne.

36 European Commission (2002) *The EU's Relations with Australia: Overview*, available <http://ec.europa.eu/comm/external_relations/australia/intro/index.htm> (Accessed 23 March 2004); Department of Foreign Affairs and Trade, Market Information and Analysis Section, Australian Government, *Australia's Trade with the European Union*, 2004.

37 European Commission, *The European Union and New Zealand: An Overview*. Available <http://www.delaus.cec.eu.int/newzealand/EU_NZ_relations/EU_New_Zealand_Overview.htm> (Accessed 4 June 2007).

38 European Commission, *The European Union and Thailand: An Overview*. Available <http://www.deltha.ec.europa.eu/Thailand/thailand_overview.htm> (accessed 4 June 2007).

39 European Commission, *The European and the Republic of Korea*. Available <http://ec.europa.eu/external_relations/south_korea/intro/index.htm> (Accessed 31 July 2004).

40 Brad Jones, 'The EU and Public Opinion in the Asia-Pacific', in N. Chaban and M. Holland (eds), *The EU through the Eyes of the Asia Pacific: Public Perceptions and Media Representations*, NCRE Research Series, 4, Christchurch, National Centre for Research on Europe, 2004, pp. 7–62.

41 Delegación de La Comisión Europea (Bolivia), *The European Union: A Global Player*. Available <http://www.delbol.ec.europa.eu/sp/eu_global_player/4.htm> (Accessed 11 January 2007).

42 'Trade 2004', a statement by Mark Vaile, Minister for Trade, Australian Government, Department of Foreign Affairs and Trade, 2004, p. 50.

43 Jones, 'The EU and Public Opinion'.

44 C. de Vreese, S. Banducci, H. Semetko and H. Boomgaarden, 'The News Coverage of the 2004 European Parliamentary Elections Campaign in 25 Countries', *European Union Politics* 7 (2006), 477–504.

45 See e.g. M. Holland and N. Chaban, 'The EU through the Eyes of Asia: a Comparative Study of Media Perceptions and Public Opinion in 2006', available <http://esia.asef.org/FeatureArticles.htm#2ndinterim> (Accessed 4 June 2007).

46 P. Shoemaker and S. Reese, *Mediating the Message: Theories of Influences on Mass Media Content*, 2nd edn, White Plains, NY, Longman, 1995.

47 M. Doidge, 'East is East: Inter- and Transregionalism and the EU–ASEAN Relationship', thesis for Doctor of Philosophy in Political Science, University of Canterbury, New Zealand, 2004.

48 The other two groups are Australian Provincial Newspapers (APN) and the Rural Press group. See Ketupa.net, 'Media Profiles: Australia', available <www.ketupa.net/australia.htm> (Accessed 10 November 2006).

49 Kevin, *Europe in the Media*.

50 W. Lippmann, *Public Opinion*, New York, Harcourt, 1922, p. 29.

51 N. Postman, *Technopoly*, New York, Vintage, 1993.

52 A. Shin, 'Newspaper Circulation Continues to Decline: Internet, Cable Cited as Competition', *Washington Post* (3 May 2005).

53 *Ibid.*

54 R. Gozzi, *The Power of Metaphor in the Age of Electronic Media*, Cresskill, NJ, Hampton Press, 1999, p. 44.

55 *Ibid.*

56 *Ibid.*, p. 97.

57 *Ibid.*, p. 26.

58 B. Cohen, *The Press and Foreign Policy*, Princeton, NJ, Princeton University Press, 1963, p. 13.

59 Nares Prabtong, news editor, TV News1, interviewed in Bangkok, June 2005.

60 Rowan Callick, Asia Pacific editor, *Australian Financial Review*, interviewed in Melbourne, 7 June 2005.

61 J. Tully, cited in J. Black, 'Read All about it!', *Listener* (26 August–1 September 2006), 14.

62 Chaban and Holland (eds), *The EU through the Eyes of the Asia Pacific*, p.48.

63 Cohen, *The Press*, pp. 12–13.

64 A. Stille, 'Italy: The Family Business', *New York Review of Books* (9 October 2003), 25.

65 J. Habermas, *The Structural Transformation of the Public Sphere: An Inquiry into the Category of Bourgeois Society*, Cambridge, MA, Cambridge University Press, 1989.

66 See e.g. M. Anning, 'Missing the EU Story', *CESAA Review* 32 (2004), 4–5.

67 Tony Hill, head of international coverage, ABC News, interviewed in Sydney, 17 June 2005.

68 *Ibid.*

69 C. Moisy, 'Myths of the Global Information Village' *Foreign Policy* 107 (1997), available <http://search.epnet.com.ezproxy.canterbury.ac.nz/login.aspx?direct=true&db=anh&an=9708190354> (Accessed 21 July 2006). Other observers (e.g. R. Rieder, 'Ripples of September 11: And what they Mean for Journalism', *American Journalism Review* 24 (2002), 6) communicate a cautious optimism that September 11, a 'dreadful reminder of how interconnected the world really is', has also resuscitated the notion that what goes on in the rest of the world might well be worth knowing about. Results from a survey among 218 editors of US newspapers indicated that some 95 per cent of editors said reader interest in foreign news increased after September 11, and 78 per cent said their space for foreign news had increased. (S. Seplow, 'Closer to Home: Long Related to the Margins, Foreign News has Experienced a Modest Resurgence since September 11. But Much of the Coverage has Focused on the War on Terrorism and the Middle East. Will the Blackout Return After the Crises Ebb?', *American Journalism Review* 24 (2002), 20). Arguably, trends observed in foreign news in the US are at least partially applicable to other countries, since the shocking event of September 11 did spur interest to international news worldwide. Although it is not likely to become chronically weak again in the foreseeable future, the dominant expectation among journalists and scholars of communication is that the recent upsurge in interest towards the international news will eventually wane (T. Ginsberg, 'Rediscovering the World: September 11 Showed All Too Clearly what

a Terrible Mistake it was for America's News Media to Largely Ignore Foreign News', *American Journalism Review* 24 (2002), 48–53).

70 M. Holland, N. Chaban, K. Stats, J. Bain and P. Sutthisripok, *EU in the Views of Asia-Pacific Elites: Australia, New Zealand and Thailand*, NCRE, December 2005.

71 Emma McDonald, political reporter, *Canberra Times*, interviewed in Canberra, 15 August 2005.

72 Nares Prabtong, news editor, TV News1, interviewed in Bangkok, June 2005.

73 Tony Hill, head of international coverage, ABC News, interviewed in Sydney, 17 June 2005.

74 Mark Jennings, director of news, TV3, interviewed in Auckland, 20 July 2005.

75 Holland *et al.*, *EU in the Views of Asia-Pacific Elites.*

76 Cohen, *The Press*, pp. 12–13.

77 T. van Dijk, 'Principles of Critical Discourse Analysis', in M. Wetherell, S. Taylor and S. J. Yates (eds), *Discourse Theory and Practice: A Reader*, London, Sage, 2001, p. 358.

2 The European Union in Metaphors

Images of the EU Enlargement in the Asia-Pacific News

Natalia Chaban, Jessica Bain,
Katrina Stats, Paveena Sutthisripok
and Yoon Ah Choi

Introduction

Constant transformations of the global environment are often associated with complex, distant, and sometimes seemingly irrelevant concepts of international politics, making these already challenging events even more confusing and difficult for the general public to grasp. The European Union (EU) is the epitome of constant change and transformation. Once perceived as an exclusive Western European 'club', the EU was rendered almost unrecognizable by the addition of ten new members, including eight Eastern European ex-communist countries, in 2004. Yet, even this new profile was only transitory; in January 2007, the Union opened its doors to two new members, Bulgaria and Romania and it continues to look east- and southwards, contemplating the possibility of accession for the Muslim state of Turkey, for the Balkan states of Croatia, Serbia, Bosnia and Herzegovina, Montenegro, and Albania, and for the former Soviet states of Ukraine, Moldova, Georgia, Armenia, and Azerbaijan.

Indeed, such is the complexity of the EU's constant evolution that average European citizens know very little about the Union to which they belong, apart from what they read in the press or see on the television news.[1] Such a lack of understanding creates a gap between the EU and its citizens. The resulting democratic shortfall has been acknowledged by the Union and attempts have and are being made to address this issue as it is perceived to undermine the EU's legitimacy. Legitimacy, though, is not only internally generated, but is also reflected in the way the polity is perceived by its external interlocutors.[2] Unsurprisingly, the Union's changing profile is even more challenging to comprehend when viewed from the outside. Since the majority of information on the EU in the Asia-Pacific – the EU's 'Other' that is the focus of this book – comes from the news media (see also Chapters 3-5),[3] radical 'makeovers' such as the 2004 enlargement, the event under investigation here, must be presented to news consumers in a skilful and efficient manner. The newsmakers' goal is to ensure that the international publics are able to comprehend, and keep pace with, the ongoing transformation of Europe and, indeed, the global geopolitical configuration.

The very different backgrounds and political contexts of the four Asia-Pacific nations participating in this project – Australia, New Zealand, South Korea and Thailand – dictated divergent approaches for dealing with the EU's fifth enlargement in 2004. In Australia, the enlargement was cautiously welcomed. Despite speculating on how Europe's "ambitious agenda…[would] impinge upon Australia's interests" and suggesting that Australia must be "an alert and active" partner of the EU,[4] the Australian government officially expressed its support of the fifth enlargement, observing the positive achievement of the rapid and successful transitions of the ten new Member States to democratically-governed market economies, and the symbolic healing of Cold War rifts that was facilitated by the development and expansion of the Union.[5] A "strong and united Europe"[6] was seen as providing an opportunity to more effectively tackle problems of increasing importance to Australia and its citizens that escape the jurisdiction of the nation-state alone, particularly, terrorism and security, trade and the international drug market; areas "where Australia's interest are strongly engaged"[7] and intertwined with those of the EU.

The New Zealand government predicted that the enlargement would have important consequences for New Zealand's interests in Europe, and New Zealand's relations with the EU.[8] One of the main concerns was "the risk that the EU would be heavily preoccupied with internal concerns, and that it would be harder to make New Zealand's voice heard."[9] To face this challenge, the government worked hard to create new links with the new Member States.[10] These efforts are reflected in the opening of New Zealand's Embassy in Warsaw which has responsibility for New Zealand's relations with Poland and three other EU newcomers – the Baltic nations of Estonia, Latvia and Lithuania. Commenting on Poland's 2004 entry into the EU, New Zealand Prime Minister Helen Clark stated that membership in the EU means that the new member countries now operate from within a system with which New Zealand is very familiar.[11] Ms Clark expressed her confidence in the stimulation of new trade and investment links between New Zealand and the new Member States of the EU; trade and investment being the areas where New Zealand's interests in the EU are the most focused.

South Korea's official attitude towards the recent enlargement of the EU was optimistic. The enlargement boosted EU economic interests in South Korea by providing opportunities for new markets in Europe for South Korean products, and there was a positive outlook on strengthening economic and trade relations between the two regions. According to Ban Ki-Moon, the South Korean Minister of Foreign Affairs and Trade, since the EU is South Korea's largest foreign investor, the 2004 EU enlargement would only "generate further momentum and reasons for Korea to expand cooperation in every field."[12] In addition to the largely economically-fuelled support for the 2004 enlargement, South Korea also supported the event because of its concerns for maintaining a peaceful and secure relationship with North Korea, and because the EU plays a key role in securing such stability.[13]

From the Thai point of view, the 2004 EU enlargement was viewed with greater ambivalence than it was in the other three countries of this study. On the one hand, the enlarged EU market presented new opportunities for Thai exports, comprising mainly of agricultural and processed food products, to reach new markets in Central and Eastern Europe. On the other hand, the new Member States directly compete with Thai products in a number of sectors, especially in manufacturing and processed foods. It was acknowledged though, that the effects of enlargement on these Thai trade sectors would be more gradual than sudden, since the candidate countries were already very well integrated with the Common Market by the time of their entry in May 2004.[14] Aside from trade, the enlargement was viewed as having few political consequences for Thai–EU relations. Thailand enjoys good relations with all the new Member States, except on the contentious issue of Myanmar which has clouded EU–ASEAN relations for over a decade.[15]

Research Questions

While Chapter 1 used a news item as the unit of analysis, this Chapter focuses on a sentence as the respective unit, in order to provide a more detailed and comprehensive insight into media content. To attain a better understanding of the meanings assigned by the international media to the EU, this study attempted an intensive and panoramic view of the metaphorical categorizations used to describe EU enlargement. Metaphors in news are seen here as vivid and compelling means, able to implicitly influence an audience's awareness and image of, and attitudes towards, important international counterparts. Specifically, a relatively novel tool of content analysis was employed – conceptual metaphors (discussed below). Conceptual metaphors are believed to be instrumental in the studies of foreign news discourses when these introduce unknown and unfamiliar concepts,[16] and thus provide the opportunity to 'probe below the surface of the text'.[17] Adopting an intertextual approach in the analysis allowed a comprehensive view on the process of aggregated meaning construction through the use of metaphors in news texts, explicating country-specific strategies within texts.

In addition, this chapter seeks to contrast and evaluate the metaphorical categorizations of the EU's largest enlargement as profiled in the daily news of four of the EU's distant partners, when compared from the point of EU news 'domestication'. The 'domestication' of foreign news is a newsmakers' strategy which attempts to ground a portion of international news in the domestic discourse, thus bringing the 'foreign' closer to home and indicating the immediate consequences of international developments for local audiences.[16] In the competitive world of news media, competition exists not only between different media (as discussed in Chapter 1), but also between news items in those media. 'Hard' political international news must vie with domestic news, other international news, and the ever-flashy 'soft' sports and entertainment news for space and coverage. To ensure that international news about any global actor, including the EU, survives such a struggle, newsmakers often resort to this strategy of 'domesticating foreign news. Although this strategy risks overlooking international developments that have no obvious connection to the domestic discourses, it provides a means of raising the visibility and salience of a country's Others for local audiences.[17] It has been observed that the predominance of this 'home news abroad' style of news reportage in part,

> reflects specific journalistic attempts to create national relevance (often at the expense of other perhaps more important news values) and to make international news more palatable, i.e. more meaningful and assimilable for home audiences by building in frequently weak and sometimes irrelevant connections to domestic issues. However, 'own country' concern may indeed be seen as a useful learning and even politicizing device.[18]

This study of metaphorical categorizations employed by the Asia-Pacific news media to describe EU enlargement was thus guided by three research questions:

RQ1   What images of the enlarging EU surface in the dominant metaphorical categorizations in the four Asia-Pacific countries when reporting EU enlargement from a *local* perspective?

RQ2   What images of the enlarging EU surface in the dominant metaphorical categorizations in the four Asia-Pacific countries when reporting EU enlargement from *outside* the domestic context?

RQ3   What pragmatic and ideological implications are apparent from the dominant metaphorical categorizations of EU enlargement in the Asia-Pacific media discourses (if compared from the point of news 'domestication')?

Theoretical Framework

Theories investigating the phenomenon of metaphors have abounded. In the production of meaning, metaphors appear to be an important element, since people frequently employ metaphors to make sense of the world and communicate their individual conceptions to others by contrasting new experiences against existing knowledge.[19] In addition to their use in everyday conception, various empirical studies have also shown the importance of metaphors in the political realm.[20]

This chapter employs the cognitive model of conceptual metaphor which illustrates how people process new phenomena by applying existing, known concepts to the unknown; in the words of Lakoff and Johnson, the "essence of metaphor is seen in understanding and experiencing one kind of thing in terms of another."[21] Usually a relatively abstract or inherently unstructured subject matter (the *target*) is understood in terms of a more concrete or, at least, a more highly structured subject matter (the *source*) (See Figure 2.1).[22] For example, the abstract subject of TIME (*target*) is often understood in terms of the very concrete subject matter of MONEY (*source*): "You are *wasting* my time," "This gadget will *save* you hours," "How do you *spend* time these days?" or "I've *invested* a lot of time in her," etc.[23] The conceptual mapping that is applied to any given

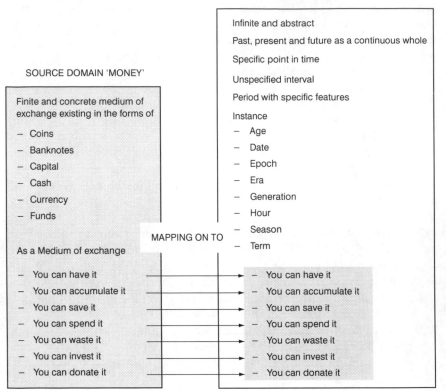

Figure 2.1 Metaphorical mapping

source–target pairing produces a *conceptual metaphor* – in the example above it was the conceptual metaphor TIME IS MONEY.

This study distinguished between *conceptual* and *linguistic* metaphors, also respectively referred to as *deep* and *surface* metaphors.[24] The *conceptual* (*deep*) metaphors are described as "super-ordinate, epistemic and semantic mappings."[25] The *linguistic* (*surface*) ones are seen as being "motivated by conceptual metaphors and are the realisations that appear in everyday written and spoken forms."[26] The *conceptual* metaphor, therefore, is a conceptual framework that underlies the *linguistic* metaphor while *linguistic* metaphors are "the main sources of evidence cited for conceptual metaphors."[27]

Several scholars have highlighted the structuring aspect of conceptual metaphors.[28] Through this process of categorization, the relations between numerous surface metaphors produce *clusters* or groups of metaphors that share a similar *source domain*. Systematically identifying clusters of linguistic metaphors in a process of close and sensitive reading is viewed as a gateway to the reconstruction of deep conceptual metaphors and revealing the underlying assumptions inherent to them. The latter underlie the former, providing mental structures to interpret the phenomenon under categorization. The awareness of those conceptual forms and their pragmatic implications provides discourse scholars and critical audiences with a "blueprint, or a ground plan, guiding the discourses,"[29] and enables them to "examine, critique, and suggest alternative ways of looking at the situation."[30]

Data

The data on the media coverage of the 2004 EU enlargement was derived from the content analysis of 20 newspapers and eight prime time newscasts on the most popular television networks in the four countries that was discussed in Chapter 1. In 2004, two significant 'spikes' in EU coverage were observed in both forms of media in the four countries; namely, April–June and October–December. Both peaks in EU reportage were primarily attributable to the topic of enlargement. The first and most significant of these spikes was triggered by the largest and most controversial EU enlargement to date, which took place on 1 May that year. Enlargement coverage was not limited to the actual accession date; the topic was also raised in connection with a number of other prominent associated events accounting for the length of the period of heightened coverage. Preceding the 1 May reportage, there was abundant coverage of the failed referendum to reunite Cyprus in March, an event cast as all the more dramatic, and thus more visible, in the context of Cyprus's eventual accession to the EU, and Turkey's vigorous, though still unrequited, desire to join the European 'club'.[31] In addition, the European Parliament elections in June were frequently discussed in the light of the recent additions to the Union. The second observed spike in EU coverage was also caused by the topic of enlargement, but this time focused on EU discussions about Turkey's membership application in September–October 2004 and the eventful Ukrainian presidential election in December 2004, the so-called 'Orange Revolution', and Ukraine's sudden emergence as a likely candidate for future EU accession. Enlargement was thus both a prominent topic and a consistent theme in the Asia-Pacific media, contributing substantially to the EU's overall visibility in the region. Indeed, it was the most prominent topic in the media discourses of all four countries (see Table 2.1).

The figures shown in Table 2.1 are relatively high considering the short length of the actual event and the number of other significant EU events in 2004 such as the European Parliament elections, the election of a new Commission president,

Table 2.1 Proportion of EU coverage devoted to EU enlargement in 2004 (in %)

	Australia	New Zealand	South Korea	Thailand
Newspapers	9	9	18.8	13.5
Television	33	41	9.5	8.5

Note
Due to a technical problem, Thai television news items during 1–5 May 2004 were missing. It is assumed that the actual percentage of EU enlargement news on monitored Thai television news was higher than is indicated here.

the constitutional debate and terrorist attacks in Madrid, among others, and the significant events in the Asia-Pacific involving or impacting relations with the EU such as the avian flu in the region and the WTO trade talks.

This chapter zooms in on the 'acute' period of the enlargement coverage, a three month period encompassing one month either side of May 2004. While centring in on the actual event, this acute period also includes some of the pre-enlargement promotion as well as some post-celebration analysis. The five Australian newspapers were found to have published 102 news items on the subject of EU enlargement in April–June 2004. In the New Zealand sample, 53 articles were located, 28 in the South Korean sample and 117 in the Thai sample. The television sample contained 5 news items from Australia, 9 from New Zealand, 4 from South Korea, and 2 from Thailand.

In this study, *EU enlargement* is the target concept of the conceptual metaphors. The located metaphors are assumed to be used to interpret concepts and actors that were tightly bound to the system of that time: EU institutions and officials involved in the enlargement process; the pre-enlargement EU-15 (Austria, Belgium, Denmark, Finland, France, Germany, Greece, Ireland, Italy, Luxembourg, Netherlands, Portugal, Spain, Sweden, United Kingdom); the ten enlargement candidates for accession in 2004 (Cyprus, the Czech Republic, Estonia, Hungary, Latvia, Lithuania, Malta, Poland, Slovakia and Slovenia); EU candidates for 2007 accession (Bulgaria and Romania); delayed candidates (Turkey); possible candidates (Croatia, Ukraine, Serbia); and the citizens and policy-makers of those countries.

Four comprehensive sets of metaphoric expressions located in the newspaper texts were compiled: 616 metaphorical instances from Australian newspapers articles covering the various aspects of the EU enlargement, 219 from New Zealand, 167 from South Korea, and 211 from Thailand. A database of 96 metaphorical instances was compiled from the eight television outlets: 31 from the Australian outlets, 36 from New Zealand, 17 from South Korea, and 12 from Thailand.

The EU's fifth enlargement was predominantly discussed in the Asia-Pacific media from two angles. The first reported EU enlargement as being *external* to the Asia-Pacific, either as an event impacting the EU itself or a third party (neither Asia-Pacific nor the EU). The second angle of reporting presented EU enlargement in relation to the monitored countries. The first perspective, a *pure foreign* angle in news reporting, presents information intended to educate the news audience on world affairs and highlights a more cosmopolitan orientation of the media outlet.[32] The second perspective, in which a *local angle* is employed in reporting the EU, is viewed in the relevant literature as that which brings the 'foreign' closer to home and indicates the immediate consequences of international developments for local audiences.[33] Both angles of reporting have different implications and suggest a different set of responses to international events and actors. Since this focus of domesticity is one of the key contextual factors contributing to the framing of important international counterparts in foreign news, the distribution of identified linguistic metaphors according to the angle of reporting the EU in the monitored

Table 2.2 Distribution of identified linguistic metaphors describing EU enlargement in the Asia-Pacific news (according to the angle of reporting), April–June 2004

		Pure foreign angle		Local angle	
		Number of linguistic metaphors	%	Number of linguistic metaphors	%
Newspapers	Australia	481	78	135	22
	New Zealand	192	88	27	12
	South Korea	141	84	26	16
	Thailand	184	875	27	13
Television	Australia	31	100	0	0
	New Zealand	36	75	12	25
	South Korea	17	100	0	0
	Thailand	19	100	0	0

texts is shown in Table 2.2. In all countries, the most visible perspective in framing EU enlargement metaphorically was from a *pure foreign angle*.

Results

Australia: EU enlargement reported from a pure foreign angle

The dominant metaphors in the Australian media depicting the enlargement from a *pure foreign* angle of reporting contained a number of conceptualizations of this historic EU event. Enlargement was often portrayed as problematic, while the EU itself was framed as a difficult relationship, a large unwieldy creature, a strange plant, an exclusive club, a broken and divided entity, and a triumphant war hero, among other depictions.

Problematic movement forward

The *pure foreign* angled Australian representations presented enlargement in terms of fast movement or a vehicle speeding ahead – concepts that did not allow stagnation. Images of a "*shift*,"[34] a "*big leap*,"[35] an "*enhance[ed] pace*"[36] of economic development, as well as of the EU "*gearing up* for enlargement" were detected in abundance.

Yet, the Australian media warned its audiences of the possible consequences of this move forward. When conceptualized as a move along a "*road* to integration,"[37] extensive examples appeared of metaphors conceptualizing this ambitious European integration project as a politically, economically and socially challenging historic "*journey*"[38] where the "*direction*"[39] of the journey remained the subject of hard bargaining for the 25 members of the EU, and where "*roadblocks*"[40] still lay ahead. When compared to a ship, the EU was seen as embarking on a perilous voyage. On May 1 the EU 'ship' was seen as "*entering into uncharted territory*."[41] "*Taking on board*"[42] new countries, the larger EU was seen as a vessel that was now more difficult to "*steer*."[43] Moreover, it was in danger of "*sinking* under the weight of a vast, unmanageable bureaucracy and its own, inevitable, internal divisions."[44]

Fragmented in space

The frequent image of the EU uniting suggests a whole that is (or was) fragmented in space. The set of spatial metaphors tracked in the Australian *pure foreign* angled news highlight the theme of reunification of a continent "*bitterly divid[ed]*"[45] by an "*Iron Curtain*"[46] in the past. The 2004 enlargement, in which eight former communist nations joined the EU, was seen as a force which finally closed Europe's "*east-west divide*."[47] Though typically carrying positive connotations, reunification was not entirely unproblematic. Heavily symbolic as it was, the reunification of East and West Europe was seen as "*bring[ing] together* two unequal and often *fractious* sides";[48] two halves of a whole that did not quite fit back together properly. 'New' Europe's unity was seen by Australians as "*fragile*" and potentially ending up "*in pieces*."[49] Both print and television news audiences in Australia saw that the new members brought with them "a disturbing wealth *gap*",[50] a "*gulf*"[51] between levels of technology, and a "new Europe/old Europe *rift* over the Iraq war."[52] There remained "cultural *gaps*,"[53] and "clear *divisions*"[54] were depicted as having emerged on the issue of the new constitution.

An exclusive club for the wealthy

Related to the images of a journey and of space, the conceptual metaphor of a 'highly desirable space to enter' was identified. The accession of the new Member States was described as a "*return*"[55] to a "*place where [they] belong*."[56] Exclusivity carries with it a certain degree of contradiction. On the one hand, it suggests a desirable space that people "*crave*"[57] to enter. On the other hand, it also suggests a closed space of privilege with tightly guarded doors. New Member States were involved in a "*struggle to be admitted*"[58] while the old EU-15 was depicted as a 'doorman' who was able to "*deny*"[59] access to the newcomers prompting one Australian commentator to ask if the EU would "ever be *willing to open its doors*" to 60 million Turkish Muslims.[60] The image of the EU as an entity closed to outsiders, inward-oriented, and protectively separated was reinforced by the repeated description of the EU as a "*rich man's club*"[61] of "*privileged, highly affluent* countries."[62] Alternatively, the EU-15 was described in Australia as "a *cultural club* of Christian or post-Christian nations,"[63] or as "*Club Euro*."[64]

Half-opened doors

The opening up of the EU and of Central and Eastern Europe to the rest of the world inspired many references to doors in the Australian media. As with those of an exclusive space, metaphors of doors also have the potential to be both positive (opening) and negative (closed). In the Australian media, the latter was considerably more prominent. The EU was seen as opening its doors to the new members – "*but not too far.*"[65] Rather than "*welcoming* [entrants] with open arms" they were seen as "*welcoming them with the door half open.*"[66]

Fragile architecture

The EU was often depicted in the Australian press as a "*structure*"[67] designed by "*architects.*"[68] The alternative political design of the newcomers – communism – had "*collapsed.*"[69] A "*[n]ew European architecture*"[70] was necessary since the previous construction of the EU-15 required "*fundamental* changes"[71] and "*structural* reform."[72] Moreover, the "*fragile architecture*"[73] was depicted as being in danger of "*collapsing*"[74] or "*imploding.*"[75]

Family

The Australian *pure foreign* angled news presented the accession of the Central and Eastern European states as their "return to [the] European *family.*"[76] Members were seen to be welcomed back with fervour, as they were "*embraced*"[77] by their older cousins. With the "*youthful* political systems"[78] of the prodigal new Member States however, there was an implied need for a parental figure. Some European politicians auditioned for that role; former German chancellor Helmut Kohl was labelled "one of the *fathers* of European reunification"[79] while French President Jacques Chirac "*berated*"[80] the new nations in a parental fashion for their backing of the United States and Britain in the Iraq conflict. The European family was not without its problems. For example, the family 'inheritance' was described as consisting of little more than a "series of territorial and ethnic *disputes.*"[81]

Difficult relationship

The Australian press reporting enlargement from a *pure foreign* focus frequently employed the metaphor of romantic relations. Proclamations such as "Europe's *getting reunited*"[82] and "[t]oday, Europe *unites,*"[83] implied the celebration of marriage, or re-marriage, as the case may be. Keen to consummate the union and start a family, the new members were looking into "*adopting* the euro."[84] Yet, this European affair was not presented in the Australian media as an easy one. While the new Member States were "determined to maintain their *partnership* with the EU,"[85] the old Member States were less committed. Ongoing political instability in the new Member States made them "*difficult* negotiating *partners*".[86] The newcomers were also noted to be partners of "*unequal standing*";[87] *The Economist*, for example was cited by an Australian newspaper as saying "it will be decades before the new entrants become *as rich as their partners* to the west."[88] The 'wannabe' members were sometimes seen as engaged in romantic squabbles. For example, 2007 enlargement candidates, Bulgaria and Romania, were seen as "lobbying for *divorce*,"[89] Bulgaria wanting its negotiations to be "*decoupled* from Romania."[90]

Triumphant victor

Positive associations emerged through images such as the EU as a liberating force for the former Soviet states, previously "*struggling* under communist rule and the soul-crushing ills of police states and command economies."[91] As a result of these depictions, the EU was seen as a growing army – with new Member States as its "*willing recruits*,"[92] joining its "*ranks*,"[93] and the enlargement was seen as "a *triumph*"[94] for the victor – European integration.

Mixed feelings

In the Australian *pure foreign* angled news, EU citizens from both the Union's old and new Member States were reported as having "*mixed feelings* about what this change will mean for them and for Europe."[95] While some commentators observed that "*joy* has given way to *apprehension* and even *hostility*"[96] on the part of both the old and new Member States, it was predicted in Australian reports that "*enthusiasm* should vastly outweigh"[97] the anxiety. The accompanying enlargement "*anxiety*" was seen as inevitable.[98] For some newcomers (e.g. Poland), enlargement resulted in a feeling of being "*betrayed* by the EU's decision to postpone the full extent of subsidies for new members for 10 years."[99] For some old EU states, the reunification of the European continent brought a "*fear*"[100] of migrants from the former communist states. This fear resulted in a public "*hysteria*" about the inability of the old EU governments to restrict access to public housing and benefits for newcomers.[101] Naturally, some existing EU members were observed to be in a "*grudging*" mood[102] and many of those states became "*much less confident*"[103] about enlargement.

Mixed diagnosis

Metaphors of well-being, both positively and negatively rendered, were especially prominent particularly in the Australian press presenting enlargement from *pure foreign* angle. Europe was pictured as being healed by enlargement. The new Member States were considered to be an "*infusion of new blood*" and "*energy*" "*invigorating*" the EU.[104] The impact of the EU's largest expansion was seen to "*inject some much-needed energy*" into the euro zone economies;[105] it was a "*lifeline*"[106] "*strengthening*" the Union as a whole and its new members individually.[107]

Yet the Australian media prognosis was not entirely positive. The EU was described as "*weak* economically, and *weak* on the world stage"[108] and was said to be "*suffering from growing pains*"[109] as a result of the enlargement. These sufferings were exacerbated by the fact that enlargement coincided with "the final *throes of a painful* debate about the Union's new constitution."[110] The enlargement process was sometimes portrayed as a premature baby – "the *birth* of the world's biggest trading bloc"[111] had come *"too soon."*[112] It was likely then, in the opinion of the Australian media at least, that "more *pain* lies ahead" for the EU Member States.[113] Moreover, the Central and Eastern European newcomers were shown as suffering "all sorts of *hangover problems* of the communist era"[114] immediately after independence. After a *"shock therapy"*[115] treatment in the form of market-oriented reforms, the eight ex-communist states had *"gradually revived* their economies."[116] But they were also learning that "there's still *a lot of pain* associated with joining the EU."[117] The old Member States, themselves suffering from economic *"sclerosis"*[118] and "political *paralysis"*[119] were seen to be in need of *"revival,"*[120] *"resuscitation"*[121] and a *"boost."*[122]

The metaphors of well-being also included related images of food and consumption – concepts that were, as it transpired, inherently connected to the health and well-being of the EU. For example, *"digesting* the latest batch of members"[123] was likely to take the EU some time. If it recovered from its most recent meal, the Union's possible future consumption of Turkey would be the *"toughest of all to digest."*[124] Thus, the huge task of integrating the 10 new members was predicted to *"dampen any appetite"* for further growth.[125]

Facelift for Europe

While the future of Europe was *"not a pretty sight"*[126] according to some Australian observers, others felt that the enlargement had given the EU a *"new face"*[127] worth celebrating. After its *"facelift,"* it was suggested that the EU might be able to find work on the global catwalk, acting as a model for other "regional power blocs in Asia, the Pacific, South America and Africa."[128]

Hybrid plant with growth problems

The Australian press frequently presented EU enlargement in terms of *"development"*[129] and *"evolution."*[130] While the EU tree was *"growing"* and *"branching out,"* it was an odd *"hybrid,"*[131] that had grown *"too big for its roots"* and was thus in danger of toppling over.[132] The new Member States, for their part, were described as weak grafts to the EU tree, *"not immediately flourish[ing]."*[133]

Large animal

Enlargement also inspired images of a living creature with a *"beating heart."*[134] According to the Australian media, the EU was already "an unwieldy, fractious *beast"* with 15 Member States and post-enlargement[135] it was a *"giant"*[136] or massive *"behemoth"*[137] which had grown into a *"fuzzy"*[138] creature.

Australia: reporting the EU enlargement from a domestic angle

In the *domestic angle* of reporting on the EU, the dominant metaphors in the Australian case were similar to those in the *pure foreign* angle; the EU was depicted as an exclusive space, as a whole that was fragmented in the past, as an expanding material and as a structure, while enlargement was pictured as organic growth, movement forward (fast and slowly) and upwards and as a journey. The metaphor of romantic relations was among the leading metaphors in the Australian *domestic* angle of reporting enlargement.

Aggressive Flirting

Australia was said, for example, to have been "in a *ménages à trois* [sic]" with America and Asia in the past, while Europe could not even "*get in the bedroom.*"[139] It had been hard for Europe to "*get a look-in*" under the shadow of Asia, but now Europe had become "too big *to ignore.*"[140] The "newest EU *debutants*"[141] with their business potential were "*wetting* the corporate *lips* of Australian business."[142] The 'debutants' were also seen as becoming an "even *closer and a more attractive partner* for Australia in political, economic and cultural domains."[143] Little wonder then Australian politicians such as Foreign Minister Alexander Downer and (the then) shadow Foreign Minister Kevin Rudd were embarking on a post-enlargement mission to "*court* Europe."[144]

New Zealand: EU enlargement reported from a pure *foreign* angle

Foreign-angled reports of EU enlargement in the New Zealand media created a negatively loaded image of this major Union transformation. Several dominant metaphorical conceptualizations contributed to this particular assessment, namely, a premature move forward, an exclusive and divided space, an unhappy family, poor health, negative emotions, and cataclysmic events among others.

Too far too soon

Metaphors of fast movement used in the New Zealand news were rather critical in tone. Enlargement was seen as having "*gone too far too soon.*"[145] The "*run-up* to enlargement"[146] had resulted in a "rash of rules,"[147] that were designed to protect workers in the existing Member States against unfair competition from low-paid Central and Eastern European labour. In a number of specific references to vehicular movement, the enlargement was again seen in a negative light. For example, the enlargement was "*driven* more by political consideration than common sense."[148] The shifting of gears was not smooth, with "the business of *running such a complex assemblage* of still-sovereign states get[ting] ever more *cumbersome.*"[149]

Physical barriers

An image of a physical barrier was often used by New Zealand newsmakers to describe a Europe that had been divided in the past and was possibly dividing in the future. In the past, 'Old Europe' was seen as a continent *"divided by fences and walls*."[150] The present reunification of Europe in the form of the EU was shown as a process of removing a *"jagged fence of steel, concrete and barbed wire*"[151] and *"dismantl[ing]* geographical *barriers* to the free movement of people and goods."[152] In the future, however, the EU-15 – representatives of the Old Europe – would be seen *"busily erecting fences* faster than Brussels [could] *tear them down*."[153] The EU's trajectory was predicted to "move more towards *discord* and *division* than towards unity"[154] with foreseen wealth gaps that would *"take decades to close*."[155]

Fortress Europe

Occasionally an inclusive space, *"welcom[ing]*"[156] and *"throw[ing] open its doors to newcomers* from Eastern Europe,"[157] the EU was more frequently painted in the New Zealand media, as in the Australian media, as an exclusive space; the EU was depicted as a heavily guarded *"fortress*"[158] looking for any opportunities to *"restrict*"[159] access to it in spite of the recent opening of its 'gates'. The enlargement candidates were required to wait patiently in a *"queue*"[160] to access the so-called *"garden* of Europe."[161] New Member States were seen to be disrupting "the cozy days of a close and like-minded European *club*"[162] members and *"old timers*"[163] (ie. the EU-15) and, in a further disruption to the peace, outsiders could now be heard *"banging on the door*."[164]

Problems in the neighbourhood

Images of the expanded EU conceptualized as a house in a *"community* that shares the same values and visions"[165] were visible in the New Zealand print news discourse. In this depiction the enlarged EU acquired some new attributes – new neighbours on its *"doorstep*"[166] (Russia), a *"new backyard [in] a morass* of failing states"[167] (Ukraine, Belarus, Moldova), while a new *"back door*"[168] (poorer Eastern European countries, e.g. Romania) was being used by US firms to access a reluctant European Union (used particularly when discussing issues of genetically modified organisms).

Poorer cousins and unhappy family

Images of the "European *common house*"[169] were supported by images of the EU enlargement described in terms of human relations between the house's inhabitants – the new Member States were seen to be *"returning home*."[170] The New Zealand *pure foreign* angled reports also extensively framed enlargement in terms of family relations. While New Zealand television reporting showed the warm welcome that the new Member States received – to the extent that parties were thrown in their honour[171] – newspaper commentators predicted that future problems awaited the "enlarged European Union *family*."[172] References to the EU as a family inevitably invoked descriptions of the new Member States as the "*poorer cousins*"[173] vying for a place at an already overcrowded "*table*."[174] "*Anything but a happy family*," the EU-15 was seen welcoming the new member in a "*chilly manner*,"[175] The members of this new, larger family were involved in "*spats*,"[176] "*squabbling* over budgets and subsidies"[177] and "*tackling* looming disputes over power and money."[178]

Indifferent or afraid

The New Zealand media was dominated by images of mutual fears ruling relations between old and new Member States. Citizens in the 15 established EU nations were described as "*indifferent* [to] or *afraid*"[179] of the enlargement, which inspired "more *angst* than *euphoria*."[180] Possible immigration from the new Member States put some old Member States (e.g. the UK and Ireland) into a state of "*hysteria*."[181] The citizens of the EU-15 were reported to be "*spooked by hysteria* over a migration wave."[182] To "*calm frayed nerves*," the Geneva-based International Organization for Migration (IOM) was reported to be releasing a series of studies on the impact of EU enlargement on both acceding and existing members of the Union.[183] New states were shown as being similarly uneasy about the outcomes of enlargement, albeit for different reasons. Populist politicians in Eastern Europe were seen to be "*stirring up worries*."[184]

Catastrophes and cataclysms

Most of the fears regarding enlargement in the established Member States stemmed from the threat of the "*flood*"[185] of immigrants – one of the most prominent *nature* metaphors in the New Zealand *pure foreign* angle discourse. This metaphorical categorization depicted the "*unmanaged surge*"[186] of migrants from poorer EU newcomers into the wealthier old Member States in terms of an "*influx*"[187] or even "*tidal wave*."[188] Regardless of the assertions by politicians and scholars that the older members were in fact "far from being *swamped*,"[189] the citizens of the EU-15 were nevertheless expecting "a migration *wave*."[190]

The New Zealand press also frequently used the concept of 'the Big Bang' to describe EU enlargement in the *pure foreign* angle of reporting.[191] Unlike the hypothesised scientific event, the May 1 enlargement was characterized not as an exception in the European universe's evolution, but as just one of its "*periodic Big Bangs*."[192] With the EU's membership "*explod[ing]* from 15 countries to 25 on May 1,"[193] the EU's latest Big Bang was said to be "*redraw[ing] the map*."[194]

Poor health

New Zealand's *pure foreign* angled news focused mostly on the enlargement outcomes for the EU-15, and the diagnosis was largely gloomy. Old Member States were seen as most likely to *"suffer* from enlargement" in terms of rising unemployment and overloaded social-welfare systems.[195] Their prosperity was seen as being *"at threat, hemorrhaged* by an exodus of jobs to the East."[196] Pre-enlargement support for the process on behalf of the established members was *"fading fast"*;[197] the EU-15 was giving birth to a baby that was *"premature."*[198] With the old members' economies perceived as weak, the fear of migrants, it was claimed, could cause Europe to "miss out on its biggest chance for *a shot of energy* in years."[199] Moreover, with ten *"fledgling"*[200] new members incorporated into the EU body, it was feared that the enlarged Union would wind up with *"paralysis."*[201]

Healthily growing plant

Predictably, the 2004 enlargement was also framed in terms of organic growth. In the New Zealand media, the EU attracted comparisons to growing organisms and the new Member States were described as fast-growing grafts. Jean Monnet was depicted as the 'God' of the European Union declaring, *"It must be created."*[202] Having thus been 'created', the EU *"grew,"*[203] and "it *grew."*[204] In particular, the EU was repeatedly conceived of in terms of a plant, "the original *seed* of European integration" having been sown by the United States in the post-war era in the form of the Marshall Plan.[205] Though typically a positively evaluated frame, organic growth was not always depicted in a wholly positive fashion in the New Zealand media, and this European 'plant' was seen to sometimes display *"prickly* issues."[206]

New Zealand: reporting the EU enlargement from a *domestic* angle

Metaphors located in the New Zealand *domestic* angle of reporting paralleled the *pure foreign* angle – the EU was depicted as an expanding substance and a growing body, and enlargement as a forward movement (slow and fast). The description of the EU's expansion in the New Zealand *domestic* context also prioritized images of forces of nature, such as oceans, earthquakes or storms.

Cataclysmic forces of nature

Even though the event was occurring halfway round the world, the 'waves' of enlargement were *"washing up* on the South Pacific,"[207] and its *"repercussions"* would be felt even in New Zealand.[208] Yet, New Zealand was said to have "nothing to fear and a lot to gain from the growth and development of the European Union" since the South Pacific nation would now never again be *"sucked into* any more intra-European civil wars."[209] Despite these positive predictions however, New Zealand's interactions with the enlarged EU were forecast to "certainly *not be plain sailing.*"[210]

South Korea: EU enlargement reported from a *pure foreign* angle

In contrast to the Australasian media discourses, which featured a substantial load of negatively charged metaphorical conceptualizations in their *foreign-angled* news, South Korean news reported EU enlargement in this angle using a relatively high share of neutral and positive conceptualizations. Among these were continuous movement, construction, and performance on the stage. Yet, negative assessments were not totally absent, and were observed in the dominant metaphor of war.

Constant movement

The Korean news reports constructed an image of the enlarging EU as a constantly moving entity. The EU was described as *"going* inside"[211] to fulfil its task while diplomats and lobbyists who dealt with the EU were described as being "busy, *running* around."[212] The EU was also conceptualized in the South Korean media as a cause of movement. The enlargement appeared to prompt foreign enterprises to *"pile into*"[213] the EU 'grounds' and, in another instance, the EU was encouraging cooperation between external countries and research and development to *"go forward.*"[214] The South Korean press went further with this description, advocating a mechanism, which would ensure the "continuous *moving forward*"[215] of EU cooperation.

As in the Australian and New Zealand media, the image of enlargement as a journey was also evident in the South Korean press discourse. The term *"ahead*"[216] was frequently used by South Korean newsmakers to depict the state of Hungary's quest for membership to the EU, for example, and to also locate the enlargement itself. An initial EU *"departure point*"[217] was described by South Korean media, thus illustrating the starting point of EU as a six member-state entity. The continued use of the journey metaphor in representing the issues surrounding EU enlargement indicates the incomplete and ongoing nature of the EU integration process.

In representing the EU's enlargement as a journey, South Korean newspapers also often used a ship metaphor (*"pulling up an anchor*"[218]) to describe the EU's actions. An additional metaphorical depiction associated with sea travel was also used in the South Korean reporting on enlargement. In the Korean language, the meaning of the word 're-departure' – found in the phrase, "the *re-departure* of enlarged super EU"[219] – is commonly associated with sailing.

Movement up

The depictions of the EU embarking on sea travel were contrasted with imagery in the South Korean media of the EU as having "many mountains *to climb*."[220] Furthermore, with the changes to the geo-political map of Europe post-enlargement, there was a need identified by the Korean media to "*heighten* mutual understanding between Asia and Europe."[221]

A building to live and work in

The EU was often portrayed as a confined space in the Korean media, which was emphasized by the press' depiction of it as a building such as a house or a factory. In one occurrence, the EU was conceptualized as a "*tower* of Babel"[222] and in another Eastern Europe was characterized as the EU's "*factory*."[223] In most cases, the EU as a whole was conceptualized as a house, complete with a roof ("Europe is entering *under one roof*"[224]), and windows ("the *window* of Europe"[225]).

Stage performances

The Korean press reporting on the EU from a *pure foreign* news angle associated many of its actions with the theatre. The 10 new EU members were described as playing "a major *role*"[226] on the economic market. Additionally, the EU was now seen to be playing a "*more active role*"[227] in North Korea's nuclear issue. Right-wing political groups were depicted as making appearances and the European Union Chamber of Commerce in Korea (ECCK) was portrayed as "*disguising*"[228] itself as a mediator. As well as its on-stage role, the EU was sometimes identified as the stage-crew. One newspaper, for example, stated that the GDP growth of the EU resulting from the development of the new members' economies was "*projected*"[229] by the European Commission, and the 'show's' audience was constituted by foreign EU investors who were "*turning their eyes*"[230] to new investments in South Korea.

Warring with external enemies

War metaphors occurred frequently in the South Korean media discourse reporting on the EU enlargement. However, not all of these conceptualizations were directly representing the process of the EU enlargement. War metaphors were applied to depict the impact of the enlargement also. For example, the press stated that the EU is "weak"[231] and will need to become "fuller"[232] in order to "*face up*"[233] to the US who is currently "*surrounding*"[234] it. Arguably, a sense of heroism was suggested by the representation of the enlarging EU proposing a competition policy and thus "*fighting* cartels and abuses of dominant positions"[235] as well as "*defending*"[236] its own values. The EU "created instruments to *defend*"[237] its values and to "present new *challenges*."[238] In this battle, however, the EU was at times portrayed as being injured, often being the recipient of repeated "*blow*[s]."[239]

Birth and an active infancy

The dominant image of EU health in the South Korean media was the metaphor of 'birth' which was applied to conceptualize the enlargement. In numerous occurrences, both in newspapers and on television, the EU was *"re-born"*[240] and one newspaper described the enlargement as being *"conceived"*[241] by the goals of the European Coal and Steel Community.[242] Next, the growing EU was described as being about to take its *"first step."*[243]

Cultivating nature

The enlargement was represented as a major historical event which had the effect of "completely *uprooting"*[244] the remnants of the Cold War that had divided the European continent. The enlargement process was described as something that had "come to *fruition"*[245] while the enlarged EU was depicted as *"cultivating"*[246] a shared role with the US in the field of global politics and responsibility.

South Korea: reporting the EU enlargement from a *domestic* angle

Metaphors depicted in the South Korean media coverage of the EU enlargement from a *domestic* angle of were similar to those used in the *pure foreign* coverage, particularly in the use of movement metaphors (featuring mostly positive assessment). The domestic angle of reportage also activated the conceptual metaphor of an aggressive attack (possessing a distinctly negative tone).

Constant movement

The South Korean press constructed an image of the EU as a constantly moving entity which tended to cause other parties to *"run* around"*[247]; an image which was paralleled in the *pure foreign* news discourse. South Korean businesses were also represented as *"advancing into"*[248] the EU and they were described as "busy, *moving* about"*[249] due to the EU's enlargement. Moreover, the ECCK was depicted as *"stepping forward"*[250] towards the enlarged EU.

Attack and invasion

War metaphors in the South Korean enlargement reports from the *domestic* angle also reflected the imagery used in the *pure foreign* news items, however, the *domestic*-angled news tended to perceive the enlargement as an opportunity for South Korea to *"invade"*[251] the EU. According to the South Korean printed press, "a gap"[252] exists in the EU for South Korean exporters to 'invade' and in fact, South Korea's small businesses had already *"set out to invade"*[253] the EU market. The enlargement was thus depicted as having positive effects on trade, causing a new market to open up for South Korean enterprises. But the enlargement was also considered a *"threat"*[254] and was depicted as having some negative effects on South Korea, such as expected difficulties in strengthening economic relations with the EU, as opposed to the new Central and Eastern European Member States who would automatically have closer economic relations with the EU due to their accession.

Thailand: EU enlargement reported from a *pure foreign angle*

Thai enlargement reports from the *pure foreign* perspective featured more metaphorical conceptualizations of a negative evaluation. Among them are images of division in space, difficult access, quarrels and fights, and poor health. Yet, a positive connotation was traced in the categorization of a successful move forward.

Successful progress

Thailand's portrayal of EU enlargement presented it as a successful process, as the EU took "a big *step*,"[255] in fact, its "most significant *step*"[256] on "the *long journey* Europe has taken since World War II."[257] Applicant states were encouraged to try not "*to stray*" from the path of integration. Yet there was a warning that "[*the path of*] enlargement has just begun and it seems to be rather thorny."[258] Enlargement was also portrayed as a 'vehicle' driving the EU into the future, however it was suggested that this vehicle may not take the EU in the right direction: "Rather than *propel* Europe into global leadership, expansion could *lead* to a long period of introspection as the EU struggles to digest the newcomers."[259]

Separated in space

Thai news audiences were shown that enlargement would not only create "*a gap*"[260] between the old and new members but would also force the EU to change its policies and priorities in order to close the gap.[261] EU membership was constructed as an "opportunity to *catch up*" for the energetic new Member States.[262]

An entry pass that is difficult to gain

In becoming members of the EU, the new states seemed to Thai newsmakers to be better off, as they were given the status of *"members"* of the club, in contrast to the status of *"satellites"* or *"minions"* they were afforded while they were in the communist camp.[263] Although the EU promised that after the May enlargement the EU's door *"remained open"*, those who wish to enter had to work hard to gain an entry pass, by pursuing dramatic political and economic reform.[264] New members were depicted as having to continue to work hard in order to "live up *the demanding criteria* of the EU."[265]

Battles and rows

In the Thai news discourses, members of the EU family were frequently said to be having "*hot* and *spicy rows*".[266] These "routine *rows*" among club members[267] quickly escalated, at least in the minds of Thai journalists, to "an ill-tempered *battle*" in which the poor were pitted against the rich, new against old.[268] Yet, enlargement was sometimes also seen as "*a reward* for a *hard-fought* and long *battle*."[269]

Celebrations

A common description used by the Thai media in reporting enlargement news was a theme of "*big parties*"[270] and "*celebrations* with fireworks and champagne"[271] on May 1, but these jubilations were clouded by "fears"[272] and "anxiety"[273] among people in both old and new Member States. Prominent European leaders, such as Gerhard Schröeder and Tony Blair were reported as trying to allay the fears of these people.[274]

Threats to health

Imagery of health was also found in the Thai *pure foreign* angle reports, though the message transmitted to Thai audiences was a mixed one. The Thai press reported that while the EU "rose out from the *trauma* of World War II,"[275] it would soon suffer from "*slow suffocation*,"[276] a "political *hangover*" or "*heartburn*."[277] It was suggested that "the EU [would be] in for a bout of *indigestion after it swallows* 10 new Member States."[278]

Thailand: reporting the EU enlargement from a *domestic* angle

Whereas some of metaphors located in the Thai *domestic* angle of reporting paralleled the *pure foreign* angle – the enlargement as a forward movement (slow and fast) and as something to be celebrated – the most visible imagery of EU enlargement in the *domestic* angle of reporting featured mostly negative images of the EU as an adversary of Thailand, particularly in terms of being a fortress, a harsh authority, a rival and an offender in a business court case.

Exclusive club or protected fortress?

Images of EU enlargement in the Thai domestic context introduced some new sets of images, as well as reinforcing some of the images employed in news items reported from the *pure foreign context* with a domestic twist. The reinforced images that appeared most frequently were those of the EU as an exclusive space or a club. The Thai media reported that enlargement strengthened the "*Fortress*

Europe." However, new Member States were seen as "*gateways*"[279] or "*portals*" to "*penetrate*" this protected 'fortress'.[280]

Stronger threatening authority

One of the most frequently shown metaphors within this domestically contextualized coverage was the image of the EU as an authority, however it was not described as a benevolent one. Instead, the EU was stern and almost 'Big Brother'-like in its behaviour: an enlarged EU was seen by the Thai media as being a body with "*more eyes on Thailand.*"[281] Moreover, the EU was reported to be an unfair authority, as it employed "*a double standard*" [282] in its admission process for new members (namely, Myanmar) to the fifth ASEM summit in Vietnam. Thailand, therefore, had to push for justice by urging Vietnam "*not to give in*" to the EU's attempts to exercise authority on this matter and the South-East Asian nation "*fought* for reciprocal" treatment concerning the expansion of the ASEM.[283]

Enlarged EU as a rival to Thailand

The EU was also frequently personified by the Thai media as a rival of Asia in general and of Thailand in particular. Enlargement would result in Thai firms facing "*increased competition*" from those in the new Member States.[284] Enlargement would also make the EU stronger and, hence, it would become "*a fearsome rival ... of the rising Asia.*"[285]

Man-made damages

Finally, the impact of the EU enlargement was depicted in the Thai *domestically*-focused news as man-made "*damages*"[286] resulting in business losses for Thailand. With the damages being caused by human actions, rather than forces of nature (see, for example, the conceptual metaphors in the case of the New Zealand *domesticated* news), Thailand, hence, was presented as being entitled to claim "*reparation,*"[287] demanding compensation from the EU. The Thai press reported that if the EU failed to pay this "*compensation,*" that the government would "*bring the case*" [288] to the WTO. The enlarging EU was thus depicted in the Thai *domestically*-focused news as an offender in a business-related court action.

Discussion

Key patterns

Metaphors are sometimes claimed to "only be understood in relation to their particular context."[289] As Tully advises, this study therefore compared a series of texts from the same period (that of the fifth EU enlargement in 2004) and dealing with the same issue (namely the enlargement from both an internal and external point of view) produced in four different contextual environments. Considering a larger political context, namely the attitudes and official reactions of four Asia-Pacific countries to the fifth EU enlargement, this study attempted to detect, cluster and compare leading country-specific metaphorical categorizations offered by national media systems to frame the dominant images of the EU. Inter-textual analysis can provide crucial insights in the study of discourses responsible for constructing the world of international relations since, as Doty notes, when "the same kinds of subjects, objects, and relations are found to exist in different texts, this is indicative of a particular logic at work."[290] Moreover, "if differences are constructed according to the same logic in a variety of texts, we can reasonably suggest that there is a dominant discourse."[291]

Several key findings emerged. Firstly, this analysis revealed that the imagery of the EU enlargement was often ambivalent and contradictory and it frequently featured extensive negative evaluations across the four media discourses. It was also observed that news outlets from four very different countries existing in different political contexts and with different patterns of media ownership (as discussed in Chapter 1), reported the topic of EU enlargement by drawing on parallel sets of conceptual metaphors which thus produced similar metaphorical clusters. Similarities were most obvious in the *foreign-angled* news, arguably due to the fact that most of this news was sourced from common sources (e.g. international news agencies). Yet, predictably, the similar metaphorical clusters in different countries highlighted slightly different aspects of the related categorizations. The most dramatic difference in metaphorical imagery was observed when EU enlargement was covered from the *domestic* angle of reporting.

Ambivalent imagery

It was assumed that the novelty and uniqueness of the 2004 EU enlargement, namely, the voluntary and peaceful accession of not one or two, but ten countries into the supranational entity, would mean that conceptualizing this event would be somewhat challenging for the international public and governments worldwide. It was furthermore assumed that factors external to the news production process (such as the specific features of a country's internal and foreign policies, as well as its trade orientations) would provide a background for media representations. The results of this study seem to support these assumptions. The official reactions of the governments of the four Asia-Pacific countries were shown to feature both positive feedback on the ongoing European integration project, as well as cautious remarks on possible (mostly economic) consequences of enlargement for their own region. This official ambivalence was reflected in the mixed and often contradictory media framing of enlargement; within each identified cluster of metaphors, each positive metaphor was accompanied by a negative counterpart. The EU was seen as 'liberating' the Central and Eastern European states but it was also engaging in battle with them. While dismantling some fences it was building others. Doors were only half-opened and embraces half-hearted. Welcomed as members of the family, the new members were nevertheless left feeling like second-class citizens. People in both the old and new Member States celebrated the fifth enlargement and yet feared what might come.

Limited set of conceptual metaphors in play

A second major finding of this analysis was a similarity of conceptual metaphorical imagery of EU enlargement found in the four very different news discourses (discourses that vary politically, economically, culturally and linguistically) (see Table 2.3). The first of these shared conceptual metaphors was that of *spatiality*. Spatial metaphors described the EU enlargement in terms of movement (both organic and mechanical), a journey along a route, and the EU as an exclusive space to enter. The second group of linguistic metaphors was underlined by the conceptual metaphor of *personification*, which rendered the EU and the Member States as persons involved in relations (whether they were romantic or family relations, or relations that had eroded into battles and war) and as persons possessing emotions (such as happiness, anger and fear) and experiencing health issues. The third group of identified metaphors was framed by the conceptual metaphor of *organisms* and included the concepts of organic growth, plants and animals. The fourth group of metaphors was underlined by the conceptual metaphor of *structure*, and within this category, the list of linguistic metaphors describing EU enlargement included images of houses, structures, construction and reconstruction. The final group of linguistic metaphors was produced by the conceptual metaphor of *nature*, and more specifically, by metaphors describing cataclysmic and natural forces as well as a cultivated nature.

Of this limited list of conceptual metaphors, spatial metaphors and the metaphors of personification were the most common methods of representing EU enlargement to the Asia-Pacific audiences. While metaphors of *spatiality* were equally common and similar in form in both the Pacific and Asian pairs, the metaphors of *personification* were represented quite differently in the two cases. Within the *relationship* cluster, references to family and to feelings and sentiments abounded in the two Pacific news media discourses. These two sets of images, however, were not strong in the Asian media discourses; indeed, the 'family' metaphor did not occur in the South Korean newspaper articles at all.

Arguably, the fact that similar conceptual metaphors underlined the imagery in four very different media discourses could be explained by a universally strong cognitive appeal of those metaphors, irrespective of cross-cultural differences and contextual factors. Firstly, with the tendency of associative thinking to conceptualize in terms of both movement and space,[292] *spatial* metaphors of movement and space are among the most typical metaphorical mappings used by the human cognitive system.[293] They are used widely in various discourses, including media discourses. Secondly, one of the major metaphors underlying foreign policy concepts is the metaphor of *personification*.[294] Within this categorization, states (or international entities) are considered to perform as 'real' people, possessing characters and inherent dispositions and being involved in social relations within the world community.[295] Within the *personification* cluster, metaphors implying

Table 2.3 Distribution of the dominant metaphors

Angle of reporting EU enlargement	Pacific case				Asian Case			
	Australia		New Zealand		Thailand		South Korea	
	Pure foreign angle	Domestic angle	Pure foreign angle	Domestic angle	Pure foreign angle	Domestic angle	Pure foreign angle	Domestic angle
	Problematic movement forward	movement forward (fast and slowly) // movement upwards	Too far too soon	movement forward (fast and slowly)	Successful progress		Constant movement // Movement up	Constant movement
Spatial	An expanding material	An expanding material	An expanding material	An expanding material	An expanding material		an expanding material	
	Fragmented in space	Fragmented in space	Physical barriers		Separated in space			
	An exclusive club for the wealthy	Club	Fortress Europe		An entry pass difficult to gain	Exclusive club/fortress		
	Half-opened doors							
Structure	Fragile architecture	Structure					Building to live and work in	

	1	2	3	4	5	6	7	8
Personification	Fathers and sons; Difficult personal relationship; Triumphal victor in a battle; Mixed feelings; Mixed diagnosis; Facelift for Europe	Aggressive flirting	Poorer cousins and unhappy family; Community with problems in the neighborhood; Indifferent or afraid; Poor health		Internal battles and rows; Celebrations and fears; Threats to EU's health	A threatening to Thailand authority; A rival to Thailand; Threat to Thailand's health	A war with external enemy; Birth and active infancy; Performance on the stage	Attack and invasion
Organic	Hybrid plant with growth problems		Healthily growing plant	A growing body				
Nature	Giant animal		Catastrophes and cataclysmic events	Cataclysmic forces of nature			Cultivating nature	

that politics is war and metaphors of health (and illness in particular) are noted to be frequently employed in political and media discourses since they are easily comprehended by the readers and viewers, effectively inducing the feelings of aggression in the former case and anxiety in the latter case.[296] Finally, as mentioned before, similarities in metaphors used in the *foreign-angled* news reports could be attributed to overlaps in international news sources.

Differing accents of similar metaphors in the foreign-angled news

Despite the common ambivalent attitudes towards EU enlargement, each country in the study had its own unique set of interests and concerns surrounding the EU's expansion. It is argued that as a result of these contextual differences, the parallel conceptual metaphors generated differing linguistic metaphors (see Table 2.3). For example, in the enlargement categorizations related to the concept of *movement*, the Australian media highlighted a theme of movement forward along a road blocked by obstacles, as well as images of a ship on a perilous voyage; the New Zealand media in turn stressed images of a hasty dash forward in addition to an awkwardly assembled large vehicle moving along; the South Korean media illuminated images of constant movement (not necessarily forward) and movement upwards; and the Thai media underlined ideas of successful progress.

In another instance, the Australian media presented a proportion of metaphors describing EU enlargement in terms of the EU's good and bad well-being, while the New Zealand media stressed the imagery of poor health of the expanded EU. In this same example, the South Korean media represented the EU-25 in terms of a newly born and actively growing baby, and the Thai media highlighted the theme of potential threats to the EU's health as a result of enlargement.

In the case of the conceptual metaphor of *organic growth*, the Australian media drew an image of the enlarged EU as a hybrid plant with problematic growth. In contrast, the New Zealand media introduced the image of a healthy growing plant. In yet another example – this time of *natural phenomenon* – the New Zealand media portrayed enlargement in terms of cataclysmic forces of nature, contrasting the South Korean examples which highlighted the theme of cultivated nature.

In using metaphors of *war*, the Australian media underlined the image of EU enlargement as a battle resulting in a triumph for the EU, while the Thai media stressed images of the internal rows and squabbles over the enlargement that the EU Member States were involved in, and the South Korean media compared enlargement to a war with external enemies (be they the US or financial cartels) defending its values.

Finally, in using the metaphor of *family*, differences were detected between the two Pacific countries: in an Australian example, the relationship between the old and new Member States was described in terms of a filial relationship with the old members cast as parental figures for younger prodigal children, the new members. In comparison, the New Zealand news metaphors highlighted images of poorer cousins, an unhappy family and a chilly welcome into a bigger family.

Divergent domesticized reporting on the enlargement.

While there were subtle differences in the portrayals of EU enlargement from a *pure foreign* angle of reporting, a more marked difference in imagery was evident in the *domestic* angle of reporting, an angle that is argued to bring 'foreign' closer to home. Arguably, in this angle, national interests and official guidelines in constructing relations with the enlarging EU were more apparent in providing a background for the media framings.

In Australia, where the then government preferred bilateral strategies in its dealings with the EU Member States and was reluctant to recognize the EU as a unified actor,[297] the metaphorical imagery seemed to advocate a more proactive approach to Australia's relations with the enlarged EU. This was evident, for example, in imagery of the possible romantic pursuit of (if not aggressive flirting with) the enlarged EU on behalf of the Australian government and businesses.

For New Zealand, its size and geographical distance from Europe created the possibility of disappearing from the radar of the enlarged EU. A bigger Union was seen as likely to turn its attention ever-inwards in order to accommodate its newcomers. Such a development was viewed likely to have disastrous effects for the New Zealand economy if the small Pacific state did not undertake an active position towards both Brussels and the new Member States. In light of such prospective threats, it seems reasonable then, that the New Zealand *domestic* angle of reporting introduced enlargement and its impact on New Zealand in terms of powerful natural forces and disasters. The inventory of images included tidal waves, sailing across oceans, and earthquakes happening half way across the globe. These images arguably reflect the New Zealand reality of being a group of islands in a seismically active zone, and also echoed the dominating proactive attitudes existing in New Zealand's society towards the need to prepare for coping with a major natural disaster.[298]

South Korea, in contrast to the other three countries in the study, presented the least ambivalent and the most optimistically-coloured imagery in its domestically focused reporting. This could be attributed to the fact that of the four countries in the study, South Korea does not need to engage with the EU in the problematic area of agricultural subsidies, but instead interacts with the EU mostly in the open and internationally competitive fields of industry and business. Official South Korean discourses framed EU enlargement as another opportunity for increasing Korean economic interactions with the EU as South Korean businesses were presented with new possibilities of trading with the new Member States. Correspondingly, the most visible metaphors specifically found in the *domestic* angle of reporting in the South Korean news media included imagery of a growing EU that was constantly moving, as well as being a cause of constant movement for Korea. The categorizations also included images of the enlarged EU as a place to be conquered by Korean business.

Thailand, as a part of the ASEAN community, has, in the past, often displayed sensitive attitudes towards the actions of the EU in the political, economic, and social arenas, most notably in response to the EU's reaction to the bird flu epidemic in the region, its stance on agricultural policies, and its involvement in the Myanmar (Burma) issue. The EU enlargement was considered to be a real threat to the economy of Thailand due to the increased competition of Thai products against the produce from the Eastern European countries for Western European markets. Notably, the most visible metaphors located in the domestic context of reporting in the Thai media seemed to solidify the image of opposition and threat – the enlarging EU was personified as an opponent who held Thailand in a stronghold from which Thailand was fighting to be released, a fearsome rival of Asia, and an unfair authority against whom Thailand had to stand up to and fight for justice. The Thai media saw the impact of EU enlargement not as a natural threat like New Zealand, but primarily as human-wrought damage.

Preference for negatively-charged imagery

Another important finding was a preference for negativity in the metaphorical images of enlargement. Both the print and television news reports monitored in this study presented a significant set of metaphorical images coloured with negative evaluations to the audiences in the four countries. For example, the metaphors of argument and war suggest mostly negative connotations. They carry images of opposition, conflict, aggression and fight which are usually disliked and feared. Images of confrontation were reinforced by the negatively-loaded images of a fragmented whole. Highly negative associations were also brought to the fore by images of physical sickness; such images have been demonstrated to induce anxiety.[299] In addition, many metaphoric examples of EU enlargement described it as a source of emotional discomfort for both new and old members. Since negative emotions are known to have a detrimental effect, the evaluations of EU enlargement as a source of fear and anxiety were interpreted as highly negative. Finally, images of natural disasters form an image of despair, depression and aggression, and are often used in an apocalyptic sense.[300]

While these evaluations are argued to be partially influenced by ambivalent attitudes towards enlargement, this study also argues that the 'commodification' of news observed across the studied news discourses triggers a constant search for dramatic and controversial in news production. Arguably, the "cynical obsession of the national press with trivia, scandal, and negativity"[301] to sell copies has resulted in the prevalence of negative imagery which tends to be much stronger and more pervasive than the corresponding positive imagery. Certainly, this argument was supported by the media producers interviewed in each country as part of this project. When asked to describe what made an item newsworthy, conflict was the most frequently cited news value, an observation also supported by our media analysis.

Pragmatic Implications

Metaphors assist news audiences to comprehend and interpret the complex and vague concepts of international politics by depicting them in familiar, everyday terms. They can be used to both strengthen culturally-shared concepts and to create new ways of seeing the world.[302] In representing EU enlargement to Asia-Pacific audiences, conventional and recognizable metaphorical categorizations were instrumental in negotiating and popularizing the understanding of a new and complex concept on the international stage. Arguably, the "conventional metaphorical routines"[303] dominating Asia-Pacific media representations of EU enlargement were employed by the regional newsmakers as an efficient means of introducing this new complex concept of the international reality. Familiar metaphorical representations allow news producers to economize on audiences' cognitive resources of image-formation since complicated and unfamiliar imagery could potentially avert readers and viewers from news on the otherwise complex and unprecedented EU.

This study recognizes that metaphorical categorizations in media discourses are just one type of categorization (consider, for example, the literal categorizations of the concept 'EU' which were explored in detail in Chapter 1 of this volume). Yet, categorization using metaphors seems to be extremely powerful. Metaphorical categorization, according to Broström, works in a unique way by "focusing on some properties of a [source concept] to the exclusion of others by using a category which brings precisely those properties together, in a compact cognitive form."[304] Conceptual metaphors thus offer extremely powerful interpretations of actors and events reported in the news and "lead to certain implied conclusions."[305] Such conclusions are influenced by the evaluative charge of the metaphorical categorizations. By subtly introducing a negative or positive evaluative dimension which serves to praise and recommend, or to criticize and denounce, metaphors act not as factual, but rather emotive devices. By stressing some properties, de-emphasizing others and concealing yet others, and by assigning perceptible assessments to those highlighted properties, this particular form of categorization serves to reinforce established stereotypes and support conventional beliefs.[306] In this case, the set of metaphors from each country was predominantly negative, suggesting to the respective audiences that the EU integration project is an inherently flawed one.

Ultimately, metaphors may not only provide a way of thinking about complex foreign policy concepts and actors, but also a way of acting towards them. The possibility that media images of the enlarged EU could modify official attitudes and thus lead to a change in behaviour – both of states acting towards and with the EU and correspondingly, the national publics in their understandings and evaluations of those state-EU relationships – is considered to be a realistic outcome from the *domestic* angle of reporting of the enlargement. While the *pure foreign* angle of reporting is ultimately intended to introduce events and people in distant lands by contextualizing them in the outside environments, the *domestic* angle is instead argued to bring 'foreign' closer to home by indicating immediate consequences to the domestic shareholders. However, this study also acknowledges a certain pitfall of 'domesticated' foreign news that was identified by Ginsberg, namely, the risk that the media will uncritically render a government position on an international actor through this particular angle of reporting.[61]

Indeed, this chapter argues that there are certain parallels in the imagery specific to the *domesticated* reporting of the EU enlargement and the nature of actions undertaken by the respective governments towards the expanding EU. For example, in the lead-up to, and wake of, the recent enlargement, the Australian government repeatedly expressed a commitment to pursuing a closer and more meaningful relationship with its European partner. In the annual Schuman Lecture on Europe Day in Canberra in 2007, the Australian Foreign Minister, Alexander Downer, welcomed the EU's increasing external engagement and suggestions that the EU and Australia look at ways of improving cooperation.[307] It could be argued that such actions and statements are somehow in line with the imagery of 'flirting' and 'courting' the newly expanded EU, imagery which uniquely surfaced in the Australian *domestic* angle of reporting enlargement if compared across the four countries.

In New Zealand, the categorizations from the *domestic* angle highlighted the properties of a cataclysmic natural event and hinted at the necessity for the New Zealand government and business sector to prepare themselves to handle 'potential disasters' arising from enlargement and to minimize the consequences. In parallel to such imagery, the current New Zealand government claims a commitment to maintaining a regular dialogue with the enlarging EU. As a 'preventative measure', New Zealand, a small Pacific state, secures its visibility of on the 'radars' of a ever expanding Union through a chain of official and ministerial trips to Europe (a mode of interaction which keeps New Zealand alert to the latest changes on the European continent) and through activated business attention towards new Member States.[308] Those official visits now include not only traditional stops at Brussels and London, but also visits to the new EU members. After the 2004 enlargement, New Zealand government and parliamentary officials visited three Baltic states, Hungary, the Czech Republic, Poland, and Malta.[309]

In South Korea, the imagery in the *domestic* angle depicted the enlarged EU as a source and cause of constant movement, thus suggesting that the Korean side will be kept busy 'running around' 'keeping up' in their dealings with the expanded EU. Moreover, the enlarged EU was shown as a place ready to be 'invaded' by South Korean businesses, thus prompting an idea of proactive stances on behalf of the South Korean business community in relation to the EU-25. In consonance with this imagery, in 2005, the South Korean Minister of Foreign Affairs and Trade Ban Ki-Moon underlined the importance of further cooperation between the EU and South Korea – an official view on the enlarged EU is that the recent EU expansions mean more room for South Korean products within the European market. With the enlarged EU becoming South Korea's largest investment partner and the third largest market for its exports, co-operation between the two is increasing also in numerous information technology and scientific projects (eg. the Galileo satellite project). In December 2005, Korea signed a Free Trade agreement with EFTA (European Free Trade Association).

Finally, in Thailand, the *domesticated* metaphorical categorizations of the enlarging EU brought to light the properties of a health threat, rivalry, exclusivity, harsh authority, and man-made damages – properties that led to the conclusion that interactions with such a partner could be rather difficult for Thailand. Notably, in order to improve the state of the EU–Thai interactions, the Thai government has been trying to move the relationship to a new level by means of concluding a formal Partnership and Cooperation Agreement with the growing EU. At present, the EU–Thai relations are conducted through the EU–ASEAN framework, on the basis of the EC–ASEAN Agreement of 1980. The dialogue at the bilateral level takes place through an EC-Thailand Senior Officials Meetings – an informal, though regular, process. By establishing a formal bilateral relationship between the EU and Thailand upon the basis of the aforementioned Partnership and Cooperation Agreement, it is hoped that the two parties will find it easier to foster closer cooperation, minimize key problems and differences and achieve a better understanding. The negotiation process, launched in November 2004, is ongoing.

Conclusions

As outsiders with no voice in the process and yet with much at stake, members of the international community outside of the EU's borders closely observed the enlargement of the EU through the respective lenses of their national media. As the general public of the four Asia-Pacific countries in our study typically have limited first-hand experience of the EU and its Member States, (an assumption supported by public surveys conducted in each country as a part of this same research project, discussed in Chapters 3, 4, and 5 of this volume), it is argued that the media, as the primary source of information, is an influential mediator of public and official discourse about the EU. According to McCombs' agenda-setting theory, the media influences both "what we think about and how we think about it".[310] *What* we think about is influenced by what is given salience in the media. *How* we think about it is influenced by the way it is portrayed in the media. In terms of visibility, the May 2004 enlargement of the EU was clearly earmarked as an important event even for Europe's distant partners in the Asia-Pacific. Its heightened prominence in the Asia-Pacific print and television media points to its international significance as both a high point in the idealistic European integration project and as a dramatic symbol of a changing global landscape. It also reveals the perceived domestic importance of the event for the four Asia-Pacific economies of this study.

This chapter has argued that, in order to introduce the rapid and constant evolution of the EU to international audiences, Asia-Pacific newsmakers extensively resorted to metaphorical categorizations as a discursive tool. The metaphorical representations of the EU in the context of enlargement in the Asia-Pacific news media were revealed to be ambivalent, confused and contradictory. The EU's relative youth and novelty may be a partial cause of such images. But it is these very same things – youth and distinctiveness – that make the study of such imagery so important. The new Member States in particular, but also the EU more generally, are for many people 'blank spots' on their mental maps. Studying metaphors that were repeatedly employed by the media at the time of enlargement provides a rare opportunity to witness the construction of stereotypes. The repetition and consistency of the identified conceptual metaphors in the two most popular and powerful news media forms – reputable newspapers and national prime time television newscasts – across different media outlets in four different countries means there is a high chance of such images anchoring in the audiences' minds. Theories of meaning construction argue that categorization is easier than re-categorization; initial impressions are therefore the most important since these have a stronger chance of becoming cemented.[311] As result, the degree of flexibility for EU images presented in the future may thus become increasingly limited. Once stereotypical meanings are primed in audiences' minds, it becomes ever easier to 'sell' such ideas and the stereotype is perpetuated. Thus, developing a strong and cohesive identity and communicating it effectively both inside and outside the Union's borders becomes a more urgent task for the EU as it continues to grow and develop.

Notes

1 Bell, L. (2004), 'Push More Pens – Europe – A Worldwide Special Report – The Bureaucracy', *The Australian*, May 3, p. T1.
2 D. Beetham and C. Lord, *Legitimacy and the European Union*, Essex, Addison Wesley Longman, 1998, p. 8.
3 N. Chaban and M. Holland (eds), *The EU Through the Eyes of the Asia-Pacific: public perceptions and media representations,* NCRE Research Series No.4, University of Canterbury: NCRE, 2005, p.48.
4 Downer, A. (May 1, 2004), 'Australia Welcomes EU enlargement', *Department of Foreign Affairs and Trade*, Available HTTP <www.foreignminister.gov.au/releases/2004/fa061_04.html > (accessed April 7, 2004).
5 *Ibid.*
6 *Ibid.*
7 Downer, A. (April 16, 2003), 'EU Enlargement: Meeting the Challenges of the Global Security and Trade Environment', *Speech at the National Europe Centre Conference on EU Enlargement*, Canberra, Available HTTP <www.foreignminister.gov.au/speeches/2003/030416_eu.html> (accessed April 7, 2004).
8 Goff, P. (May 9, 2005), 'NZ and the EU, 12 months after enlargement', *Europa Lecture at National Centre for Research on Europe*, University of Canterbury, Available HTTP <http://www.europe.canterbury.ac.nz/europa/pdf/2005_goff_address> (accessed July 23, 2005).
9 *Ibid.*
10 NZ Ministry of Foreign Affairs, (May 1, 2004), 'Goff Welcomes Enlargement of EU', Available HTTP <http://www.beehive.govt.nz/ViewDocument.aspx?DocumentID=19621> (accessed May 12, 2006).
11 Clark, H. (April 21, 2004), *Address at State Luncheon in Poland.* Available HTTP <http://www.beehive.govt.nz/ViewDocument.aspx?DocumentID=22797> (accessed May 12, 2006).
12 H.E. Ban Ki-moon, (19 March 2004), 'Korea's Major Security Issues and Korea-EU Cooperation', Luncheon Speech by the Minister of Foreign Affairs and Trade of the Republic of Korea at the European Union Chamber of Commerce in Korea, Available HTTP <http://www.mofat.go.kr/me/me_a002/me_b006/1158488_980.html> (accessed 31 March 2007).

13 European Commission, (April 2006), 'The EU's relations with The Republic of Korea', Available HTTP <http://ec.europa.eu/comm/external_relations/south_korea/intro/index.htm> (accessed 31 March 2007).

14 Anonymous interview with Thai diplomat at the Royal Thai Embassy, Brussels, 8 November 2006.

15 *Ibid.*

16 Ginsberg, T., (2002) 'Rediscovering the World: September 11 Showed All too Clearly what a Terrible Mistake it was for America's News Media to Largely Ignore Foreign News', *American Journalism Review* 24, no.1.

17 Sreberny-Mohammadi, A., *et al.* (eds.) (1985), 'Foreign News in Media: International Reporting in 29 Countries', *Reports and Papers on Mass Communication* 93, UNESCO, Paris, pp. 38-39.

18 *Ibid.*

19 G. Lakoff and M. Johnson, *Metaphors we Live By*, Chicago, University of Chicago Press, 1980.

20 Chilton, P. and Ilyin, M. (1993), 'Metaphor in political discourse: the case of the "common European house"', *Discourse & Society* 4: 1, pp. 7-31; Chilton, P and Lakoff, G. (1995), 'Foreign Policy by Metaphor', in C. Schäffner, and A. Wenden (eds.), *Language and Peace*, Dartmouth, Aldershot, pp. 37-59; Chilton, P. (1996a) *Security Metaphors: cold war discourse from containment to common house*, New York, Peter Lang; Chilton, P. (1996b) 'The Meaning of Security', in: F. Beer and R. Hariman (eds.), *Post-Realim: the rhetorical turn in international relations*, East Lansing, Michigan State University Press, pp. 193-216; Schäffner, C. (1996), 'Building a European House? Or at Two Speeds into aDead End? Metaphors in the Debate on the United Europe', in A. Musolff, C. Schäffner, and M. Townson, (eds.), *Conceiving of Europe: diversity in unity*, Dartmouth, Aldershot, pp. 31-60; Straehle, C. et al. (1999) 'Struggle as metaphor in European Union discourses on Unemployment', *Discourse & Society* 10: 1, pp. 67-99.

21 G. Lakoff and M. Johnson, *Metaphors We Live By*, Chicago, University of Chicago, 2003, p. 5.

22 Lakoff, G. (1993), 'The contemporary theory of metaphor', in A. Ortony (ed.), *Metaphor and Thought*, New York, Cambridge University Press, pp.202-251

23 Lakoff and Johnson, *Metaphors We Live By*, p. 7-9

24 Gozzi, *The Power of Metaphor in the Age of Electronic Media*, pp. 59, 64-6.

25 Bailey, R. (2003), 'Conceptual Metaphor, Language, Literature and Pedagogy', *Journal of Language and Learning* 1: 2, p. 59.

26 *Ibid.*

27 A. Deignan, "Linguistic Metaphors, Grammar and Conceptual Metaphor Theory: Evidence from the Bank of English". Paper at the 8th International Cognitive Linguistics Conference *Language between Mind and Text: The Use of Corpora In Cognitive Linguistics*, July 20–25, 2003, La Rioja, Spain, Available HTTP <http://people.freenet.de/iclc2003/iclc_deignan.html> (accessed May 10, 2005).

28 Pepper, Stephen C. *World Hypotheses: A Study in Evidence.* Berkeley, University of California Press, 1942; Lakoff and Johnson, *Metaphors We Live By*, 1980; Lakoff and Johnson, *Metaphors We Live By*, 2003.

29 Gozzi, *The Power of Metaphor in the Age of Electronic Media*, p. 59.

30 *Ibid.*

31 The images of Turkey in its interactions with the EU in the context of EU enlargement, Cyprus referendum and the fall entry negotiations were investigated in greater detail in the article: Chaban, N, et. al. (2005), 'Past Imperfect, Present Continuous, Future Indefinite?: Images of Turkey in the Context of EU integration in ANZAC Media', *Insight Turkey* 7: 3.

32 Shulz, W., (May 24-28, 2001), 'Foreign News in Leading Newspapers of Western and Post-Communist Countries', Paper prepared for presentation at the *51st Annual*

Conference of the International Communication Association, Washington D.C., USA, Available HTTP <http://www.kwpw.wiso.uni-erlangen.de/pdf_dateien/ica_fn2001. pdf> (accessed September 14, 2004).

33 Ginsberg, 'Rediscovering the World'.
34 *ABC News*, (2004), 'The European Union has become the world's largest free trade region', May 1. ; *ABC News*, (2004), 'There's opposition to EU policies in former communist states which have just joined the EU', May 2.
35 *The Australian*, (2004), 'Flights of fancy: EU expansion clears the way to exotic locations', May 21, p. B1.
36 *Canberra Times*, (2004), 'Bells will ring during Malta celebrations; Acceding country', April 30, p. 7.
37 *Canberra Times*, (2004), 'Slovak Republic aims for important partnerships; Acceding country', April 3, p. 14.
38 *Canberra Times*, 'A Day Of Unity'.
39 Kitney, G. (2004), 'Hard Bargaining ahead as EU Expands', *Australian Financial Review*, May 3, p. 8.
40 *ABC News*, (2004), 'EU Leaders Have Resolved Differences And Agreed On The Organisation's First Ever Constitution', June 19.
41 *Herald Sun,* (2004), 'Europe's getting reunited', May 1, p. 23.
42 *Canberra Times*, 'A Day Of Unity'.
43 Wilson, P., (2004), 'New Faces - Regional Overview - Europe - A Worldwide Special Report', *The Australian*, May 3, p. T1.
44 *Sydney Morning Herald*, (2004), 'Uniting States of Europe', May 1, p. 42.
45 *Canberra Times*, (2004), 'A Day Of Unity'.
46 *ABC News*, 'The European Union Has Become The World's Largest Free Trade Region'.
47 Moskwa, W. (2004), 'Joy as Europe Swells by 10', *Sunday Herald Sun*, May 2, p. 4.
48 Fray, P. (2004), 'Europe's biggest gamble', *Sydney Morning Herald*, May 1, p.39.
49 *Sydney Morning Herald*, (2004), 'Just Too Big For Its Roots', May 1, p. 40; Fray, P. 'Poles Apart', *Sydney Morning Herald*, May 1, p. 34.
50 *Sydney Morning Herald,* 'Uniting States of Europe'.
51 Fray, 'Poles Apart'.
52 Wilson, 'New Faces - Regional Overview'.
53 *The Australian*, (2004), 'Push More Pens - Europe - A Worldwide Special Report - The Bureaucracy', May 3, p. T1.
54 Fray, P. (2004), 'France and Germany No Longer Fulcrum Of Expanded Europe, Says Blair', *Sydney Morning Herald*, May 1, p. 4.
55 Moskwa, 'Joy as Europe Swells by 10'.
56 *Canberra Times*, (2004), 'Estonia in a Place Where It Belongs; Acceding Country', April 30, p. 14; *Canberra Times,* (2004), 'EU Expansion A Historic Step', May 1, p. B13.
57 *Sydney Morning Herald*, (2004), 'The Cyprus Countdown', April 22, p. 1.
58 *Canberra Times*, (2004), 'A Motley Lot: Good, Bad And The Ugly', May 1, p. 1.
59 Brook, S. (2004), 'Ironing Out the Curtain - Europe - A Worldwide Special Report - The Applicants', May 3, p. T1.
60 *Sydney Morning Herald*, 'Just Too Big For Its Roots'.
61 Wilson, P., (2004), 'Europe's Suffering From Growing Pains', *The Australian*, May 1.
62 Fray, 'Europe's Biggest Gamble'.
63 *Sydney Morning Herald*, 'Just Too Big For Its Roots'.
64 *ABC News*, 'The European Union Has Become The World's Largest Free Trade Region'.
65 Fray, 'Europe's Biggest Gamble'.
66 *Ibid.*

67 Wilson, 'New Faces - Regional Overview'.
68 Kitney, G, (2004), 'Old Europe Gambles On Infusion Of New Blood To Invigorate EU', *Australian Financial Review*, May 1, p. 29.
69 Moskwa, 'Joy as Europe Swells by 10'.
70 *Sydney Morning Herald*, 'Uniting States of Europe'.
71 Kennedy, A., (2004), 'Spotlight On... The European Union', *Sydney Morning Herald*, May 6, p. 20.
72 Kitney, 'Old Europe Gambles On Infusion Of New Blood'.
73 *Sydney Morning Herald*, 'Uniting States of Europe'.
74 *Sydney Morning Herald*, 'Just Too Big For Its Roots'.
75 *Ibid.*
76 Moskwa, 'Joy as Europe Swells by 10'; *Canberra Times*, (2004), 'Big EU welcome', May 11; *Canberra Times*, (2004), 'Cyprus Celebrates Accession; Acceding Country', April 30, p. 8.
77 *ABC News*, 'The European Union Has Become the World's Largest Free Trade Region'.
78 *Canberra Times*, 'A Motley Lot'.
79 Moskwa, 'Joy as Europe Swells by 10'.
80 *Canberra Times*, 'A Motley Lot'.
81 *Ibid.*
82 *Herald Sun*, 'Europe's getting reunited'.
83 *Sydney Morning Herald*, 'Uniting States of Europe'.
84 *Canberra Times*, (2004), 'Adopting the Euro', April 30, p. 8.
85 Wilson, 'Europe's Suffering from Growing Pains'.
86 Wilson, 'New Faces - Regional Overview'.
87 *The Australian*, (2004), 'Angst over EU Rookies', May 1, p. 23.
88 *Sydney Morning Herald*, 'Just Too Big For Its Roots'.
89 Brook, 'Ironing Out the Curtain'.
90 *Ibid.*
91 *Sydney Morning Herald*, 'Just Too Big For Its Roots'.
92 Kitney, 'Old Europe Gambles On Infusion Of New Blood'.
93 *Herald Sun*, 'Europe's Getting Reunited'; *Canberra Times*, 'A Day Of Unity'.
94 Kitney, G. (2004), 'Cracks Open In Euro Zone's Credibility', *Australian Financial Review*, April 20, p. 14.
95 Kitney, 'Old Europe Gambles On Infusion Of New Blood'.
96 *Ibid.*
97 *The Australian*, (2004), 'Angst over EU Rookies', May 1, p. 23.
98 *Ibid.*
99 *Ibid.*
100 *Canberra Times*, (2004), 'EU Expansion a Historic Step', May 1, p. B13; *ABC News*, 'The European Union Has Become the World's Largest Free Trade Region'.
101 Kitney, 'Old Europe Gambles On Infusion Of New Blood'.
102 *The Australian*, 'Angst over EU Rookies'.
103 Wilson, 'Europe's Suffering from Growing Pains'.
104 Kitney, 'Old Europe Gambles On Infusion Of New Blood'.
105 Kitney, G. (2004), 'Challenges On All Sides For EU', *Australian Financial Review*, April 27, p. 12.
106 Fray, 'Europe's Biggest Gamble'; *The Australian*, 'Angst over EU Rookies'.
107 *Herald Sun*, 'Europe's Getting Reunited'; Wilson, 'Europe's Suffering from Growing Pains'; *Canberra Times*, (2004), 'Economic Growth Will Strengthen Czech Republic; Acceding Country', April 30. p. 10.
108 *The Australian*, "Angst over EU Rookies'.
109 Wilson, 'Europe's Suffering from Growing Pains'.
110 *Ibid.*

111 Moskwa, 'Joy as Europe Swells by 10'.
112 Bell, 'Push More Pens'.
113 *ABC News*, (2004), 'There's Opposition to EU Policies in Former Communist States Which Have Just Joined the EU', May 2.
114 Kitney, 'Old Europe Gambles On Infusion Of New Blood'.
115 *Canberra Times*, (2004), 'Poland Boasts Economic Achievements; Acceding Country', April 30, p. 12.
116 Este, J. (2004), 'Three's Company At Russia's Door – Europe – A Worldwide Special Report - The New Members', *The Australian*, May 3, p.T10.
117 Fray, 'Europe's Biggest Gamble'.
118 *Sydney Morning Herald*, 'Just Too Big For Its Roots'.
119 Kitney, 'Old Europe Gambles On Infusion Of New Blood'.
120 Kennedy, 'Spotlight On...The European Union'.
121 *Canberra Times*, (2004), 'EU Expansion A Historic Step', May 1, p. B13.
122 *Canberra Times*, 'A Day Of Unity'
123 *Canberra Times*, 'EU Expansion A Historic Step'.
124 Wilson, 'New Faces - Regional Overview'.
125 *Ibid.*
126 Fray, 'Europe's Biggest Gamble'.
127 *Ibid.*
128 *Sydney Morning Herald*, 'Just Too Big For Its Roots'.
129 Este, J. (2004), 'Poles Going Cold – Europe – A Worldwide Special Report – New Members,' *The Australian*, May 3, p. T04.
130 *Canberra Times*, 'A Day Of Unity'; Kitney, 'Hard Bargaining Ahead As EU Expands'; Kitney, 'Old Europe Gambles On Infusion Of New Blood'; *Canberra Times*, "Poland Boasts Economic Achievements'; Wilson, 'New Faces – Regional Overview'.
131 Fray, 'Europe's Biggest Gamble'.
132 *Sydney Morning Herald*, 'Just Too Big For Its Roots'.
133 *Sydney Morning Herald,* 'Uniting States of Europe'.
134 *Canberra Times*, 'A Motley Lot: Good, Bad And The Ugly'.
135 *Sydney Morning Herald*, 'Just Too Big For Its Roots'.
136 *ABC News*, 'The European Union Has Become The World's Largest Free Trade Region'.
137 Bell, 'Push More Pens'.
138 *Sydney Morning Herald*, 'Just Too Big For Its Roots'.
139 Harcourt, T. (2004), 'More Countries Means More For Us – Europe – A Worldwide Special Report – Australia And The EU', *The Australian*, May 3, p.T08.
140 Onto, J. (2004), 'Europe Now Too Big To Ignore', *Australian Financial Review*, May 3, p. 63.
141 *Canberra Times*, (2004), 'Trade the Cornerstone of EU; Partners in Learning', April 30, p. 6.
142 *Ibid.*
143 *Canberra Times*, 'Poland Boasts Economic Achievements'.
144 Kerin, J. and Shanahan, D., (2004), 'Downer and Rudd Court Europe', *The Australian*, May 20, p. 12.
145 Espiner, C. (2004), 'Chilly Welcome Awaits New EU', *Press*, April 27, p. 11.
146 *Ibid.*
147 McHardy, A., (2004), 'Hysteria Building Over Flood Of New Migrants As EU Expands; People From Poorer Countries Look For Jobs And Better Pay', *New Zealand Herald*, May 4, p. B4.
148 Espiner, 'Chilly Welcome Awaits New EU'.
149 Dyer, (2004), 'Where to the EU? Like as Not, from Portugal to the Pacific', *Otago Daily Times*, April 29, p. 9.

150 Field, C. (2004), 'Emotions Flow as EU Welcomes 10', *New Zealand Herald*, May 3, p. B3.
151 *Ibid.*
152 Meyer, 'End of a Golden Era'.
153 Espiner, 'Chilly Welcome Awaits New EU'.
154 Meyer, 'End of a Golden Era'.
155 *Otago Daily Times*, (2004), 'Weekend of Celebration for EU', May 3.
156 *TV3 News*, (2004), 'The Formation Of The World's Largest Trading Bloc Has Been Heralded By Fireworks, Celebrations, Speeches And Singing As Ten New Members Were Welcomed Into The European Union', May 1.
157 Field, C. (2004), 'EU Vision Leaves Voters Cold', *New Zealand Herald*, June 14, p. b02.
158 Wallace, N. (2004), 'Expanding EU Impacts on NZ Trade', *Otago Daily Times*, May 1.
159 Espiner, 'Chilly Welcome Awaits New EU'.
160 Dyer, 'Where to the EU?'.
161 *Ibid.*
162 Meyer, 'End of a golden era'.
163 *TV3 News*, (2004), 'A Ceremony In Dublin Has Celebrated The Expansion Of The European Union', May 2.
164 Dyer, 'Where to the EU?'.
165 Field, 'Emotions Flow as EU Welcomes 10'.
166 Field, C. (2004), 'Big Bang' Redraws the Map', *New Zealand Herald*, April 28, p.B4.
167 Meyer, 'End of a Golden Era'.
168 Marinas, R. (2004), 'Romanian Farmers All for GM Soya', *Otago Daily Times*, June 14.
169 Meyer, M. (2004), 'End of a Golden Era', *New Zealand Herald*, May 1, p. B1.
170 Field, 'Emotions Flow as EU Welcomes 10'.
171 *TV3 News*, 'The Formation Of The World's Largest Trading Bloc...'.
172 *Otago Daily Times*, 'Weekend of celebration for EU'.
173 Espiner, 'Chilly Welcome Awaits New EU'.
174 *Otago Daily Times*, 'Weekend of celebrations for EU'.
175 Espiner, 'Chilly Welcome Awaits New EU'.
176 Meyer, 'End of a Golden Era'.
177 Dyer, 'Where to the EU?'.
178 *Otago Daily Times*, 'Weekend of celebrations for EU'.
179 Field, 'Big Bang' Redraws the Map'.
180 Meyer, 'End of a Golden Era'.
181 McHardy, 'Hysteria Building over Flood of New Migrants'.
182 *Ibid.*
183 Espiner, 'Chilly Welcome Awaits New EU'.
184 Field, 'Big Bang' Redraws the Map'.
185 *Ibid.*
186 Espiner, 'Chilly Welcome Awaits New EU'.
187 *Ibid.*
188 Espiner, C. (2004). 'National identity key to migration worries', *New Zealand Herald*, June 26, p. 17.
189 Espiner, 'Chilly Welcome Awaits New EU'.
190 *Ibid.*
191 The 'Big Bang' is the dominant scientific theory for the creation of the universe, and according to the theory, a single point of intensely focused energy erupted in a tremendous explosion, thus causing the gradual expansion of the universe.
192 Meyer, 'End of a Golden Era'.

193 Field, C. (2004), 'EU Sees an End to Gridlock over New President's Post', *New Zealand Herald*, June 28, p. b02.
194 Field, 'Big Bang Redraws the Map'.
195 Espiner, 'Chilly Welcome Awaits New EU'.
196 Field, 'Emotions Flow as EU Welcomes 10'.
197 Espiner, 'Chilly Welcome Awaits New EU'.
198 *Ibid.*
199 *Ibid.*
200 Field, 'Big Bang' Redraws the Map'.
201 *Otago Daily Times*, 'Weekend of Celebration for EU'.
202 Meyer, 'End of a Golden Era'.
203 *Ibid.*
204 Dyer, 'Where to the EU?'.
205 Meyer, 'End of a Golden Era'.
206 Meyer, 'End of a Golden Era'.
207 Wallace, 'Expanding EU Impacts on NZ Trade'.
208 *Ibid.*
209 Schouten, H. (2004), 'EU Expansion Good For NZ', *Dominion Post*, April 29, p. 10.
210 Wallace, 'Expanding EU Impacts on NZ Trade'.
211 박혜윤, (2004), 'EU의 GM(유전자조작식품)식품에 대한 행동의 변화', *Donga Ilbo*, April 20.
212 박제균, (2004), 'EU 통합및 확대의 문제점의 해결 과정과 한국에 대한 걱정', *Donga Ilbo*, April 3.
213 강경희, (2004), '변화하는 친기업중심의 동유럽 국가들', *Chosun Ilbo*, April 27.
214 심재우, (2004), 'EU와 한국의 R&D분야의 교류가 활성화 위해 방한', *Jungang Ilbo*, April 16.
215 *Ibid.*
216 Associated Press, (2004), 'EU가입 앞두로 부는 헝가리의 부동산 붐', *Chosun Ilbo*, April 14.
217 이진, (2004), '25개국으로 확대되는 EU의 과제', *Donga Ilbo*, April 29.
218 김세원, (2004), 'EU의 확대와 이로인한 한국의 긍정적 효과', *Donga Ilbo*, April 30.
219 Won Jae Lee, (2004), '무력없이 확대된 유럽', *Donga Ilbo*, May 15.
220 강경희, (2004), 'EU회원국간의 빈부격차', *Chosun Ilbo*, April 27.
221 Hong Kwon Hee, (2004), '[인물]아시아유럽재단 사무총장 조원일 뉴욕총영사 선출', *Donga Ilbo*, May 29.
222 박제균, (2004), 'EU 통합및 확대의 문제점의 해결 과정과 한국에 대한 걱정', *Donga Ilbo*, April 3.
223 강경희, '변화하는 친기업중심의 동유럽 국가들'.
224 박제균, (2004), 'EU 확대의 긍정적 영향과 남은 과제 그리고 한국과의 관계', *Donga Ilbo*, April 26.
225 김세원, 'EU의 확대와 이로인한 한국의 긍정적 효과'.
226 Kim Tae Gyu, (2004), 'EU's enlargement and Korean profit', *Korea Times*, April 18.
227 Yoon Won Sup, (2004), 'Enlargement & EU to play bigger role in NK crisis', *Korea Times*, April 30.
228 Kim Yong Gi, (2004), '[산업] 주한유럽상공회의소, 외국인 한국투자 중재자로', *Donga Ilbo*, May 18.
229 Kim Tae-Gyu, (2004), 'EU's enlargement and Korean profit', *Korea Times*, April 18.
230 Bae Keun Min, (2004), 'Asian, EU investors snatch up properties', *Korea Times*, May 21.
231 차지완, "EU는 미국과 같은 한국에게 거대한 시장", *Donga Ilbo*, April 29, 2004
232 박제균, "EU 확대의 긍정적 영향과 남은 과제 그리고 한국과의 관계", *Donga Ilbo*, April 26, 2004.
233 *Ibid.*

234 *Ibid.*
235 Yoon Won Sup, (2004), 'EU's new competition rule for all around the world', *Korea Times*, April 23.
236 *Ibid.*
237 Ivan Hotek, (2004), 'EU's enlargement and Relations between Korea and Czech', *Korea Times*, April 26.
238 *Ibid.*
239 주성원, (2004), 'EU헌법에 대한 국민투표를 결정한 토니블래어 총리', *Donga Ilbo*, April 22.
240 See for eg: Lee Jin , "'빅EU'탄생..10개국 가입 총 26개국으로", *Donga Ilbo*, May 1, 2004.
241 *Chosun Ilbo*, '거대 EU탄생의 의미를 아는가?<Do you know the meaning of the birth of the huge EU?>', May 3.
242 Predecessor to the EU: the European Coal and Steel Community
243 *Donga Ilbo*, (2004), '리비아와 EU의 협력관계에 대한 회담', April 28.
244 Kang Kyoung Hee, (2004), '유럽통합 닻올린다', *Chosun Ilbo*, May 1.
245 *Chosun Ilbo*, '거대 EU탄생의 의미를 아는가?'.
246 Kang Kyoung Hee, '유럽통합 닻올린다'.
247 박제균, (2004), 'EU 통합및 확대의 문제점의 해결 과정과 한국에 대한 걱정', *Donga Ilbo*, April 3.
248 박용근, (2004), 'EU의 시장규제 대폭 풀림', *Chosun Ilbo*, April 23.
249 허진석, (2004), 'EU확대와 한국의 대처 방안에 대한 조언', *Donga Ilbo*, April 27.
250 Kim Sung Yeun, (2004), '유럽에 한국투자 연락사무소', *Chosun Ilbo*, May 22.
251 차지완, (2004), 'EU는 미국과 같은 한국에게 거대한 시장', *Donga Ilbo*, April 29.
252 *Ibid.*
253 강경희, (2004), '유럽시장을 위한 한국 공동 물류센터 오픈', *Chosun Ilbo*, April 29.
254 현오석, (2004), 'EU확대가 한국에게 주는 득과 실', *Chosun Ilbo*, April 24.
255 *The Nation*, (2004), 'EU heading for heartburn?', 1 May, p.3.
256 Matichon, (2004), 'อียุยุคใหม่: ก้าวสำคัญที่ต้องจับตบ, 3 May, p.1.
257 *Bangkok Post*, (2004), 'EU welcomes new states', 1 May, p.6.
258 Matichon อียุยุคใหม่: ก้าวสำคัญที่ต้องจับตบ' 3 May 2004, p.1
259 . *Bangkok Post*, (2004), 'New and very different members pose test for EU', 13 April, p. 4.
260 *Bangkok Post*, 'New and Very Different Members Pose Test for the EU', 13 April 2004, p. 7.
261 *The Nation*, (2004), 'EU heading for heartburn?, 1 May, p. 1; Thai Rath " อียุสยายปีกคลุ 25 ประเทศ", 2 May 2004, p. 2.
262 *The Nation*, (2004), 'Expanding the EU-new Member State face difficult path for full integration', 10 May, p. 4.
263 *The Manager*, "ชาวเช็กเตรียมฉลองร่วมเป็นสมาชิกใหม่อีย", 1 May 2004; *Bangkok Post*, (2004), 'Macedonia mourns loss of its president', 28 February, p7
264 *Bangkok Post*, (2004), 'EU welcomes Turkish reforms, warns more needed for entry', 19 June, p. 4.
265 *Bangkok Post*, (2004), 'Turkey's future belongs to the EU', 23 December, p. 11.
266 *The Manager*, "20ภาษาทำมีน อียุตั้งงบแปลปีละพันล้าน", 11 May 2004
267 *Bangkok Post*, (2004), 'Closing the east-west divide' 2 May, p. 7.
268 *Bangkok Post*, (2004), 'Party Over', 3 May, p. 3.
269 *The Manager*, เกิดการปะทะที่ไอร์แลนด์ในระหว่างพิธีรับสมาชิกใหม่อีย, 2 May 2004.
270 *The Manager*, "เฉลิมฉลองทั่วยุโรปต้อนสมาชิกใหม่อีย", 1 May 2004.
271 *The Nation*, 'EU heading for heartburn?'.

272 *The Nation,* 'A continent once again united', 2 May 2004, p. 8A, *Thai Rath,* 'โอ้หน
     คนบนโลกที่3', p. 2.

273 *Bangkok Post,* 'Party Over', 3 May 2004, p. 3.

274 *The Manager,* "เยอรมนีฉลองต้อนรับสมาชิกใหม่อียู", 1 May 2004; *The Nation,* (2004),
     'EU prepares to usher in a new era', 1 May, p. 4.

275 *The Nation,* (2004), 'A Continent Once Again United,' DATE?? p. 8.

276 *The Nation,* (2004), 'Power bargaining within the EU decision-making', 6 March, p.
     5.

277 *The Nation,* 'EU heading for heartburn?' 1 May 2004, p. 1

278 Ibid.

279 *The Nation,* (2004), 'There are ways around expanded EU's tariffs', 21 April, p. 4.

280 *Bangkok Post,* (2004), 'Expanded EU offers greater opportunities', 30 April, p. 3.

281 *Bangkok Post,* (2004), 'Expanded EU more than a major market', 6 May, p. 8.

282 *The Nation,* (2004), 'EU has "double standards"', 25 June, p. 7.

283 *Bangkok Post,* (2004), 'VN urged not to give in to the EU', 8 Jan, p. 4. The South East
     Asian countries (and Thailand in particular) have been observed as being sensitive
     about 'equality' in their relationships with Europe, and this concern was reflected in
     the identified news items. This sensitivity has to do not only with Thailand's status as
     a 'developing country', but also with the country's 'scars' dating back to the period of
     colonization of the South-East Asian region by European imperial powers.

284 *The Nation,* 'There are ways around expanded EU's tariffs'.

285 *Thai Rath,* "อียูสยายปีกคลุม 25 ประเทศ", 2 May 2004

286 The Manager, " พาณิชย์"รองอียูชดเชยไทย", 31 May 2004.

287 The Manager, "พาณิชย์"รองอียูชดเชยไทย", 31 May 2004.

288 *The Nation,* 'There are ways around expanded EU's tariffs'.

289 Tully, James. "The Pen is a Mighty Sword: Quentin Skinner's Analysis of Politics." In
     Meaning and Context: Quentin Skinner and his Critics, edited by James Tully, 7 - 25.
     Princenton, NJ: Princeton University Press, 1988.

290 Doty, R. (1993), 'Foreign Policy as Social Construction: A Post-Positivist Analysis of
     U.S. Counter-Insurgency Policy in the Philippines', *International Studies Quarterly*
     37, pp. 308-309 in F. Rusciano, (1997), 'First- and Third-World Newspapers on World
     Opinion: Imagined Communities in the Cold War and Post–Cold War Eras', *Political
     Communication* 14: 2, p. 175.

291 *Ibid.*

292 R. Jackendoff, *Semantics and Cognition,* Cambridge, MIT Press, 1983, p. 60; P.
     Chilton, *Orwellian Language and the Media,* London, Pluto, 1988, p. 6.

293 Lakoff and Johnson, *Metaphors we Live By,* 1980

294 Gozzi, *The Power of Metaphor in the Age of Electronic Media,* p. 61; Lakoff, *Metaphor
     in Politics.*

295 This study extrapolated that not only individual states, but other international entities
     (e.g. the EU) could be conceptualized as a 'person' engaged in social relations
     within a world community. This study clearly recognized that the EU is not a state,
     nevertheless, it has been found that the media and political discourses inside and outside
     the Union extensively compared the EU to a state in their literal and metaphorical
     categorizations. Indeed, Manners and Whitman claimed that the EU is generally
     addressed and understood by its external partners in a capacity similar to that of a
     state (Manners, I. and Whitman, R. (2003), 'The Difference Engine: Constructing and
     Representing the International Identity of the EU', *Journal of Public Policy* 10:3.)

296 see for eg. Mumby D. and Spitzack, C. (1983), 'Ideology and Television News',
     Central States Speech Journal 34 in R. Gozzi, *The Power of Metaphor in the Age of
     Electronic Media,* Cresskill, Hampton Press Inc, 1999, p. 61; Cibulskien , J. (2002),
     'The Metaphorization of Election as War in the 2001 General Election Campaign of
     Great Britain', *Respectus Philologicus* 2: 7 Available HTTP <http://filologija.vukhf.
     lt/2-7/cibulskiene.htm> (accessed May 3, 2005). The ARGUMENT IS WAR schema

is also researched in detail by G. Lakoff and M. Johnson, *Metaphors We Live By*. The metaphors of health/ illness were researched by Koeller, W., *Semiotek und Metapher*, Mertzlersche Veralgs buchhandlung, Stugart, 1975, pp.289, 298, Koeningsberg, R., *Hitler's Ideology. A Study in Psychoanalytic Sociology*, The Library of Social Science, New York, 1975, p.15-29; and Edelman, M. *The symbolic use of politics, Uraban*, Ilinois. 1974, all cited in Landtsheer, C. (1991), 'Function and the Language of Politics: A Linguistic Uses and Gratifications Approach', *Communication and Cognition* 24, 3-4, p. 322

297 See K. Stats, (2006), *Framing the European Union: An Australian Case Study of the EU's Image Abroad*, unpublished MA thesis, The University of Melbourne.

298 The New Zealand government provides information on how NZ Government is prepared to deal with natural disiaters , namely earthquakes, landslides, volcanic eruptions, hydrothermal activity, tsunami and floods on its official website. See http://www.govt.nz/search?type=thes&t=service&q=%22Floods%22; (accessed Janury 31, 2007)

299 de Landtsheer, C. (1991), 'Function and the Language of Politics: A Linguistic Uses and Gratifications Approach', *Communication and Cognition* 24: 3-4, p. 322.

300 de Landtsheer, C., 'Function and the Language of Politics', p. 323

301 Blumler, J. G. and D. Kavanagh (1999) 'The Third Age Of Political Communication: Influences And Features', *Political Communication*, 16: 209–230, 1999, p 216

302 Chilton & Ilyin, 'Metaphor in Political Discourse', p. 1, in I. Hellsten and M. Renvall, *Inside Or Outside Of Politics? Metaphor And Paradox In Journalism*, Available HTTP <http://www.nordicom.gu.se/common/publ_pdf/29_hellsten.pdf> (accessed May 24, 2006).

303 I. Hellsten and M. Renvall, *Inside Or Outside Of Politics? Metaphor And Paradox In Journalism*

304 Sofia Broström, *The Role of Metaphor in Cognitive Semantics*. Lund University Cognitive Studies, 31 LUHFDA/HFKO-3003-SE, Lund, Lund University, 1994, p. 32.

305 *Ibid.*

306 Stereotype here is understood as a concept held by one social group about another and which is used frequently to justify certain discriminatory behaviours.

307 Alexander Downer, 'Australia and Europe: Sharing Global Responsibilities', The Schuman Lecture, Canberra, 11 May 2006, Available HTTP <http://www.foreignminister.gov.au/speeches/2006/060511_schuman_lecture.html> (accessed 23 May 2006).

308 Business NZ, *Export Perspectives*. 18 April 2007 Available HTTP <http://www.businessnz.org.nz/file/1190/business_nz_text-loRes%20crop.pdf>, (Accessed May 5, 2007), p.15

309 New Zealand Ministry of Foreign Affairs and Trade, 'European Union Information Paper', Available HTTP <http://www.mfat.govt.nz/Countries/Europe/European-Union.php> (accessed 24 January 2006).

310 M. Glecker, *Critique*, Available HTTP <http://oak.cats.ohiou.edu/~mg398797/agscri.htm> (Accessed August 26, 2005).

3 Exposure, accessibility and difference

How Australians and New Zealanders perceive Europe and the European Union

Bradford S. Jones

An assertion commonly made about the nature and structure of attitudes towards politics and political institutions is that individuals are largely uninformed, attitudes largely unconstrained. In the context of American public opinion, the line of research examining attitude constraint goes back more than 40 years, its canonical root being Converse's classic 1964 study, 'The Nature of Belief Systems in Mass Publics'.[1] With respect to the American public, Converse found only a small percentage of individuals who could 'constrain' – tie together – issues ideologically. Converse cast further doubt on the ability of individuals to hold meaningfully coherent opinions with the publication of his famous 'black and white' model.[2] In this, Converse essentially argued individuals offered not much more than random guesses as to their issue positions. In looking at panel data, Converse found little evidence for attitudinal stability. He treated this as indicative of the absence of meaningful opinions among all but the most highly educated.

Subsequent research has refined (or in some cases putatively refuted[3]) Converse's claims, offering instead more nuanced explanations for the apparent lack of meaningfully held attitudes among individuals. For example, in a pair of now-classic studies, Feldman and Zaller show that individuals' ambivalence over certain kinds of political and social issues *appears* as non-attitudes; however, if under some conditions respondents 'favor' an issue, and under other conditions 'oppose' an issue, then in the analysis of panel data, what appears as non-attitudes is really ambivalence.[4] The voluminous literature on political attitudes has extended beyond the sphere of public opinion on domestic issues. In a series of important articles, Hurwitz and Peffley considered the issue of attitudinal constraint on foreign policy.[5] Using structural equation models, they found substantial evidence of 'general orientations' towards foreign policy issues and foreign affairs. In short, the stark picture painted in Converse's original classics seems not to hold, generally, in subsequent research.

This chapter is concerned with 'attitude constraint'. The main question of this study is, 'how do individuals *outside* of the European Union actually evaluate the political entity?' The question is more than mere academic rumination. The nature and structure of attitudes towards the EU is incredibly important from the standpoint of a functioning democracy. The dimensions over which individuals perceive the EU may in turn have sway over political elites' willingness to pursue certain courses of action, and certain kinds of policy. To that end, the now vast literature on public opinion and the EU has shown us that individuals residing within Member States or potential Member States have a tremendous amount of attitudinal constraint. Concerns about national sovereignty, sense of community, economic self-interest and cultural threat posed by the membership in the EU have all been found to be related to attitudes and perceptions of the EU.[6] However, there is an important omission in the literature on EU public opinion. Given the EU's demonstrable role in global politics, ranging from banking and mercantile concerns to its role in international disputes, it seems natural to ask how individuals *outside* of Western and Eastern Europe perceive the EU, its role, scope and function. After all, the EU is the global counter to the United States and, as such, serves as a major trading partner to virtually every industrialized country. Further, as the euro supplants the US dollar as the international currency of choice, it is becoming increasingly apparent that sovereign governments and private industry will, out of necessity, need to work with the EU and the EU Commission.[7] Put differently, perceptions of the EU are not just a 'continental issue'; migration and immigration issues, concerns with travelling to Europe and trading with EU Member States affect the global community generally, not just Member States and potential Member States specifically. This chapter will consider how individuals from two geographically distant countries (from Europe) perceive and evaluate the EU. Specifically, survey data collected from a random sample of Australian and New Zealand citizens show consistent patterns in the nature and structure of attitudes towards the likely impact the EU will have on these countries. Indeed, as shown below, the dimensions over which Australians and New Zealanders view the EU exhibits remarkable similarity, though the factors that 'predict' attitudes over these dimensions vary between the two nations. The following section describes the social and political connections between Australia and New Zealand and presents some analyses of the perceptions of the EU among Australians and New Zealanders.

Australia, New Zealand and the European Union

As Holland and Jones note, the EU plays a central role in the economic, political and social fabric of both Australia and New Zealand.[8] Economically, the EU is among the leading trading partners of each country. For over ten years, the EU has been Australia's leading trading partner; for New Zealand, the EU is the second leading trading partner (behind Australia). The EU serves as a major economic market for commodities like coal, wool, meat (particularly lamb), produce and wine. Indeed, Australia is now the leading exporter of wine to the EU. With respect to global climate change and carbon emissions, both Australia and New Zealand are intertwined with the EU. Both New Zealand and the EU have ratified the Kyoto agreement; Australia has not. Australia's lack of ratification has rankled both the EU and many Australian citizens. Nevertheless, the issue of greenhouse gas emissions plays a central role in the dialogue between the three parties. As New Zealand Prime Minister Helen Clark said:

For countries, like New Zealand, whose economies are based on agriculture, this poses a significant threat. For some regions of Australia, already susceptible to drought and with rainfall forecast to decline further, the threat is even more severe. The President of Australia's National Farmers' Federation summed it up in August this year, when he said that climate change is possibly the biggest risk facing Australian farmers in the coming century.[9]

Politically, given Australia and New Zealand's colonial connection with England, there are natural connections between the two countries and Europe more generally, the historical gateway being Britain. Moreover, as Chaban notes, a substantial proportion of New Zealanders trace their ancestral roots to Europe, particularly Britain.[10] Similar remarks apply for Australia. With respect to Australia, the EU's relationship with the United States on matters of foreign policy is paramount. Perhaps next only to former British Prime Minister Tony Blair, former Australian Prime Minister John Howard was President George W. Bush's biggest supporter on issues pertinent to terrorism, the Middle East and Iraq in particular. How Australians view the EU *vis-à-vis* the United States would seem to be of natural interest, both academically and politically. New Zealand's relationship with the EU *vis-à-vis* the United States is equally important. On the trade front, the relationship between the two countries has been 'cool' in recent years in part due to New Zealand's declaration of being a nuclear-free zone in the 1980s. Bush administration officials, who have referred to this policy as 'a relic', have hindered efforts at liberalizing trade flows between the countries.[11]

To evaluate perceptions Australians and New Zealanders have of the EU, this investigation now turns to survey data. In December 2004, a random sample was administered to a representative sample of Australian and New Zealand residents. The survey was designed by the National Centre for Research on Europe at the University of Canterbury in Christchurch, New Zealand. The survey was part of the APP project that is the focus of this book, and which was designed to measure citizens' and elites' perceptions of the EU as well as measure media coverage of the EU.[12] The intent of this survey was to gauge evaluations of the EU, as well as other geo-political regions in the world, and to measure the extent to which individuals acquire information (both general information acquisition and specific information acquisition about the EU) as well as how information is acquired (i.e. newspapers, television, word-of-mouth, etc.). The survey was a computer-assisted telephone interview, with each survey lasting about fifteen minutes.[13] The usable sample sizes for the Australian survey and the New Zealand survey were each, respectively, 400. The composition of both samples mostly consisted of non-indigenous respondents. About 88 per cent of the New Zealand sample identified as being of 'European' or 'Pakeha'[14] descent and about 99 per cent of the Australian sample self-identified as being 'non-Aboriginal'. Both samples captured variation in education levels. About 36 per cent of the Australian sample and 28 per cent of the New Zealand sample reported having tertiary education. These estimates are consistent with OECD population estimates.[15] About 52.75 per cent of the Australian sample and 50.25 per cent of the New Zealand sample were female.[16]

To begin the analysis of the nature and structure of attitudes towards the EU, first consider Figure 3.1. This figure gives a histogram display of respondents' answers to an item asking 'which overseas countries or regions, you think, are the most important partners for (Australia) (New Zealand)?' Following this question, respondents were read a list of sixteen countries/regions, one of which was 'Europe/EU'. Responses were in the form of 'yes' or 'no'. Respondents could give multiple 'yes' answers. In the histogram, the percentage of Australian and New Zealand respondents answering 'yes' for each region is given. As Figure 3.1 shows, Australians ranked the United States as Australia's most important partner followed closely by Asia. The United Kingdom is ranked a distant third. Interestingly, despite the trade ties between Australia and the EU, only about 11 per cent of the Australian sample rated the EU as being an important partner for Australia.

With respect to New Zealand, predictably (and with accuracy), New Zealanders viewed Australia as its most important partner. About 78 per cent of respondents answered 'yes' when asked whether or not Australia is a leading partner. The US was a distant second. Indeed, the Australian and New Zealand samples are remarkably similar, particularly in one respect: like their Australian counterparts, few New Zealanders – about 12 per cent – rated the EU as an important partner, this despite the demonstrably strong economic connection between New Zealand (and Australia) and the EU. As a sidebar, it is interesting to note that while 26 per cent of the New Zealand sample rated the UK as being among the most important partners and about 12 per cent rated the EU as being among the most important, only about 2 per cent of the New Zealand sample rated *both* as being important. For the Australian data, about 3 per cent of respondents jointly rated both as being important. In stark contrast, 15 per cent of New Zealanders and 22 per cent of

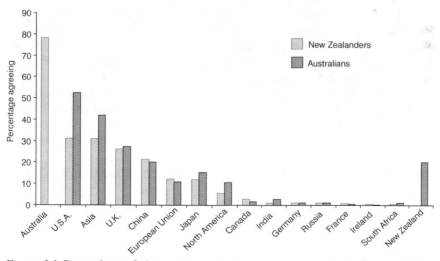

Figure 3.1 Perceptions of the most important partners among Australians and New Zealanders

Australians rated both the UK and the US as being important. At least with respect to evaluating national ties with other countries/regions, both New Zealanders and Australians clearly separate 'Europe and the EU' from the UK. Put differently, this result suggests the European 'magnet' to which Australians and New Zealanders are 'attracted' is Britain, not Europe or the EU more generally. Politically, this result surely comes with implications. As the Australian and New Zealand governments begin to work more directly with the EU, elites need to be aware that citizen perceptions of Europe are more tethered to Britain, not the EU.

Of course evaluations of Europe/EU as an important partner for each country do not directly speak to the issue of the perceived 'impact' the EU will have on Australia and New Zealand. That is, the contemporaneous assessment of Europe/ EU as an important partner in 2004 is not very informative about the prospective judgements individuals have about the likely implications of the EU for Australia and New Zealand beyond 2004. This is all the more true when one takes into consideration issues of EU enlargement and the growing authority of the EU Commission. Further, the weakening of the US's global standing *vis-à-vis* the EU makes the issue of prospective evaluations of the EU critically important.

Fortunately, we have survey items that allow some leverage on this issue. During the course of the survey, respondents were asked the following: 'I am now going to read out a number of statements about the European Union, or EU. On a scale of 1 to 10, where 1 is no impact at all and 10 is huge impact, please tell me how much impact you think the following will have on (Australia) (New Zealand) *in the near future*?' (Emphasis added.) Following this, respondents were read in rotated order a list of twenty items and asked to give ratings on them.[17] In Table 3.1, the mean rating for each item is given for both samples as well as two-sample difference-in-means t-test (along with the two-tailed p-value for the test statistic). The items are rank ordered according to the size of the t-statistic: positive t-statistics imply the mean rating among Australians was higher than for New Zealanders on the items. The last four items in Table 3.1 are for items asked only in one survey, and thus no difference-in-means test is possible. Generally, a t around 1.96 (in absolute value) is indicative of a statistically significant difference at or below a probability value of .05.

There are several interesting features of Table 3.1. First, on almost *every* common item asked about, Australians rated the impact of the EU on Australia as being greater than New Zealanders' rating of the item's impact on New Zealand. Moreover, for many of these ratings, the mean difference is statistically different from 0. For example, on issues pertaining to the EU's involvement with the Middle East and Iraq ($t = 3.917$) and the EU's dealing with the United States ($t = 3.714$), Australian respondents rated much more highly the likely impact of these factors on Australia than New Zealanders did for their country. A significant difference-in-means was also found for the EU's role on international terrorism issues ($t = 3.294$). These substantial differences are most likely related to Australia's close connection to the US, and in particular the Howard government's close ties to the Bush administration. The salience of Australia's connectivity to the US in the post-9/11 era is clearly evinced in these data. While New Zealanders rated

Table 3.1 Difference-in-means tests for EU impact items, Australia and New Zealand

Item	Mean (Australia)	Mean (New Zealand)	t-test	p-value
Middle East/Iraq	6.360	5.710	3.917	0.000
Dealings with USA	6.748	6.193	3.714	0.000
Euro currency	6.138	5.593	3.388	0.001
Trade power	6.953	6.498	3.356	0.001
International terrorism	6.858	6.308	3.294	0.001
Human rights	6.378	5.953	2.743	0.006
Economic growth	6.675	6.385	2.156	0.031
Dealings with Pacific	6.153	5.835	1.980	0.048
Anti-trust regulations	5.820	5.625	1.555	0.120
Genetic modification	6.340	6.173	1.109	0.268
Carbon emissions	6.880	6.740	0.855	0.393
EU Power	6.338	6.215	0.839	0.402
Agriculture subsidies	6.850	6.980	−0.828	0.408
EU enlargement	5.933	6.018	−0.565	0.572
EU Commission	5.360	5.300	0.443	0.658
EU migration regulations	5.713	5.653	0.402	0.688
EU Parliament	5.075	4.990	0.563	0.574
EU Constitution	5.410	5.390	0.105	0.917
Market for NZ produce	–	6.833	–	–
Economic relations with USA	–	6.118	–	–
EU banking regulations	5.640	–	–	–
EU accounting regulations	5.430	–	–	–

Data: Asia-Pacific Perceptions of the EU; $n = 400$ for each sample. Cell entries are (unweighted) means for each sample, t-test for difference in means, and p-value (2-tailed). A positive t-test implies Australian means are larger than New Zealand means. The last four items were not asked in both surveys; a t-test is not possible to compute.

the impact of the EU's dealings with the US (and with actions against terrorism) highly, the overall impact rating was significantly lower than when compared to Australians'. On these matters, the impact of the EU looms large, at least in the minds of Australian respondents.

There are commonalities across ratings, however. Both sets of respondents rated the impact of European agriculture subsidies on their respective countries as being quite high. In both Australia and New Zealand, the agricultural sector is dominant and it is clear that respondents view the prospective role of the EU in this area as being quite high. Similar remarks apply for the perception of the role of the EU in matters of trade, carbon emissions, genetic modification and economic growth. Further, for New Zealand respondents, the issue of Europe as a market for New Zealand produce is rated highly (a comparable item was not asked in the Australian survey). Taken together, these results suggest a substantial 'national self-interest' component is driving perceptions of the likely impact of the EU between both Australians and New Zealanders.

Unfortunately, simply reporting means as has been done in Table 3.1 does not permit much direct leverage on the issue of attitudinal structure and constraint, as discussed in the previous section. In an attempt to assess the structure (if any exists) of Australian and New Zealand attitudes towards the EU, an exploratory factor analysis of the items shown in Table 3.1 was conducted. Factor analysis is typically used when one is interested in data reduction or, similarly, interested in assessing commonality across different sets of survey items (or other kinds of variables). The technique is 'data reducing' because, from a large set of items, factor analysis attempts to reconstruct the original data (or correlation matrix of items) with as small a number of factors as possible. Resultant 'factors' have a qualitative interpretation, one that is usually related to the composition of items within the factor. If respondents do not 'group together' sets of items (i.e. constrain items), then it is difficult to find a small number of unique factors that describe the data. This would be the case if, over the survey, respondents were simply responding randomly *or* if individual differences in assessments 'cancelled' out any emergent patterns.

Separate factor models for Australian and New Zealand respondents were estimated. To estimate these, the twenty items from Table 3.1 were used in a principal factor analysis. From these twenty items, two factors were retained (based on analysis of eigenvalues and a scree plot).[18] To come to a final factor solution, an oblique oblimin rotation was used, which permits the factors to be correlated. The 'stylized' results from the factor model are shown in Table 3.2. The results are stylized because, for reasons of clarity, only the factor loadings of .55 or above are reported.[19] The top panel of Table 3.2 gives the factor structure for Australian respondents; the bottom panel gives the factor structure for New Zealand respondents.

One clear result emerges. Despite the difference-in-means found in Table 3.1, the structure on which *both* Australians and New Zealanders evaluated the EU's prospective role is *remarkably similar* across the two surveys. Two clear factors emerge, each having common sets of variables loading on them. 'Factor 1' clearly taps a 'domestic/threat' dimension. With the exception of the items related to the EU's dealings with the US and with terrorism, every one of the remaining items has a clear connection to economic 'national self-interest' concerns, and in particular, the EU's role in trade and economic growth. For Australian respondents, the three variables that load highest on this factor were 'trade power', 'agriculture subsidies' and 'economic growth'. For New Zealanders, the strongest factor was the EU as a 'market for NZ produce', followed next by 'trade power' and 'economic growth'. The items rounding out this first dimension related to the EU's role in greenhouse gas reduction (which, as evinced by the Helen Clark quote, ties directly into

Table 3.2 Factor structure of EU impact items, Australia and New Zealand

Item	Australian respondents	
	Factor 1	Factor 2
Trade power	0.749	
Agriculture subsidies	0.707	
Economic growth	0.682	
Carbon emissions	0.663	
Dealings with USA	0.611	
Dealings with Pacific	0.606	
International terrorism	0.600	
Genetic modification	0.591	
EU Commission		0.864
EU Parliament		0.760
EU Constitution		0.685
EU migration regulations		0.605
EU enlargement		0.557

Item	New Zealand respondents	
	Factor 1	Factor 2
Market for NZ produce	0.715	
Trade power	0.648	
Economic growth	0.641	
International terrorism	0.619	
Genetic modification	0.610	
Carbon emissions	0.609	
Economic relations with USA	0.596	
Dealings with Pacific	0.594	
Agriculture subsidies	0.593	
EU Commission		0.823
EU Parliament		0.678
EU Constitution		0.657

Data: Asia-Pacific perceptions of the EU; $n = 400$ for each sample. Cell entries are factor loadings. Estimates are from a principal factor analysis with oblique oblimin factor rotation. Not all factor loadings are reported; those having a loading less than .55 are not reported.

self-interest concerns), dealings with Pacific nations and genetic modification. Given the 'no-GM' movement in New Zealand, an issue that has also been widely publicized in Australia, it is not surprising that respondents 'tie together' this issue with other issues pertinent to economic development.

Within this dimension, there is also a 'threat' component, evinced by the linkage of concern about the US and terrorism and the EU's actions related to both.

Clearly both Australia and New Zealand have been affected by terrorist actions in the 2000s, albeit in different ways. The 2001 attacks on the United States, the 2002 Bali bombings, which killed 88 Australians (and three New Zealanders also), and the 2004 Madrid train bombings (which occurred in the same year as the survey) were all highly salient events, to say the least. The bundling of 'terrorism and EU actions' and 'EU dealings with the US' with the economic/trade items is therefore interesting. It seems clear that respondents connected the implications of terrorism with economic viability. Moreover, overseas involvement in military actions is extremely costly, particularly for Australia. A reasonable explanation for the kind of bundling of issues found here is that the economic concerns are not independent of concerns about terrorism and the interface between the EU and the US.

In addition to the 'domestic/threat' dimension a second weaker dimension emerged in the analysis of the survey items. This second factor relates to the EU as a political institution. For Australian respondents, the three highest-loading items on this factor were the roles of the 'EU Commission', the 'EU Parliament' and the adoption of an 'EU Constitution'. Additionally, Australians tied in EU 'migration regulations' and 'EU enlargement'. For New Zealand respondents, the items comprising this factor were the 'EU Commission', 'EU Parliament' and 'EU Constitution' items – again, a factor structure virtually identical to that found among Australian respondents.

What makes this factor interesting is the linkage that respondents made between the EU as a political institution and the likely impact this institution will have on Australia and New Zealand. This dimension is also interesting because it suggests that Australians and New Zealanders do, to some extent, identify the EU as a distinctive political entity.

The two factors identified in this analysis mark two distinct (though correlated) dimensions over which Australians and New Zealanders evaluate, judge and perceive the role of the EU. The strongest dimension, the first factor, has a fairly clear national self-interest component embedded within it, while the second factor illustrates that respondents do, in fact, evaluate the EU's role as a deliberative political institution.

Modelling attitudinal structure

The structure of Australian and New Zealand perceptions of the role of the EU exhibits substantial similarity. A natural extension of the analysis is to consider factors that are related to the two dimensions discussed above. Namely, can we account for factors, or covariates, that are related to 'scoring' highly or 'lowly' on the two dimensions? What factors help to predict why some respondents consistently rate each of the factor items high (or low)? In this study, a model having the functional form will be given by:

$$y = \beta' \mathbf{x} \qquad (1)$$

where **x** corresponds to a factor or covariate thought to be related to the response variable y having an effect parameter β. In this study, y will correspond to some function of issue dimensions uncovered in the factor model of the previous section; the form of the response variable, y will be discussed shortly. First, let us consider the factors that relate to the nature of attitudes toward the EU.

In the literature on attitudinal constraint, Zaller persuasively argues that among the best predictors of political attitudes is political knowledge.[20] The argument is that those who are most well informed have the wherewithal and incentive to make sense out of potentially nuanced political issues. In the survey, respondents were asked several questions about news consumption and information-seeking. Among the items was a five-point scale asking respondents to indicate how often 'you access media for foreign news'. Respondents could respond 'never', 'once a month', 'every couple of weeks', 'once a week', 'several times a week' and 'every day'. In addition to this item, respondents were asked about acquiring news from specific newspapers (i.e. *The New Zealand Herald, The Press, The Herald Sun, The Sydney Morning Herald,* etc.) and acquisition of news from specific television news programs (TV1 News, TV3 News, ABC News, Channel 9 News, etc.). Respondents could indicate that they relied on none of these sources for information or they could indicate that they relied on multiple sources for information (e.g. multiple newspaper or television programmes). Finally, two items were asked about information-seeking as it specifically pertains to the EU. The first survey question asked: 'how often do you discuss Europe/EU related issues with your family and friends?' The second question substituted the phrase 'with your colleagues at work'. Respondents could answer 'never', 'rarely', 'occasionally' and 'often'.

To derive an indicator of 'information acquisition', a summative index for the newspaper access and television programme access was first created. For example, if a New Zealand respondent was asked about reading newspapers x, y and z, and the respondent stated that she reads newspapers x, and y, then the self-reported 'score' for this respondent would be two. For those reporting no use of newspapers, the item is scored a 0. A similar index was constructed for television news programmes. In this sense, these two items are counts of the number of papers and programmes the respondent claims to use to access news.

The overall indicator of information acquisition was derived by creating a summative scale of: frequency of foreign news acquisition + newspaper count + television program count + frequency of talking about EU with family/friends + frequency of talking about EU with colleagues at work. This may seem an unduly complicated (or convoluted) way to measure information acquisition; however, this is not the case. The logic behind the indicator is straightforward: if a respondent claims to access foreign news frequently, reads many newspapers, watches many news programmes and frequently talks about the EU with family, friends, and colleagues, then putatively this respondent is highly motivated to acquire information. By extension, we might assume that this respondent is also highly informed (though we are not directly measuring the content of any information here). In contrast, a respondent who never accesses foreign news, never reads newspapers or watches news programmes and never discusses the EU with others is, putatively, a 'low incentive' information-seeker. Again, by extension, we might speculate that this kind of respondent is relatively uninformed.

The observed scale score is the average score over the five items (which is mathematically equivalent to simply taking the raw sum). The range on the information acquisition scale is 0 to 3.2. In terms of actual counts, a 0 implies the complete absence of information acquisition and a score of 3.2 implies the respondent scored '16' on the raw summative scale (16/5 = 3.2). Four respondents in total from the two samples scored 0; two respondents in total from the two samples scored 3.2. The mean scale score for the Australian sample was 1.633 (0.575) and for the New Zealand sample it was 1.776 (0.602). If information acquisition is related to the attitudinal dimensions discussed in the previous section, theory would suggest the scale should be positively related to judgements on how the EU will impact Australia (or New Zealand).

In addition to treating attitudes as a function of information acquisition, it is also useful to include in the specification of the model shown in (1) an 'importance rating' of Europe. The idea here is simple. If respondents do not view Europe as being important to Australia's (New Zealand's) future, attitudes about the EU's prospective role in Australia (New Zealand) may merely be random guesses. On the other hand, if the respondent perceives the region as being important, responses on the EU impact items discussed in the previous section may be conditioned on this 'importance rating'. To measure the importance of Europe to Australia (New Zealand), respondents were asked: 'how important to Australia's (New Zealand's) future' is Europe (including the UK)? Answers could range from 'not at all important' to 'very important'. In addition to being asked about Europe, respondents also gave importance ratings to Asia (excluding China and Japan), North America, South America, Britain, China, Japan and Russia. As with information acquisition, the expected relationship between the importance rating and attitudes about the prospective role of the EU should be positive: those who perceive Europe as being an important region may in turn view the EU as having an impact on their country.

Another factor that may be theoretically related to EU perceptions is connectivity with EU Member States. With connectivity comes a semblance of familiarity. Perhaps the respondent has visited one or many EU Member States and thus, has a sense of the socio-political context of Europe. Maybe a respondent has family or friends living in a Member State with which they discuss politics. The extent to which a respondent has had exposure to EU states may influence the extent to which he or she perceives the likely impacts the EU will have on Australia (New Zealand). Unfortunately, the 'direction' of the relationship between connectivity and perceptions of the EU cannot be clearly stated. That is, one might speculate that exposure to EU countries leads one to discount the likely impacts of the EU. On the other hand, a plausible story could be told as to why connectivity would enhance beliefs the EU will have a substantial impact on Australians and New Zealanders. For example, imagine a business person who has dealings with firms in EU states. In the course of doing business, the business person encounters, for example, EU-related bureaucratic hurdles that must be overcome. For this kind of respondent, connectivity might lead to the belief the EU will have fairly large impacts on the home country. Simply put, for the model in (1), no 'directional' hypothesis can be stated. For purposes of estimation, a scale of connectivity that simply represents a count was created. In the survey, respondents were asked if they felt 'connected' (in any way) to the twenty-five European countries. If a respondent said 'yes' then they were scored a 1; if they said 'no', they were scored a 0. Summing up and averaging these binary scores gives a scale that theoretically ranges from 0 (no connectivity) to 1 (maximal connectivity). The means for the Australian and New Zealand samples were each about .09 (which is equivalent to slightly greater than 'two' connections, on average).

To fully specify model (1), additional demographic factors are necessary. To that end, an index of socio-economic status is included and coded in the following way. Three binary variables were created: 1 if the respondent reported completing a college education, 0 if not; 1 if the respondent reported his/her family income was $70,000 (for Australians; $75,000 for New Zealanders) or greater, and 0 if not;[21] and 1 if the respondent indicated his/her occupation status was in the categories of 'business manager/executive', 'professional/senior government' and 'farm owner/manager'. Respondents not in these categories scored a 0 on the indicator. To complete the measure, an averaged summative index was created with scores 0 (implying the respondent had no college degree, had a family income less than $70,000 (NZ$ 75,000) and was not in the professional/senior government/management occupation sector; .33 (implying 'one out of three' of the indicators was a one); .66 (implying 'two out of three' of the indicators was a one); and 1 (implying the respondent scored a one on all three items). For the Australian sample, about 48 per cent of the sample scored a 0 on the scale and about 4 per cent scored a 1 on the measure. For the New Zealand sample, about 52.75 per cent of the sample scored a 0 on this item and 5.75 per cent scored a 1 on the measure. As with the connectivity indicator, a directional hypothesis for this variable as it relates to EU attitudes cannot be specified, although there is some evidence by Chaban[22] and Murray (this volume) that Australian and New Zealand *elites* tend to *downplay* or *understate* the expected role of the EU.[23] To the extent that 'high-status' respondents have attitudes similar to political elites, one might hypothesize that socio-economic status (SES) is *negatively* related to perceptions of the role of the EU. Ultimately, this is a testable conjecture (and it will be tested shortly).

The remaining demographic indicators in the model are a binary variable coded '1' for female respondents and '0' for male respondents and two dummy variables to record age of the respondent. The first is coded '1' if the respondent reported his/her age as being below 35 and '0' otherwise. The second dummy variable is coded '1' if the respondent reported his/her age as being above 55 and '0' otherwise. The theoretical motivation of these latter two indicators is to capture any age effects in EU perceptions. Since the EU has come into greater prominence in recent years, it may be the case that younger respondents actually have more solidified attitudes about the EU than do older respondents.

We have now completed the specification of the 'right-hand' side of the model in (1); what remains is specification of the response variable, y. A natural choice for the dependent variable is the use of factor scores based on the two-factor model presented in Table 3.2. Factor scores have the virtue of being (approximately) centred around 0 and so positive scores reflect high and positive scores on the dimension and negative scores reflect the opposite case. An alternative to using factor scores is the creation of an average summative scale of the items that most strongly comprise the factors. This strategy is opted for here. The reason for taking this route as opposed to using factor scores is straightforward: the average summative scale is in the same metric as the items used to comprise the scale. As such, the interpretation of regression coefficients from model (1) is more transparent. Therefore, to create the dependent variables for the Australian sample, the eight items from Table 3.2 were taken that loaded strongest on factor 1 and created an average, summative scale. The range of the scale goes from 0 to 10. Here, a '10' implies that for each of the eight items the respondent rated the likely impact to be huge (i.e. a score of 10); a '0' implies that, over the eight scale items, the respondent claimed that the EU's prospective role would have no impact on Australia (New Zealand). In the tables below and the ensuing discussion, this scale is referred to as measuring 'domestic/threat' concerns. The basis of this terminology was discussed in the previous section. For the second response variable, an averaged summative scale of the five items that load most strongly on factor 2 was created. Again, the range of this scale goes from 0 to 10. In the tables, this item is referred to as the 'EU Institutions' scale, again for reasons previously discussed.

For the New Zealand sample, the exact same procedure was followed. For the 'domestic/threat' scale, an averaged summative scale for the nine items that load most strongly on factor 1 was created; for the 'EU Institutions' scale, the index based on the three factors that loaded most strongly on factor 2 was created. Given the remarkable similarity in factor structures shown in Table 3.2, the construction of these response variables, while not identical for the two samples, conveyed common information (indeed, *very* common information since many scale items are identical between the two samples).[24] With the response variables and covariates measured, we can specify the following regression model:

$$y = \beta_0 + \beta_1(\text{Info. Acquisition}) + \beta_2(\text{Importance of Europe}) + \beta_3(\text{Connectivity})$$
$$+ \beta_4(\text{SES}) + \beta_5(\text{Gender}) + \beta_6(\text{Under 35 yrs old}) + \beta_7(\text{Over 55 yrs old}).$$

In all, four models need to be estimated, two each for the Australian and New Zealand samples. The coefficients should help inform us as to what factors predict (or fail to predict) attitudes towards the EU. To estimate the model, OLS regression was used. The standard errors for the parameters were computed based on clustering observations by geographical location.[25] The parameter estimates and standard errors are given in Table 3.3. The top panel corresponds to the models for Australian respondents and the bottom panel corresponds to the models for New Zealand respondents. The coefficient estimates on the left side of the table are

Table 3.3 Modelling domestic/threat and EU institution scales, Australia and New Zealand

Dependent variable	Australian respondents			
	Domestic/threat		EU institutions	
Covariate	Estimate	S.E.	Estimate	S.E.
Information acquisition	0.500	0.183	0.299	0.161
Importance of Europe	0.315	0.051	0.408	0.103
European connectivity	−0.403	0.468	−0.877	0.765
Socioeconomic status	−0.192	0.218	−0.766	0.327
Gender (1 = female)	0.361	0.118	0.748	0.092
Under 35 years old	−0.307	0.043	0.008	0.124
Over 55 years old	−0.543	0.108	−0.303	0.195
Constant	4.887	0.152	3.547	0.162
	New Zealand respondents			
Information acquisition	0.096	0.113	0.050	0.088
Importance of Europe	0.431	0.082	0.349	0.097
European connectivity	−0.668	1.085	−1.644	0.353
Socioeconomic status	0.210	0.200	−0.069	0.432
Gender (1 = female)	0.372	0.138	0.419	0.107
Under 35 years old	0.187	0.158	0.400	0.201
Over 55 years old	−0.155	0.240	0.002	0.119
Constant	4.525	0.263	3.753	0.470

Data: Asia-Pacific perceptions of the EU; $n = 400$. Estimates are ordinary least square estimates with standard errors (clustered on R's location).

for the 'domestic/threat' scale and the estimates on the right side are for the 'EU institutions' scale. A positively signed coefficient implies that for a unit change in the covariate, the expected scale score increases by β amount.

First consider the relationship between information acquisition and EU attitudes for Australian respondents. The parameter estimate for the 'domestic/threat' scale is .50 and is significantly greater than 0 (the one-tailed p-value is .0155). Theoretically, the result is in the expected direction and the magnitude of the effect is substantial. This parameter has an elasticity estimate of .12 implying that, at the means of y and x, the change in the 'domestic/threat' scale for a percentage change in the information acquisition scale is about 12 per cent. Put in less sterile terms, exposure to information has a substantial relationship with Australians' perceptions of the prospective role of the EU on matters of national self-interest (as measured by the domestic/threat scale). A similar story holds for the 'EU institutions' scale. The coefficient estimate of .299 has a one-tailed p of about .05 with an elasticity estimate of about .08 (or 8 per cent). Again, the positively signed coefficient implies information acquisition is strongly related to perceptions of the role of the EU as a political institution. These results are consistent with the theoretical expectation that information is associated with more highly constrained attitudes; here, we find that as information levels increase, the ability (or willingness) of Australian respondents to rate each of the items on the scale highly also increases. In simpler terms, information fosters attitudinal constraint – but only, apparently, for Australians.

Interestingly, the predicted relationship of information acquisition for New Zealand respondents simply does not hold (given the specification of the models). The parameter estimates of .096 (for 'domestic/threat') and .050 (for 'EU institutions') are much smaller than the standard errors. This result implies that information acquisition has effectively no relationship to perceptions New Zealanders have towards the EU over either of the scales. Why this effect fails to emerge is puzzling and the result will be returned to shortly.

Turning now to the European importance rating scale, we find that across all four models, the coefficient estimate is positive – the expected direction – and is significantly greater than zero. The substantive interpretation of this relationship is that, for respondents who believe Europe is important to Australia's (New Zealand's) future, perceptions of the role of EU sharpen. That is, prospective judgements of the EU's role in matters of national self-interest and its role as a political institution are substantially higher for respondents who believe Europe is important to their country's future compared to those who do not. Interestingly, in the design of the survey, the European importance rating question was asked shortly before the EU impact items (which are the items used in the 'domestic/ threat' and 'EU institutions' scales). This finding, in my view, is a virtue of the design. In the context of American public opinion, Zaller and Feldman found that when respondents were given the opportunity in a survey to 'stop and think' about an issue, the marginal distribution of survey responses were substantially different compared to respondents not given the 'stop and think' probe.[26] Clearly, in this survey, no such probe is given; however, the placement of the importance rating in the survey, it is argued, effectively serves as a 'stop and think' probe. Prior to being asked about the role of the EU, respondents have had time to (briefly) consider the role of Europe more generally. Consequently, this gives us some confidence that when called on to make judgements about the EU's prospective role, respondents have been primed to think about the issue. The strong relationship between the European importance rating and scores on the scales are consistent with this story.

Consider now the EU connectivity measure. As will be recalled, this item records the number of connections between the respondent and EU countries. No directional relationship was hypothesized, however, in looking at the coefficient estimates for the variable, we find the relationship is uniformly negative. Further, with the exception of New Zealanders' perceptions of the role of the EU as a political institution, none of the coefficient estimates are significantly different from 0. For the one estimate that is significant, the coefficient estimate of -1.644 suggests that, as connectivity increases, the perceived role of the EU as a political institution decreases. Some possible explanations of this result will be discussed shortly, although it can be noted that, in general, the pattern of the coefficient estimates for this variable suggests, at least initially, that connectivity has very little effect on attitudes towards the role of the EU.

The coefficient estimates for the demographic control variables are mixed across models, though with one major exception. The role of gender is significantly related to perceptions of the role of the EU. For each model in both the Australian and New Zealand samples, a 'gender gap' of perceptions is found. Further, the signage of the *all* the coefficients is positive, implying that, on average, female respondents rate the EU's role as being significantly stronger than do males. While this chapter does not have a theoretically motivated 'story' to 'explain' this result, it is interesting and arguably warrants future research. Given the size of the parameter estimate relative to the standard errors, the result seems fairly robust across models and samples.

The socio-economic status scale exhibits limited effects in predicting respondents' attitudes towards the role of the EU. The only instance where the coefficient estimate is significantly different from 0 is for Australians' perceptions of the role of the EU as a political institution. The coefficient estimate is –0.766, implying that, as status levels increase, views about the importance of the EU as an institution decrease. This result is consistent with Murray's finding (this volume) that Australian elites tend to downplay the EU's role in Australian politics.[27] To the extent that high-status respondents approximate Australian elites, perceptions of the EU's role diminish as a function of status. With respect to the age variables, the results are mixed. The relationship between Australian attitudes on the 'domestic/threat' scale is negative for respondents in the youngest and oldest age groups. These negative coefficients imply that compared to respondents in the age range between 35 years and 54 years, perceptions of the EU's role on domestic and threat issues are relatively lower. No significant age effects are found for Australians' ratings on the 'EU institutions' scale. For New Zealand respondents, the only significant 'age effect' is for the youngest age group. Respondents under 35 years of age tend to, on average, rate the EU's role as a political institution significantly higher than any other age group (coefficient is .40, standard errror is.20). Like the coefficient for gender, this chapter can offer no theoretically motivated story behind these age effects and the 'age gaps' found merit more systematic study.

Discussion

Let us now summarize the results to this point. The attitudinal structure of perceptions of the role of the EU is remarkably similar across countries. Two clear dimensions emerge, one measuring domestic/threat concerns, the other measuring attitudes towards the EU as a political institution. Although slightly different variables are loaded on these factors, there is substantial commonality in the factor structure. In modelling these attitudes as a function of covariates, we find considerable variability across theoretically important factors. Most noteworthy are differences found for information acquisition. For Australians, the effect is positive, pronounced and substantial: information levels are strongly related to the perceptions of the role of the EU. For New Zealanders, no effects emerge. This is curious.

To see why these differences exist, consider Table 3.4. Here, the mean levels for each of the (non-binary) covariates from Table 3.3 are given (as well as covariates not included in the model). Additionally, a two-sample *t*-test is given to test for difference-in-means.[28] Consider the information acquisition scale. The mean score on this item is significantly higher for New Zealanders than when compared to Australians ($t = -3.435$). At any conventional level, this difference is significantly different from zero. The mean difference is substantively interesting. Although the model for New Zealanders' perceptions of the EU shows *no* relationship to information acquisition, on average, New Zealand respondents have *significantly higher levels of information acquisition*. Since the information acquisition scale is a composite of five variables, one might think a significant difference on one of the five factors is driving this result. This is not the case. Look again at Table 3.4. The means given for variables not directly in the model are included in the bottom half of the table. The five variables that make up the information acquisition scale are: self-report of newspapers, self-report of television programmes, frequency of foreign news attention, frequency of talking with family/friends about the EU and the frequency of talking with colleagues about the EU. On four of five of these indicators, mean scores are *highest* for New Zealand respondents. Further, three of the items (self-report indicators and foreign news access) are significantly

Table 3.4 Difference-in-means tests selected covariates, Australia and New Zealand

Item	Mean (Australia)	Mean (New Zealand)	t-test	p-value
Domestic/threat scale[a]	6.682	6.430	2.374	0.018
EU institution[a]	5.498	5.230	2.324	0.020
Information acquisition	1.633	1.776	−3.435	0.001
European connectivity	0.085	0.095	−1.150	0.250
Socioeconomic status	0.261	0.250	0.508	0.612
Importance of Europe	3.548	3.583	−0.487	0.626
Report: TV news	1.310	1.593	−4.300	0.000
Report: newspapers	0.895	1.080	−4.026	0.000
Foreign news	3.775	4.020	−2.183	0.030
Talk at work	0.803	0.808	−0.075	0.941
Talk with family	1.383	1.380	0.038	0.941

Data: Asia-Pacific Perceptions of the EU; $n = 400$ for each sample. Cell entries are (unweighted) means for each sample, *t*-test for difference in means, and *p*-value (2-tailed). A positive *t*-test implies Australian means are larger than New Zealand means. Items above the dashed line are *t*-tests for covariates included in regression models (see Tables 3 and 4; [a] denotes dependent variables from models. The *t*-tests for variables below the dashed line are discussed in text.

higher among New Zealanders compared to Australians. It is *not* the case that mean levels on the information acquisition scale are a function of one or two of the composite items. Across almost all the items, New Zealanders showed substantially higher levels of information acquisition. And so the puzzle emerges. If, as theory predicts, information is related to attitude constraint, why does the sample for which education levels are highest show absolutely no effects for information?

One possible explanation is that for New Zealanders, the effect of information acquisition is a *conditional* effect. But conditional on what? Consider the impact of connectivity for New Zealand respondents. With respect to the 'EU institutions' scale, the estimated effect is negative, implying exposure to EU countries dampens, or lowers, perceptions of the role of the EU as a political institution. The effect for the 'domestic/threat' scale is also negative, but the standard error is huge (1.085). Suppose it was the case that connectivity 'conditioned' the effect of information acquisition? This would imply that the relationship between information acquisition and connections to Europe are not independent of one another. If such a relationship held, the results given in Table 3.3 would be misleading, for the estimated effects there are all 'unconditional'. To evaluate this possible conditioning relationship, the models from Table 3.3 were re-estimated and this time included a statistical interaction term between information acquisition and connectivity, thus leading to the following model:

$$y = \beta_0 + \beta_1(\text{Info. Acquisition}) + \beta_2(\text{Importance of Europe}) + \beta_3(\text{Connectivity}) + \beta_4(\text{Info. Acquisition} \times \text{Connectivity}) + \beta_5(\text{SES}) + \beta_6(\text{Gender}) + \beta_7(\text{Under 35 yrs old}) + \beta_8(\text{Over 55 yrs old}).$$

The parameter β_4 gives the coefficient estimate for the 'interaction' but now β_1 gives the unconditional effect of information acquisition *only when connectivity is equal to 0*. Similarly, β_3 gives the unconditional effect of connectivity *only when the information acquisition scale is equal to 0*. When neither scale is 0, the relationship is fully conditional. Table 3.5 presents the results from this model for New Zealand respondents' attitudes on the 'domestic/threat' scale.[29] The model shows that the conditioning effect in fact does hold. The parameter estimate for the interaction term is more than twice the size of the standard error. The fact the interaction term is negative is substantively fascinating. To explain: the new parameter estimate for the information acquisition variable is now .245. With a standard error of .092, we can now, seemingly, conclude that the coefficient is statistically different from 0; however, what the results *really* show is that when New Zealanders' report *no* connectivity to Europe, the estimated effect of information acquisition is .245 and *is* statistically significant. This leads to the important conclusion, one that resolves the puzzle: connectivity to Europe mitigates the effect of information acquisition. When personal exposure to Europe is nil, the effect of information acquisition is strong, in the 'correct direction' and statistically significant. However, as connectivity levels increase, the effect of information acquisition on attitudes drops. To illustrate this, the conditional

Table 3.5 Modelling domestic/threat and EU institution scales, New Zealand response on domestic/threat scale

Dependent variable	Domestic/threat	
Covariate	Estimate	S.E.
Information acquisition	0.245	0.092
Importance of Europe	0.430	0.087
European connectivity	3.748	2.399
Info. x Connectivity	−2.143	0.932
Socioeconomic status	0.181	0.198
Gender (1 = Female)	0.366	0.146
Under 35 years old	0.186	0.161
Over 55 years old	−0.166	0.234
Constant	4.261	0.301

Data: Asia-Pacific perceptions of the EU; n = 400. Estimates are ordinary least square estimates with standard errors (clustered on R's location).

effects for the information acquisition scale were computed and are plotted in Figure 3.2.

The main feature of this graph is clear: as connectivity increases, the conditional effect of news acquisition decreases, hence the downwardly sloping scatterplot. At zero on the *x*-axis, the effect of information acquisition is highest. Thus, in the absence of any countervailing information gained through European connections (i.e. connectivity is 0), the impact of information acquisition – the effect of 'the news' – is substantial. It is useful to note that 25 per cent of the New Zealand sample claims *no connectivity* to Europe, so the sample sizes here are sufficient to sustain the inference. Yet as connectivity increases, New Zealanders (on this particular scale) seem to engage in a bit of 'counter arguing'. Information gained through the media that positively affects attitudes on the 'domestic/threat' scale is offset by information gleaned from or absorbed by past and present connections with Europe. In short, information acquisition has an effect for New Zealanders; however, the effect is conditional.

Conclusion

This chapter has attempted to model the nature and structure of Australians' and New Zealanders' attitudes and perceptions of the EU. The structure of attitudes is remarkably similar between the two countries, however the pathways leading to these attitudes are substantially different. Information access through the media and talking with family/friends has a direct, strong and unconditional relationship on Australian attitudes; while for New Zealanders, the relationship is more complicated. At least with respect to concerns about domestic/threat issues (or national self-interest concerns), information effects are strongest for those having

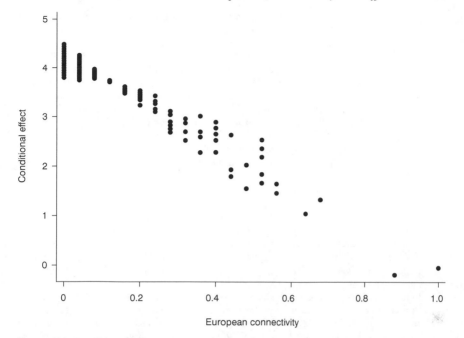

Figure 3.2 Conditional effect of European connectivity on information acquisition among New Zealand respondents

the least connectivity to Europe. Although several questions have been answered, several remain. Further exploration into the nature of European connectivity seems warranted. The results presented here hint at a 'negative effect' of connectivity; however, more detailed kinds of analysis, for example, social network analysis, might lead to deeper insights into the relationship between European connectivity and attitudes towards Europe and the EU. Ultimately, the results here suggest that both Australians and New Zealanders 'coherently' think about the EU in common sorts of ways. While perceptions of the EU's impact relative to other regions is low, it is clear that when called upon to evaluate the EU, respondents offer answers that are far from random guesses.

Notes

1 P. Converse, 'The Nature of Belief Systems in Mass Publics', in D. Apter (ed.), *Ideology and Discontent*, New York, Free Press, 1964, pp. 206–61.
2 P. Converse, 'Attitudes and Non-attitudes: Continuation of a Dialogue', in E. Tufte (ed.), *The Quantitative Analysis of Social Problems*, Reading, MA, Addison-Wesley, 1970, pp. 168–89.
3 Christopher Achen argued that once error-in-measurement of the survey items in question was accounted for, a *great deal* of attitude stability is found among survey respondents: 'Mass Political Attitudes and the Survey Response', *American Political Science Review* 69 (1975), 1218–31.

4   See S. Feldman and J. Zaller, 'The Political Culture of Ambivalence: Ideological Responses to the Welfare State', *American Journal of Political Science* 36 (1992), 268–307; J. Zaller and S. Feldman, 'A Simple Theory of the Survey Response: Answering Questions or Revealing Preferences', *American Journal of Political Science* 36 (1992), 579–616. For extended treatment of these issues, see J. Zaller, *The Nature and Origins of Public Opinion,* Cambridge, Cambridge University Press, 1992. Recent work by Jennifer Hill also argues for an ambivalence explanation. See J. Hill and H. Kriesi, 'An Extension and Test of Converse's "Black-and-White" Model of Response Stability', *American Political Science Review* 95 (2001), 397–414.

5   J. Hurwitz. and M. Peffley, 'How are Foreign Policy Attitudes Structured? A Hierarchical Model?', *American Political Science Review* 81 (1987), 1099–120; M. Peffley and J. Hurwitz, 'Models of Attitude Constrain in Foreign Affairs', *Political Behavior* 15 (1993), 61–90.

6   The literature on public opinion toward the EU is, literally, voluminous and far too vast to do justice to here. Important works finding some semblance of attitude constraint include: M. Gabel and C. Anderson, 'The Structure of Citizen Attitudes and the European Political Space', *Comparative Political Studies* 35 (2002), 893–913; L. McClaren, *Identity, Interests and Attitudes to European Integration*, New York, Palgrave, 2006; R. Rohrschneider and S. Whitefield, *Public Opinion, Party Competition, and the European Union in Post-Communist Europe*, New York, Palgrave, 2006.

7   Indeed this has been the case. The EU Commission has become involved with anti-trust regulations (most recently with Microsoft) as well as banking regulations.

8   M. Holland and B. Jones, (2006) 'Public Attitudes toward the European Union in Australia and New Zealand', in W. Gellner and M. Reichinger (eds), *Deutschland nach der Bundestagswahl 2005: Fit für die globalen Aufgaben der erweiterten EU?*, Baden-Baden, Nomos Verlag, 2006, pp. 219–30.

9   Helen Clark Address, the New Zealand-Australia Climate Change Conference, 4 Nov. 2004, available <www.beehive.govt.nz/Print/PrintDocument.aspx?DocumentID= 21402> (Accessed 4 November 2004).

10   N. Chaban, '"Constellation" or "Giant Star"? Perceptions of the European Union by New Zealand National Elites', in Gellner and Reichinger (eds), *Deutschland nach der Bundestagswahl 2005*, pp. 211–18.

11   TVNZ, 'US Diplomat's Comments Welcomed', available <http://tvnz.co.nz/view/news_politics_story_skin/712082> (Accessed 10 May 2006).

12   For examples of work on elite perceptions and media coverage, see Chaban, '"Constellation" or "Giant Star"?'; N. Chaban and M. Gibbons, 'New Zealand Newspapers' Representations of EU Enlargement between January 2000 and May 2004', in Gellner and Reichinger (eds), *Deutschland nach der Bundestagswahl 2005*, pp. 231–40; N. Chaban, S. N. Kim, K. Stats and P. Sutthisripok, 'When Enough is Enough? Dynamics of the EU Representations in Asia-Pacific Print Media', *Asia-Pacific Journal of EU Studies* 2 (2002), 173–93.

13   N. Chaban and M. Holland (eds), *The EU through the Eyes of the Asia-Pacific: Public Perceptions and Media Representations*, Christchurch, NCRE Research Series 4, 2006.

14   The New Zealand Maori word for non-indigenous people, specifically used to refer to people of European origin.

15   OECD, 'Education Levels Rising in OECD Countries but Low Attainment Still Hampers Some', available <http://www.oecd.org/document/31/0,2340,en_2649_201185_33710751_1_1_1_1,00.html> (Accessed 12 November 2005).

16   For further information on the demographic from the samples, see Chaban and Holland (eds), *The EU through the Eyes of the Asia-Pacific.*

17   The items asked about were: EU actions as a political power, EU enlargement, adoption of EU constitution, appointment of the EU Commission, elections to EU Parliament,

EU role in Middle East and Iraq, EU dealings with the USA, EU dealings with Pacific countries, EU actions against international terrorism, EU support for reducing carbon gas emissions, EU economic growth, EU actions as a world trade power, EU and European agriculture subsidies, EU as a market for NZ produce (NZ survey only), EU economic relations with the US (NZ survey only), EU role in genetic modification, European common currency, EU anti-trust regulations, EU migration regulations, EU advocacy of human rights, EU banking regulations (Australian survey only), EU accounting regulations (Australian survey only), EU actions on human rights.

18 The statistical software package Stata (v. 9.2) was used. The data and code to replicate the results can be found at <http://psfaculty.ucdavis.edu/bsjjones/euproject>.

19 No chicanery is intended. The full factor pattern matrix can be produced using the data and code referenced in the previous endnote. Results are presented this way to illustrate the dominant variables that load on factors 1 and 2.

20 Zaller, *Nature and Origins*.

21 In the Australian survey, respondents were given income levels. For this variable, if a respondent said they were in income categories $70,000 or above, they were score a '1' on the indicator. For New Zealand respondents, the income category level was $75,000 (the income items are not directly comparable).

22 Chaban, ' "Constellation" or "Giant Star"?'

23 Ibid. P. Murray, 'What Australians Think about the EU: National Interests in an International Setting', in M. Holland and N. Chaban (eds), *Public, Elite and Media Perceptions of the EU in the Asia-Pacific: Conceptualizing EU Public Diplomacy*, London, Routledge, 2007.

24 The Cronbach's alpha for these scales was above .80 indicating that the items scale together with a high degree of reliability.

25 Clustered standard errors were used in order to account for the potential of nonspherical errors. In general, the model with clustering produced slightly larger standard errors than models without clustering. Also, alternative estimators were considered. Specifically, the 'domestic/threat' and 'EU institutions' models were estimated simultaneously using a SUR estimator. The standard errors reported from the SUR estimates were actually smaller than those reported here; to err on the conservative side, the standard OLS estimates (with cluster-based standard errors) were opted for.

26 Zaller and Feldman, 'Simple Theory of the Survey Response'.

27 Murray, 'What Australians Think'.

28 As a sidebar, note that mean levels for the two dependent variables are significantly higher for Australians compared to New Zealanders. This was consistent with what we saw in Figure 3.1: on all items, Australians perceive the role of the EU as being greater than do New Zealanders. Strictly speaking, the scales are not directly comparable as they are a function of different items; however, the scales are on the same metric and since the factors from which the scales are derived are so similar, the tests given in Table 3.4 are a reasonable approximation of mean differences in attitudes.

29 This model was estimated for each of the response variables; however, the model only holds for New Zealanders' attitudes on the 'domestic/threat' scale. This is not surprising. The Australian data give no suggestion that information acquisition is anything other than a main effect.

4 Bringing public opinion back in

Public perceptions of the EU in Thailand and South Korea

Kenneth Ka-Lok Chan

Introduction

Most commentaries on the European Union's strategy towards Asia have concentrated on the promotion of trade, democratic values, civil society development, human rights dialogue, as well as programmes on economic, commercial and development cooperation. In recent years, security and political cooperation have contributed to a much wider spectrum of European Union–Asia relations, presenting new opportunities for diplomatic manoeuvre. But a key of aspect of the European Commission's 2001 Communication has been 'to strengthen further the mutual awareness between Europe and Asia and to reduce persisting stereotypes'.[1] However, given the conventional emphasis on the activities and importance of political elites, mass public opinion has received little attention in existing analyses of trade figures, tourist numbers, policy issues, common stances or areas of discord.

This chapter seeks to fill this gap by examining what Europe and the European Union (EU) mean to citizens in Thailand and South Korea. Interviews with representative samples of 411 Thai citizens and 401 Korean citizens were successfully completed in 2005 under the auspices of Chulalongkorn University in Thailand and Korea University, respectively.[2] The main findings of this study suggest the presence of reasonably strong images about the EU as a strong actor in areas of economics, trade and agriculture. While trade partnerships between the EU and these two Asian countries were not without difficulties, public perceptions on the EU were found to be largely positive. A vast majority of respondents in both countries felt that their country's relationship with the EU was improving or steady. However, the EU was regarded as far less important than the United States, Japan and China to the future of the two nations in question.

Notwithstanding the inherent shortcomings of one-off opinion surveys which capture the contours of public attitudes at a fixed point of time, one must bear in mind that the formation of public attitudes towards the EU does not take place in isolation from the historical context and the political process. In the following sections, the range of public attitudes in Thailand and South Korea towards the EU must be spelt out systematically and contextually. For that, an overview of the developments of EU–Asian relations will be in order. It is hoped that these findings enable us to trace the image of the EU in public opinion, and to explore what ties, if any, there are between Europe and ordinary citizens in Thailand and South Korea.

Moreover, it is important to note that cognition, affect and evaluation are interrelated aspects of public attitudes.[3] To make sense of the general patterns of public attitudes found in this study requires further delineation with regard to the following issues:

1   current images of the EU in contemporary Thailand and South Korea and their foundations;
2   the perceptions and attitudes towards the EU and individual European countries among Thai and Korean citizens;
3   the degree of knowledge and understanding of the EU and its evolution within the general public of Thailand and South Korea; and
4   Thai and Korean citizens' sources of information about the EU and the degree of personal connections with the EU.

Last but not least, to the extent that political leaders pay attention to public opinion in the process of foreign policy formulation,[4] we believe that the findings of this study may be a more than useful accompaniment to the formation of the EU's policy towards the two Asian nations, and may assist in identifying problems and opportunities in earlier stages where actions are most effective.

Building strategic partnership with Asia

Interregional relations between the EU and Asia date back to the 1970s, when the European Community (EC) began to establish diplomatic contacts with a number of nations in Asia through multilateral dialogue and development assistance. But it was during a period of extraordinary changes in Asia that it was deemed necessary for the European leaders to establish a more coherent and differentiated policy towards the Asian peoples.[5] The processes of liberalization, democratization and, most important of all, seemingly incessant economic growth have increased Asia's strategic value to the Europeans. Thus, beginning with the adoption of the Korea Strategy in 1993, the EU successively adopted strategic policies towards Asia (1994, 2001), China (1995, 1998, 2001, 2003, 2006), South Korea (1996, 2001), Japan (1991, 1995, 2001), as well as Southeast Asia (1996, 2003), to name but a few.[6] The steady development of the relationship with Southeast Asian nations through a long-standing cooperation with the Association of South East Asian Nations (ASEAN) was a case in point. EC–ASEAN dialogue was launched in 1972. In accordance with the 1980 EC–ASEAN Cooperation Agreement, both sides have continued to strengthen their ties on commercial, economic and development fields. Commercial cooperation commits the parties to cooperate in promoting interregional trade flows, improving access to one another's markets and consulting one another over new measures that may affect such ties. Economic cooperation aims at encouraging investment, scientific and technological progress, job creation, as well as equitable treatment for business and capitals. Development cooperation recognizes that ASEAN is a developing region and therefore commits the EC and its Member States to provide ASEAN countries with Overseas Development Aid (ODA) on projects concerned with food production and supplies, rural development, education and training facilities, and the promotion of ASEAN regional economic development and cooperation.[7] Describing ASEAN as 'a key partner' for Europe, EC/EU foreign ministers meet with their ASEAN counterparts for political dialogues every second year. A joint cooperation committee was set up to oversee and ensure the implementation of the agreement's aims. The European Commission Communication, 'A New Partnership with South East Asia', presented in 2003, reaffirmed the importance of the EC–ASEAN partnership.

At the Maastricht summit, EC leaders expressed their commitment to work together towards a Common Foreign and Security Policy (CFSP), which came into existence when the EU was established in 1993. The CFSP has provided the EU with a range of foreign policy instruments including humanitarian aid, trade policy, development assistance and cooperation, confidence-building, preventive diplomacy and conflict resolution. Against this background, the Essen European Council of 1994 endorsed a 'New Asia Strategy' to strengthen the EU's economic presence in the region and to contribute to its political stability, thereby achieving a higher profile of the EU in Asia. In 1997, the Council of Ministers reiterated this line of thinking by stating that 'Asia continues to constitute a key priority for the CFSP'.[8] EU leaders realized that their main strategic interest in Asia was related to economic matters, namely (a) to maintain the EU's leading role in the world economy and (b) to promote the economic development of the less prosperous countries and regions in Asia. In the words of the paper, 'the Union needs to select priority sectors for economic cooperation which reflect its own competitive advantage, e.g. banking, energy, environmental technologies, transport equipment, telecommunications, etc.'[9]

It goes without saying that regional security was of equal importance to economic development in the EU's interests in Asia. For that, the 1994 Strategy suggested that the EU participate in the ASEAN Regional Forum (ARF) which provided for a wide-ranging dialogue on security concerns. The ARF has been the largest and the most visible security forum in the region whose activities, in the view of the EU, would be coordinated with work done under ASEAN. Essentially, the Forum has provided participating nations with some confidence-building measures and a platform for exchange of ideas and values. It is hoped that, over time, the Forum will help bring about a more favourable atmosphere for preventive diplomacy and conflict resolution.

The 1994 Strategy Paper took into consideration Asia's size and the diverse nature of the region, thus encouraging a 'dialogue of equals' with its Asia partners bilaterally and with multilateral organizations. Two years later, the Asia–Europe Meeting (ASEM) was launched in Bangkok as an informal process for interregional and intergovernmental dialogue and cooperation between the EU and ASEAN countries, plus China, Japan and South Korea.[10] The ASEM Vision Group was initiated by South Korea at the first summit to consider mid- to long-term strategies. At the third ASEM Summit in Seoul, the 'Asia–Europe Cooperation Framework 2000' was adopted. This document set out the vision, key principles, objectives, priorities and coordination mechanisms of the ASEM process for the first decade of the twenty-first century.[11] ASEM is an informal interregional process of dialogue and cooperation initiated in 1996 and constitutes the most visible interregional linkage between Asia and Europe. By and large, ASEM summits are regarded to have contributed to a stable, ongoing dialogue platform with pertinent agendas for the peace and prosperity of the two regions. To mark the tenth anniversary, the 'Declaration on the Future of ASEM' was adopted at the sixth summit in Helsinki in 2006.[12] Among the areas identified for further deliberations included global threats, globalization and competitiveness, sustainable development and intercultural and interfaith dialogue. But the progress on institutional development and a more cohesive regional security structure remains slow as long as ASEM participants continue to emphasize ASEM's informal nature.

Over the years Europeans have developed at least three complementary layers of relations with their Asian counterparts. First is a bilateral relation at the interstate level. The second type is a bilateral relation between the EU and individual Asian countries such as South Korea, China and Japan. The third type is a multilateral relationship at the interregional level through ASEM, ASEAN and ARF. Multilateral interactions may also take place in other international organizations and forums devoted to dealing with nuclear proliferation, anti-terrorism, human rights, health, environment, trade poverty alleviation, human trafficking and crimes. Table 4.1 shows membership of ASEM and other regional organizations in Asia and Europe. Depending on the nature of specific agenda and interests, it is not uncommon for Europeans to be engaged in multilevel interactions with Asians in a concomitant manner. Thus, the first EU–China Summit took place before the opening of the ASEM Summit in London in 1998, and in Helsinki in 2006, EU–China and EU–South Korea summits took place before the ASEM Summit.

As far as Asia is concerned, the EU's strategy towards Asia has expanded from 'aid and trade' into an 'enhanced partnership' encompassing regional security, social, political and cultural fields.[13] The EU has engaged its Asian partners on global agenda such as free trade, environmental protection, climate change, conflict prevention and human rights dialogue. The EU's presence in Asia is also felt in regional security architecture and confidence-building mechanisms such as the ARF and ASEM. In recent years, the EU has also begun to step up its campaign for 'strengthening the awareness of Europe in Asia (and vice versa)'.[14] In all, Europe has every interest in forging a partnership not only with the leaders but also with the peoples of Asia.

Despite its aspirations to promote democracy, civil society development, human rights, free trade and good international governance, it has been argued that the EU is a 'soft', 'civilian' force rather than a power in international relations because it does not have at its disposal traditional means of statecraft.[15] For one thing, the CFSP depends on the inner consensus of the Member States. For another thing, swift and decisive actions have been rare because of the procedural and

Table 4.1 Membership of ASEM and regional organizations in Asia and Europe

	ASEM	Enlarged ASEM*	ASEAN	ARF	ASEAN +3	ASEAN PMC 10+10	EAS	APEC	SAARC	SCO
EU25		Y		Y		Y				
EC	Y	Y								
Bulgaria		Y								
Romania		Y								
Brunei		Y	Y	Y	Y	Y	Y	Y		
Indonesia	Y	Y	Y	Y	Y	Y	Y	Y		
Malaysia	Y	Y	Y	Y	Y	Y	Y	Y		
Philippines	Y	Y	Y	Y	Y	Y	Y	Y		
Singapore	Y	Y	Y	Y	Y	Y	Y	Y		
Thailand	V	Y	Y	Y	Y	Y	Y	Y		
Vietnam	Y	Y	Y	Y	Y	Y	Y	Y		
Cambodia	Y	Y	Y	Y	V	Y	Y			
Laos	Y	Y	Y	Y	Y	Y	Y			
Myanmar	Y	Y	Y	Y	Y	Y	Y			
ASEAN Secretariat		Y								
Timor Leste				Y						
China	Y	Y		Y	Y	Y	Y	Y		Y
Japan	Y	Y		Y	Y	Y	Y	Y		
S. Korea	Y	Y		Y	Y	Y	Y	Y		
N. Korea				Y						
Mongolia		Y		Y						
India		Y		Y		Y	Y		Y	
Pakistan		Y		Y					Y	
Bangladesh				Y					Y	
Nepal									Y	
Bhutan									Y	
Sri Lanka									Y	
Maldives									Y	
Hong Kong								Y		
Chinese Taipei								Y		
USA				V		Y		V		
Canada				Y		Y		Y		
Australia				Y		Y	Y	Y		
New Zealand				Y		Y	Y	Y		
Papua New Guinea				Y				Y		
Chile										
Mexico								Y		
Peru										
Russia				Y		Y		Y		V
Kazakhstan										Y
Kyrgyzstan										Y
Tajikistan										Y
Uzbekistan										Y

Source: http://ec.europa.eu/comm/external_relations/asem/asem_process/asem_organisations.pdf.
ASEM: Asia-Europe Meeting; ASEAN: Asssociation of Southeast Asian Nations; ARF: ASEAN Regional Forum; ASEAN PMC: ASEAN Post Ministerial Conferences; EAS East Asia Summit; APEC: Asia-Pacific Economic Cooperation; SAARC: South Asian Association for Regional Cooperation; SCO: Shanghai Cooperation Organisation.
* Bulgaria, Romania, India, Mongolia, Pakistan and the ASEAN Secretariat will start participating in ASEM activities upon completion of the necessary procedures in their respective regions. They will formally become ASEM partners at the ASEM 7 Summit in 2008.

logistical complexities of intergovernmental coordination. In reality, the EU is mostly a regional rather than a global force. The EU has been quite successful in promoting, through dialogue, cooperation, assistance and simply by the prospects of accession into the Union, transformation in the former communist countries in post-Cold War Europe.[16] Outside Europe, however, the EU has relied mainly on soft security tools to exert its influence and to maintain its visibility. In any case, the so-called 'capabilities–expectations gap' has remained a critical issue in the EU's ability to exercise influence and shape the international order.[17]

Against this background, one must probe further into country-specific issues that may have rendered bilateral relations better or worse. The cases of Thailand and South Korea are considered here, followed by an investigation into the public's perception of the comparative importance of the EU and its Member States with regard to both nations.

The case of Thailand

Thailand's approach to the EU is indicative of a perceived partnership with the European countries based on equality and mutual respect for their differing policies towards regional issues and interregional ties.[18] European–Thai relations can be traced back to the seventeenth century, when European influences were strongly felt in the modernization process of nations in Southeast Asia. Thailand was exceptional in the sense that it was never colonized by European powers. Official EC–Thai relations were first established in 1972 through the EC–ASEAN dialogue. The EC–Thailand Framework Agreement was concluded in 1981, the year after its EC–ASEAN equivalent. Since then, EU–Thai relations have been developed within the regional and interregional context under the auspices of both the ASEAN–EU and ASEM frameworks.

Against the background of the shift, during the early 1990s, from development aid to economic cooperation, EU-Thailand bilateral relations have been broadened to cover a wider range of areas ranging from trade, new market development, intellectual property rights, education and trainings to public health, AIDS and the environment. The European Commission has maintained a delegation in Bangkok since 1979. When a confederation of bilateral Chambers of Commerce was formed in 1993, the European Business Information Centre, forming part of it, was supported by Commission funding. A joint Thai–EU Small and Medium Enterprises Development Project operated in southern Thailand from 1998 onwards.

Economically, the EU is the third most important trading partner for Thailand (after the US and Japan). Since 1995, EU has accounted for approximately 15 per cent of Thailand's total trade volume and during the 1999–2003 period Thailand enjoyed a trade surplus with the EU. Major Thai exports include machinery products, agriculture, textiles and clothing. The major Thai imports from the EU are machinery and chemicals. Periodic EU bans on Thai shrimps and poultry on food safety grounds have caused major problems for Thai exporters since 2000.

Despite annual growth rates in Thailand of around 9 per cent from 1992 to 1996, the late 1990s brought problems of corruption, rural poverty and social tensions. The Asian economic debacle of 1997–8 and the tsunami of December 2004 took a heavy toll on Thailand. Thus, a number of EU-supported programmes and projects in Thailand have continued to provide ODA to the distressed areas to boost economic recovery and rural development. The EU has also supported Thailand in providing relief for hundreds of thousands of Burmese refugees on the Thai–Burma border. In September 2006, in the wake of a military coup which ousted the unpopular Thaksin government, the EU called for a 'speedy return to democracy and constutitional order' and spoke out on human rights issues.

The case of Korea

The EC and South Korea have been at odds over trade issues and market access for decades. South Korea has been one of the main targets of the EC/EU's anti-dumping measures, minimum price regulations and imposition of quotas, safeguards and countervailing duties, even a temporary suspension during 1989–92 of the Generalized System of Preference (GSP) preferences for Korean goods. The EU has in particular targeted Korea exports of textiles, clothing, steel, electronics and footwear, and has expressed particular concerns about the widespread counterfeiting of expensive luxury goods and the protection of intellectual property rights in Korea. The five-year-long dispute between Korea and the EU over the growth of subsidized shipbuilding in Korea ended with a WTO panel ruling in December 2004.[19]

But the steady growth of the EU–South Korean trade and investment flows eventually provided strong enough incentives for both parties to reach the Korean–EU Framework Agreement for Trade and Cooperation in 1996, as well as the Telecommunications and Customs Cooperation agreements. These agreements contained a number of concessions from Seoul, which had been anxious to secure EU backing for its application to join the OECD. Among these agreements was a Korean commitment to end discrimination against access to its domestic markets, including its financial services markets.

With South Korea being the eighteenth largest exporter to the EU and Europe's third largest export market in Asia, a new EU–Korea Trade and Cooperation Framework Agreement entered into force in April 2001. Moreover, there has been a growing consensus that a Korea–EU free trade agreement (FTA) could provide further opportunities to strengthen strategic complementarities. There are other areas in which the EU and Korea are seen to share common interests, and thus there is potential for a wider scope of cooperation. South Korea–EU Joint Committee Meetings have been held to deal with common challenges in the areas of political, security, economic and commercial relations.

In terms of the partners' respective contribution to regional security and interregional dialogue, South Korea has been actively involved in the ASEM process from the very beginning. South Korean leaders have developed many new ideas in the ASEM process including the Vision Group, the Trans-Eurasia

Information Network, Iron Silk Road, DUO ASEM Fellowship Program and so forth.[20]

For its part, the EU's involvement in the Korean Peninsula has grown substantially in recent years. In 1995, the EU forged a partnership with South Korea, Japan and the USA in the Executive Board of the Korean Peninsula Energy Development Organization (KEDO), whose immediate aim was the closure of North Korea's Russian graphite-moderated nuclear reactors, which are capable of producing weapons-grade plutonium. The Commission communication, 'EU Policy towards the Republic of Korea' (1998), as well as the Council conclusions of 19 July 1999, stated the EU's stance on democratization, reform and support for the multilateral talks over the long-drawn-out division. The EU adopted the 'EU Lines of Action towards North Korea' in November 2000 and put forward guiding principles that the EU Member States and the Council of Ministers should follow:

1. The future of the Korean Peninsula is a major challenge for the EU, meaning the EU is not an outsider and Member States must adopt consistent lines of action with regard to North Korea;
2. The policy of the EU and the Member States will be based on regular evaluation of the positions of North Korea,
3. The EU will endeavor to intensify its political consultations with South Korea, whose efforts at rapprochement between the two Koreas it supports, in order to identify common areas for action, including in the fields of technical assistance and economic cooperation with North Korea, and,
4. Partners who are interested in establishing diplomatic ties with North Korea will coordinate among themselves and inform the Council of the content of their discussions with Pyongyang.[21]

In practice, the EU's policy towards North Korea has become a dual-track approach, combining a relatively hard-line position on the North's nuclear and human rights issues with the provision of EU humanitarian assistance and aid from mid-1990s.

Public perceptions of the EU in Thailand and South Korea compared

Spontaneous images of the EU

One way to understand what South Korean and Thai people think of the EU is to identify the spontaneous images they hold of the EU. In our 2005 surveys, respondents were asked to list three thoughts that came to mind when they heard the phrase 'the European Union'. The generated list of such spontaneous images of the EU included 756 entries in Thailand and 474 entries in South Korea, respectively. The most frequently mentioned ones are presented in Figures 4.1

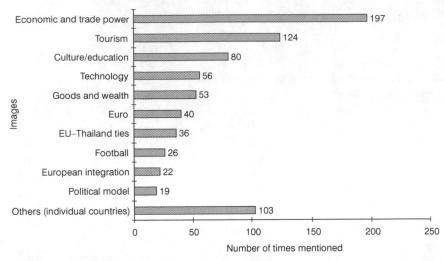

Figure 4.1 Spontaneous images of the EU (Thailand)

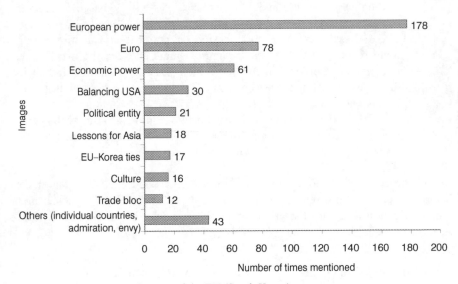

Figure 4.2 Spontaneous images of the EU (South Korea)

and 4.2. Clearly, there were different concerns and feelings towards the EU in both countries. Respondents in Thailand largely saw the EU in the positive light. The Union stood for a strong economy, a powerful trading bloc with a single currency, prosperity, democracy, human rights and rule of law, the welfare state, good education systems, culture, technological innovations and, quite interestingly, football teams. However, the EU's restrictions on Thai products (in response to the outbreak of bird flu in 2004) received most complaints.

Respondents in South Korea tended to view the EU's economic power and growing political influence with mixed feelings. For some respondents, the EU, together with the process of European integration, constituted a positive model for Asian integration. For others, the EU was seen as an exclusive club for a number of economically powerful countries, thus reinforcing the division between those who were in and those who were not. While the EU was seen as a powerful international actor, South Koreans paid little attention to its material wealth, culture and industries. Some respondents expected the EU to act as a counterbalance to the hegemonic position of the US.

The comparative importance of the European Union

The 2005 survey results show that the most important partners for South Korea were considered to be (in order of significance) the US (65 per cent), China (47 per cent), Japan (44 per cent), North Korea (10 per cent), the UK (5 per cent) and EU (3.5 per cent). For Thailand, the most important partners were the US (48 per cent), China (38 per cent), Asia (30 per cent), Japan (24 per cent), Europe/EU (12 per cent), the UK (8.5 per cent) and Malaysia (5 per cent).

Notably, both the United States and Japan continued to be regarded as the leading actors in the Asian region. Overall, the survey findings suggest that awareness of the EU as an important partner was at a reasonable level, occupying fifth place in Thailand and sixth place in South Korea. Over the last two decades, China has rapidly emerged as global player. With its robust economy and growing confidence in international affairs, the China factor could hardly be ignored in neighbouring nations. Consequently, in comparison the EU was seldom seen to be *the* power to reckon with in this part of the world.

Regions important to the future of Thailand and South Korea

The surveys further measured people's perception of major world regions' importance to the future of Thailand and South Korea using a scale from 1 to 5, where 5 was considered very important and 1 not important at all. The regions concerned were Asia, Britain, the EU (including the UK), North America and South America. In Thailand, the regions that were considered to be most important to the country's future were China (4.2), Japan (3.8), both Asia (excluding China and Japan) and the EU (excluding UK) occupied third place (3.6), while the UK came fourth (3.5), followed by North America (3.2). In South Korea, the most important regions to the country's future were considered to be China (4.3), Japan (3.7) and North America (3.5), followed by the EU (excluding UK) (3.3), Asia (3.2) and Russia (3.1). The rise of China as a regional power was widely expected, whilst Japan appeared to maintain its position as an economic powerhouse in the region. The EU took third place in Thailand and came fourth in South Korea. Europe's increasing relevance to the future of both Asian nations is somewhat encouraging, indicating some room for deepening and widening cooperation with the EU. This expectation was supported by an additional question in the surveys in which respondents were asked to evaluate the state of their country's relationship with the EU.

State of relationship with the EU

A vast majority of respondents in both countries felt that their country's relationship with the EU was improving or steady. Respondents in Thailand were generally positive about this relationship, which was regarded as steady (39 per cent) or improving (49 per cent). Similarly, in South Korea, most respondents considered the relationship between South Korea and the EU as steady (49 per cent) or improving (37 per cent). However, 7 per cent of South Korean respondents interviewed did not have a clear idea about their country's relationship with the EU, whilst another 7 per cent described the EU–South Korean relationship as worsening. On the other hand, 10 per cent of respondents in Thailand regarded the Thailand–EU relationship as worsening. Thus, as the EU was generally seen to be increasingly important to both nations, it is fitting to consider what aspects of the EU other than being just an economic power had been considered to have some relevance to the region. Moreover, we shall probe further into factors that shaped the contours of the public attitudes towards the EU in Thailand and South Korea.

Impact of the EU on Thailand and South Korea

To further understand respondents' evaluations on the levels of the EU's impact on South Korea and Thailand, participants were presented a common list of issues covering a wide range of areas including: EU actions as a political power, EU enlargement, the adoption of an EU Constitution, the appointment of the new European Commission, European Parliament elections in 2004, the EU's role in the Middle East and Iraq, EU dealings with the US, the EU stance against international terrorism, EU support for the Kyoto protocol, EU economic growth, EU actions as a world trade power, EU agricultural subsidies, the Euro, the EU's role in debate about genetically modified organisms, EU anti-trust regulations, EU migration regulations and EU advocacy of human rights and democracy.

In addition, there were also a few country-specific issues. For Thailand, these included the EU's dealing with ASEAN, the EU computer and IT industry and the EU dealings with bird flu. For South Korea, these included the EU's dealing with North Korea (generally seen in South Korea as too accommodating), competition with the EU's car industry and investments in South Korea. The interviewees were then asked to rate each issue using a ten-point scale. The findings are presented in Figures 4.3 and 4.4. The nature and levels of EU's impact on both nations can be summarized by grouping the twenty-three issues into three categories:

Economic, trade and agricultural issues

It is not surprising that respondents in both Thailand and South Korea viewed the EU's significance first and foremost in economic terms. More specifically,

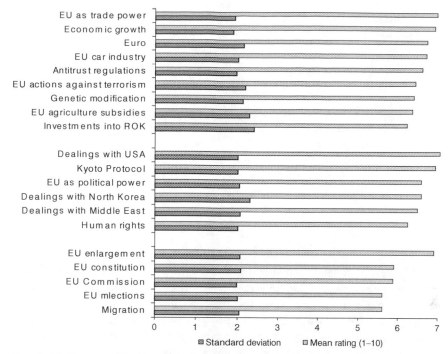

Figure 4.3 Nature and levels of perceived impacts of the EU on Thailand

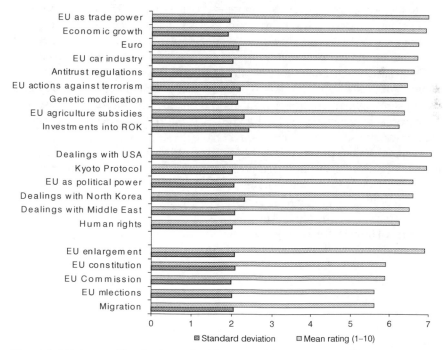

Figure 4.4 Nature and levels of perceived impacts of the EU on South Korea

South Koreans were concerned about their competition with the EU car industry and EU investments in South Korea. The issues with the most perceptible impact on Thailand were trade issues, the EU's stance on eliminating trade barriers and widening trade access.

International role

The EU's international roles in eastern and south-eastern Asia received significant attention as well. Respondents in South Korea were mostly concerned with the EU's dealings with the US and the prospects of the Kyoto Treaty, followed by the EU's dealings with North Korea. Thai respondents tended to see Thailand's relationship with the EU developing in the broader context of EU–ASEAN and EU–US relationships, as well as the EU's actions against terrorism.

Internal issues

The EU's institutional growth and internal development received relatively less attention in Thailand and South Korea. The one notable exception to this was the perceived impact of EU enlargement on the two nations.

Respondents were also asked to list any other issues relating to the EU that could have a significant impact on their country. In Thailand, 107 issues were listed, and within this list trade, economic and agricultural issues remained the most emphasized items. But Thai respondents were also concerned about inflation due to high EU import prices, environmental issues and the EU's interference in Thai political affairs (such as human rights abuses and civil society development). In South Korea, 163 issues were listed. Korean respondents were most concerned about trade-related issues and the growing economic and political powers of the EU. The EU's dealings with North Korea and the humanitarian crisis there naturally raised serious concerns and some critical comments. There was also some interest in the 'European model' and lessons for South Korea and Asia. The most frequently mentioned entries for both Thailand and South Korea are given in Figures 4.5 and 4.6, respectively.

In some sections of the Asian population, the EU seemed to have managed to capture people's imagination as a positive model for regionalism and regional integration in Asia. There was some discussion from respondents about adopting at least part of the European model. In particular, the EU came across as a reference point for integration for ASEAN members in their desire for regional stability and prosperity. This may partly be because the processes of globalization have brought about economic, political and security challenges which are considered to require regional responses. Additionally, European integration offers rich experiences of state-led regional cooperation to demonstrate how sovereignty pooling might work for mutual benefit.

Despite this public perception of the possibilities of an EU-inspired Asian regional integration, countries embarking on regional cooperation in Asia have not reached any consensus on an agreeable degree of institutionalization. Since

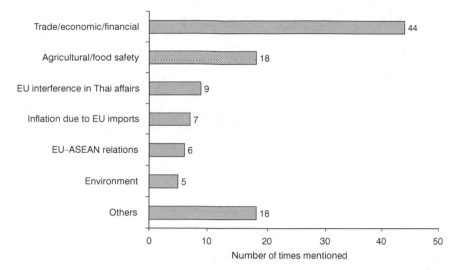

Figure 4.5 Other EU issues that impact (Thailand)

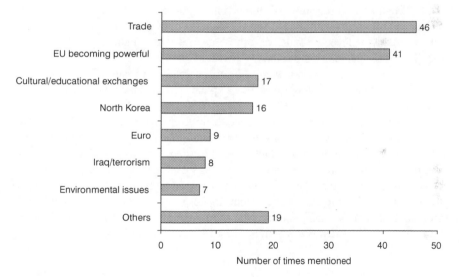

Figure 4.6 Other EU issues that impact (South Korea)

its foundation in 1967, ASEAN has adhered to the doctrine of non-intervention in the domestic affairs of Member States. The Treaty on Friendship and Cooperation in South East Asia of 1976 introduced elements of arbitration that remain largely on paper. 'The ASEAN Way' has been limited to quiet diplomacy and attempts to 'mediate' between members. ASEAN has never imposed sanctions for the poor conduct of any of its member states. In economic terms, intra-ASEAN trade had risen to only 22 per cent during the 1990s, which was small compared with the

EU's internal trade of more than 50 per cent. Some Asian countries, Japan, Korea and China, constitute ASEAN's main trading partners, accounting for 50 per cent of its export market and providing the region with 60 per cent of its imports. None of the three Northeast Asian countries, individually or collectively, has acquired the status of an indisputable leader that is arguably necessary for the institutional development of a new regional order.

It is unlikely that the European model of regional integration will be actively pursued by Thailand, South Korea and their neighbors in the foreseeable future. A consistent and assertive leadership has been missing to turn visions into realities. Consequently, the EU's participation in interregional forums such as ARF and ASEM under the rubric of 'enhanced cooperation' has yet to produce visible results for authentic regional integration.

Personal and professional contacts with the EU countries

It is possible that connectivity to European countries may motivate individuals to think more about the EU. But the conducted surveys showed that neither Thai people nor South Koreans had strong personal and professional ties with many of the EU Member States. Figure 4.7 shows that respondents in Thailand had slightly stronger connections with the EU than did their South Korean counterparts. The UK, Germany, France and Italy were the countries with which respondents were the most personally and professionally involved.

The new Member States were largely unknown to survey respondents. Historical and commercial reasons may explain why Asians were more familiar with Western Europe than with the east. As Europe attracts tens of thousands of students and tourists from Asia every year, this apparent vacuum of knowledge about the new Member States may not be a lasting phenomenon. Among the new Member States, the more prosperous central European states of Poland, Hungary and the Czech Republic were better known than the others to our respondents.

With regard to the types of connections that respondents claimed to have with the EU Member States, Figure 4.8 shows that the ties were mostly general knowledge, tourism, family and friend connections and business in nature. None of our Thai or South Korean respondents was born in or had ancestors from Europe.

Sources of information about the EU

For a vast majority of South Korean and Thai citizens, information about the EU is usually obtained via the mass media. Figure 4.9 shows that our respondents primarily gained information about the EU through television news (73 per cent in South Korea and 87 per cent in Thailand), newspapers (52 per cent in South Korea and 61 per cent in Thailand), other television programmes (12 per cent in South Korea and 37 per cent in Thailand), and the internet (41 per cent in South Korea and 22 per cent in Thailand). Moreover, 53 per cent of Thai respondents and 43 per cent of South Korean respondents accessed the media for international or foreign news everyday.

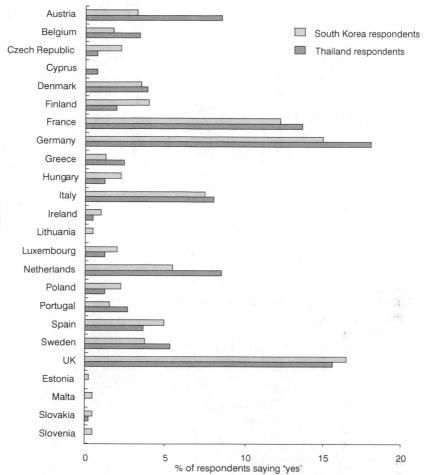

Figure 4.7 Personal and professional connections with EU member states

According to the survey results, in Thailand, the most popular television news programmes for accessing information about the EU were ITV News (60 per cent of respondents), and Channel 7 News (48 per cent), followed by Channel 9 News (34 per cent) and Channel 3 News (33 per cent). The most popular television news programmes for accessing EU information in South Korea were KBS News at 9pm (57 per cent of respondents), MBC News at 9pm (57 per cent), and SBS News (23 per cent) (Figures 4.10 and 4.11).

Newspapers then, were the second most popular source of information about the EU in the two studied countries. In Thailand, the most popular newspapers for those who wanted to obtain information on the EU were *Thai Rath* (46 per cent of respondents) and *Delinews* (26 per cent). The most popular newspapers in South Korea for obtaining EU news and information were *Chosun Ilbo* (26 per cent of respondents), *Joongang Daily* (23 per cent) and *Donga Ilbo* (18 per cent) (Figures 4.12 and 4.13).

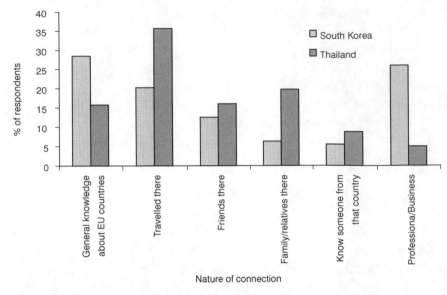

Figure 4.8 Nature of connections with EU member states

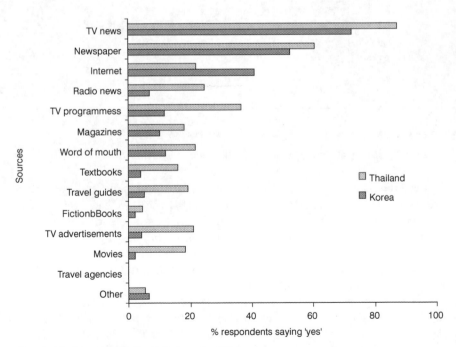

Figure 4.9 Sources of information on the EU

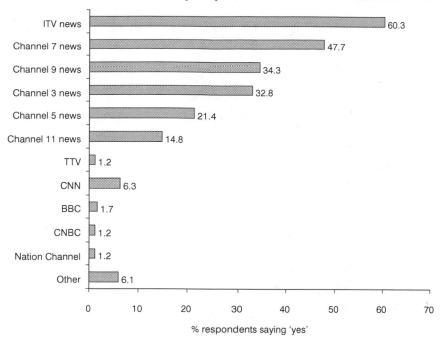

Figure 4.10 Television news accessed for information on the EU (Thailand)

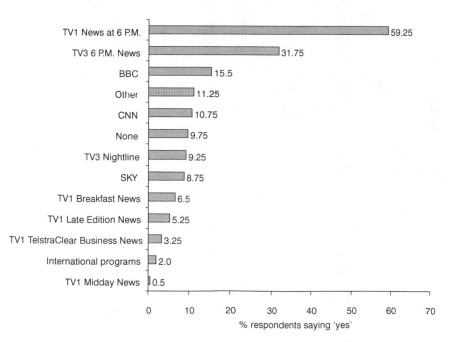

Figure 4.11 Television news accessed for information on the EU (South Korea)

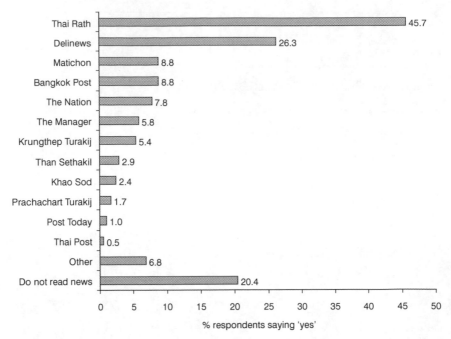

Figure 4.12 Newspapers accessed for information on the EU (Thailand)

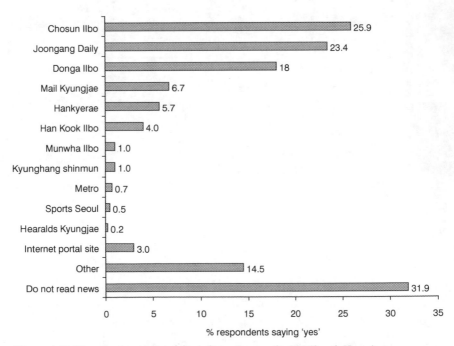

Figure 4.13 Newspapers accessed for information on the EU (South Korea)

Interpersonal communication

The discussed findings thus far have shown that Thai and Korean respondents were interested in a multitude of issues concerning the EU. In Thailand, the most talked about subjects included the war in Iraq, terrorism, EU–Thailand relations (especially the EU's restrictions on Thai exports), the euro, tourism in Europe and, quite commonly, football. In South Korea, respondents were reported to have discussed further education in Europe, football, the war in Iraq, as well as trade and economic situations in the EU.

However, only 4 per cent of respondents in Thailand and South Korea discussed EU-related issues often with their family and friends. Of the interviewees in Thailand 28 per cent never discussed the EU in their personal circles, 37 per cent rarely and 30 per cent occasionally. In South Korea, 15 per cent of the interviewees never discussed the EU in their personal circles, 51 per cent rarely and 29 per cent occasionally.

EU-related issues received limited attention at the workplace, too. In Thailand, 18.5 per cent of respondents never discussed the EU at work, 22 per cent rarely and 18 per cent occasionally. In South Korea, 4.2 per cent of respondents never discussed the EU at work, 20.2 per cent rarely and 16.7 per cent occasionally. Merely 3 per cent of Thai respondents and 2.2 per cent of South Korean respondents claimed to have often discussed EU-related matters with colleagues at work.

Conclusion: enhancing the presence of the EU in Asia

In the field of international relations much of the emphasis is on the political elites whose visions and conducts shape the course of the contemporary world. The findings of this study have somewhat filled the gap in the current literature on EU–Asian relationships by looking at how the EU has been perceived in Asia by the general public. We believe it is both necessary and helpful for political elite to understand the popular basis of their actions, namely how the public view their actions and where public opinions are likely to have an impact on the legitimacy of those actions.

In Thailand and South Korea, our respondents' knowledge about the EU was at a reasonable level. They were primarily concerned with the EU's economic roles in trade, agricultural issues and monetary areas to which they could relate more or less directly. A high proportion of respondents in both countries also paid attention to foreign or international news on daily basis. Respondents relied on the mass media (namely television news, newspapers and general television programmes) for news and information about the EU. In South Korea, the internet was another significant source of information.

In terms of dominant perceptions of the EU in Thailand and South Korea, the findings here strongly support the conventional wisdom that the EU has developed into an economic bloc using a soft power approach to international affairs. Such a stance appeared to have been welcomed by the majority of our respondents who rated the state of the relationship with the EU as 'improving' and 'steady'.

One interesting aspect in the Korean and Thai public attitudes towards the EU concerned the experiences of European integration. Here, the EU was seen to embody a positive model for regionalism and regional integration which has delivered stability and prosperity. However, our respondents showed little interest in the internal workings of the EU and its institutions such as the 2004 European Parliament elections and the ill-fated ratification of the EU Constitution. The public's focus was rather on the Economic and Monetary Union, with the euro serving as a symbol of economic integration. It is beyond to scope of this analysis to examine how much respondents understand the political and economic debates arising from the process of European integration.

Respondents interviewed were less acquainted with the Member States of the EU, except the United Kingdom, France, Germany and Italy. The enlargement of the EU to former communist countries in Eastern and Central Europe, plus the Mediterranean nations of Malta and Cyprus meant little to the respondents whose connections with and knowledge about the traditional, Western part of Europe were clearly stronger. It is fair to suggest that the enlargement was largely viewed by the Asian public through the prism of prospects of economic and trade gains with the EU.

Naturally, there were also areas of contention. In the Thai case, these included the EU's approach to dealing with bird flu during the time of the survey and other trade restrictions on Thai exports to the EU. In South Korea, these contentious areas included the EU's dealings with North Korea, the EU's car industry, its exclusivity as a trade bloc and the disputes ensuing from the Common Agricultural Policy. In other words, Thai and Korean citizens were aware of certain negative impacts of the EU on their economy and livelihood.

Thus, when our respondents were asked what issues should be kept in mind while their government was developing diplomatic ties with the EU, there appeared to be considerable room for improvement. In Thailand, some 231 suggestions were generated and of these, the most frequently mentioned issues were related to free and fair trade including of agricultural products (these references accounted for around two-thirds of the total responses), followed by fewer mentions of the importance of political relations and diplomacy, educational exchange, the fight against terrorism, the influence on tourism, monetary issues (like the value of the Thai baht), inflation caused by EU imports and jobs for Thai citizens in the EU. In South Korea, some 251 suggestions were generated and were again primarily concerned with trade (a little more than half of the references), economic competition and investments. They were also concerned about cultural and educational exchanges between South Korea and Europe, and the EU's dealings with the US and North Korea were also high on the agenda. Finally, there were calls for better treatment for Koreans in Europe.

Looking to the future, the EU's soft power approach to international relations has clear limitations in dealing with various long-standing security issues which persist in Asia.[22] Moreover, it is not uncommon for the EU and its Member States to be seen as junior partners of the US. In point of fact, the EU's policy towards Asia does not appear to confront or challenge the US leadership. To make a virtue out of necessity, the EU may act consciously to complement efforts made by other members of the international community who share the EU's foreign policy values. For the EU, this would mean further efforts in line with preventive diplomacy, reinforced political dialogue regarding the state of democracy and human rights, as well as extended economic and humanitarian assistance. All this requires the EU and its Member States to pursue a more visible political profile in parallel with its better-known economic profile.

Notes

1 European Commission, 'Europe and Asia: A Strategic Framework for Enhanced Partnerships', available <http://ec.europa.eu/comm/external_relations/asia/doc/com01_469_en.pdf> (Accessed 31 January 2007).

2 In Thailand, 51 per cent of respondents were between 25 and 44 years old, 56 per cent had obtained a university degree and/or university/technical institute diploma, 60 per cent of respondents were full-time employees and self-employed, 32 per cent of respondents had a household income over B30,000 per year, and 78 per cent voted in the last election. In South Korea, 48 per cent of respondents were between 25 and 44 years old, 45 per cent obtained a university degree and/or university/technical institute diploma, 40 per cent of respondents were full-time employees and self-employed, 48 per cent of respondents had a household income over KRW2.5 million per year, and 76 per cent voted in the last election. Other aspects of the samples are presented in Appendix III.

3 G. Almond and S. Verba, *The Civic Culture: Political Attitudes and Democracy in Five Nations*, Princeton, NJ, Princeton University Press, 1963.

4 R. Sinnot, 'Bringing Public Opinion back in', in O. Niedermayer and R. Sinnott (eds), *Public Opinion and Internationalized Governance*, Oxford and New York, Oxford University Press, 1995, pp. 11–32.

5 G. Wiessala, *The European Union and Asian Countries*, London and New York, Sheffield Academic Press, 2002.

6 European Commission, 'The EU's Relations with Asia: An Overview', available <http://ec.europa.eu/comm/external_relations/asia/index.htm> (Accessed 31 January 2007).

7 From 1976 to 1991, the EC and its Member States were the second biggest provider of ODA to Asia, making available just under $30 billion in aid compared to Japan's $35.2 billion. See C. Piening, *Global Europe: The EU in World Affairs*, Boulder, CO, and London, Lynne Rienner Publishers, 1997, p. 144.

8 Council of Ministers, 'Annual Report CFSP 1997', available <http://www.consilium.europa.eu/uedocs/cmsUpload/rapport97EN.pdf> (Accessed 31 January 2007), point 15a.

9 European Commission, 'The Europe Asia Meeting Process: Towards a New Asia Strategy', available <http://ec.europa.eu/comm/external_relations/asem/asem_process/com94.htm#0> (Accessed 2 February 2007).

10 ASEM, 'ASEM Bangkok 1996', available <http://asem.inter.net.th/> (Accessed 18 December 2006).

11 European Commission, 'The ASEM Process: The Asia–Europe Cooperation Framework (ACEF) 2000', available <http://ec.europa.eu/comm/external_relations/asem/asem_process/aecf_2000.htm> (Accessed 3 January 2007).

12 ASEM, 'Helsinki Declaration on the Future of ASEM', available <http://ec.europa.eu/comm/external_relations/asem/asem_summits/asem6/asem6_future.pdf> (Accessed 3 January 2007).

13 It should be noted that the European Union reacted rapidly and generously to countries affected by the tsunami which took place in December 2004. The total amount of EU aid was estimated at €473 million for 2005 and 2006.

14 European Commission, 'Europe and Asia: A Strategic Framework for Enhanced Partnerships'.

15 H. Maull, 'Europe and the New Balance of Global Order', *International Affairs* 81 (2005), 775–99. See also M. Telò, *Europe, A Civilian Power? European Union, Global Governance, World Order*, New York, Palgrave, 2006.

16 G. Pridham, *Designing Democracy: EU Enlargement and Regime Change in Post-Communist Europe*, New York, Palgrave, 2005.

17 See e.g. J. Peterson and H. Sjursen (eds), *A Common Policy for Europe?*, London and New York, Routledge, 1998; S. Nuttall, *European Foreign Policy*, Oxford and New York, Oxford University Press, 2000.

18 European Commission, 'The EU's Relations with Thailand', available <http://ec.europa.eu/comm/external_relations/thailand/intro/index.htm> (Accessed 4 March 2007).

19 For further details, see H. Kim, 'The Development of Korea–EU Relations: A Multi-Dimensional Approach', *EU–Asian Relations: State of Affairs, Problems and Perspective*, NESCA Series No.1, November 2006, Macau, Institute of European Studies of Macau, pp. 215–46.

20 European Commission, 'The EU's Relations with the Republic of Korea', available <http://ec.europa.eu/comm/external_relations/south_korea/intro/index.htm> (Accessed 2 June 2007).

21 European Commission, 'The EU's Relations with Democratic People's Republic of Korea (North Korea), available <http://ec.europa.eu/comm/external_relations/north_korea/intro/index.htm> (Accessed 1 June 2007).

22 See e.g. M. Smith, 'Between Two Worlds? The European Union, the United States and World Order', *International Politics* 21 (2004), 95–117.

5 Europe from within, Europe from without

Understanding spontaneous perceptions of the European Union in the Asia-Pacific

Michael Bruter

Introduction and theoretical framework

Perceptions, evaluations, and identities: internal and external perspectives

The politics of identity, of likes and dislikes between peoples and nations, has fascinated historians, social psychologists and political thinkers alike for generations. How much do we really know about the perceptions, images and prejudices – be they positive or negative – that individuals hold about members of their own groups and about outsiders?

The Asia-Pacific Perceptions (APP) project constitutes a unique attempt to understand how the European Union is viewed by the media, elites and the mass public from the other side of the planet. This particular chapter will investigate the spontaneous perceptions of the European Union expressed by the masses via the open-ended question modules of our comparative questionnaire.

The chapter will first consider the theoretical bases that we can use to understand the various possible meanings of Europe as an entity and the way in which they can be measured and organized. It will then explore insights into the way the European Union is primarily perceived by Europeans themselves, and will use this as a benchmark to analyse the Asia-Pacific data. Finally, the chapter will examine the findings of the empirical study and the way in which the mass public in the Asia-Pacific sees, perceives and understands what the European Union is.

Europe: continent, political system or project?

Unlike many continents, Europe, because of its historical, economic social, and political developments and significance is a fundamentally polysemic object; in turn continent, civilization, tourist destination, economic and diplomatic power, political system and ever-changing project.

At first, of course, Europe is quite simply, a continent. But even as a continent, Europe remains mysterious. The relevant literature shows that the borders of

Europe have been contested by geographers ever since cartography emerged as a discipline.[1] This uncertain border has implications for the equally uncertain 'centres' that Europe could claim: a number of cities, from Germany to Lithuania via Poland claim to sit at the geographical centre of Europe, joining only a few other pretenders on institutional (Brussels) or symbolic (Strasbourg, Geneva) grounds.[2] Even more topically, twentieth-century geo-strategic divisions have left a significant part of the world's population believing that Europe was or is limited to its Western half and that the Central and Eastern parts of the European Union truly belonged to another grouping which Europe naturally excluded. These variations – which affect the conceptions held by Europeans as well as outsiders – have left deep marks in the way Europe is perceived.

At the same time, next to these strictly geographical conceptions, Europe, because of its historical role, is also often perceived as a civilization and/or a consistent touristic and cultural ensemble by a significant proportion of foreigners. Young Americans may well indulge in a celebratory trip to Europe after their schooling years, and indeed are more likely to do so than to go to Spain, Germany or Poland. Even more importantly, however, the nature of Europe as one of the civilizations that has shaped many modern national cultures means that, to a certain extent, the ownership of European civilization may be claimed by a large number of other countries and regions, from North and South America to Oceania. Despite the geographical distance between these regions and Europe, 'Europeanness' may be more characteristic of the heritage of some parts of the local population than of others and may, as a result, have been internalized as a distinctive category. Similarly, in countries where little or no part of the population feels connected to a European heritage, 'Europeanness' may still represent a whole world and system of values which may extend well beyond the borders of Europe *per se*.

Apart from being a continent, a civilization and the approximation of a certain system of values and ideas, over the past thirty years in particular, Europe has progressively become synonymous with the European Union. As such, this new reference is itself characterized by multiple meanings and facets. As has been shown in previous studies,[3] the evolution of European integration over the past sixty years, from diplomatic achievement, to policy integration, institutionalization and the development of a mass identity, has resulted in changing perceptions of the European project in the eyes of public opinion. For some, the EU is first a set of existing policies (the euro, Common Foreign and Security Policy, etc.), for others it is a major international economic player, perceived as unified in that it is represented in a unique way at major international forums. At the same time, other citizens may perceive the European Union as a political system with its own institutions, or even as an identifiable super-state.

These multiple dimensions are not only interesting in themselves. They also create a series of complex procedures and modes of citizens' perceptions and identification. Before developing a model which will be relevant to the Asia-Pacific case, this chapter will now consider which aspects of our more advanced knowledge of the European case should be taken into consideration.

Europe from the inside: citizens and the European Union

The progressive emergence of a mass European identity

The first important insight from the literature on how Europe is perceived from the inside is that, as far as European citizens are concerned, Europe exists! By and large, research has shown that a mass European identity has progressively emerged since the 1970s.[4] One study in particular has found that, despite significant differences across countries, this continuous progress of the European identity of citizens has affected all the Member States of the European Union over time, except for Luxembourg (which started very high) and Germany (which saw a decline in aggregate levels of European identity after the far less 'Europeanized' Eastern part of Germany integrated into the federation).[5]

Civic and cultural dimensions

Among the important distinctions drawn by political scientists when it comes to the study of a European identity, Bruter has underlined the difference between the civic and cultural dimensions of a European identity.[6] This terminology, further adopted by Herrmann, Risse *et al.* and by Meinhof, suggests that citizens tend to identify with Europe along two distinct dimensions.[7] Civically, they relate to the European Union, which they feel partly defines their status, rights and duties as citizens; that is, as political beings. Culturally, they identify with Europe as a human community; that is, they feel closer to fellow Europeans than to non-Europeans, regardless of the way that they express their reasons for this (it might be that they feel that they share some values, a specific heritage, a taste for green apples or anything else, but ultimately, they believe that 'being European' has a human meaning).

In many ways, this distinction may be useful when considering the way citizens of Asia-Pacific countries perceive the European Union. Indeed, the civic and cultural dimensions largely cover the different objective realities of Europe as defined in the past few pages. Even more interesting, however, will be to compare the way Asia-Pacific citizens relate to these two dimensions of Europe as compared to the way European citizens do. Indeed, studies have found that for European citizens, on the whole, European identity is a predominantly civic affair.[8] A majority of citizens in the countries comprised in these studies indeed thought of themselves as predominantly 'civically' European, although this was not true in Britain and Sweden, or amongst right-wing voters, all of whom defined themselves as predominantly 'culturally' European.[9]

What is Europe for Europeans? Evidence from focus group discussions and narratives

Similarly, previous research also shows how European citizens talk about Europe in a free unprompted context. One study showed that when asked what Europe means to them in the context of focus group discussions, European citizens overwhelmingly referred to the right to cross borders without any form of passport or customs control (the Schengen agreements) and the single currency (the euro), two eminently civic symbols.[10]

These findings emphasize the importance of a mixture of closed and open-ended questions in establishing the way in which citizens perceive a political community. Indeed, without contradicting each other, the answers to closed survey questions and open-ended focus group discussion prompts validate each other and respectively add robustness and precision to each other to paint a clearer picture of what Europe means for its citizens.

The external dimension

Incidentally, these insights into the way Europeans perceive (and identify with) Europe reveal a very clear lack of interest in the external dimension of Europe, or of its external perceptions. In fact, it seems that Europeans have gone such a way in ceasing to see Europe as something exterior to them and to domesticate it that they do not realize that Europe can still mean something to non-Europeans.

Of course, this attitude singularly contrasts with the attempt of European institutions in general and the European Commission in particular to try and give the European Union an international image as a unified economic, political and diplomatic actor.[11] This contrast probably underlines some of the contradictory messages received by non-Europeans about what the European Union is and what it stands for. It may thus explain why some confusion exists in the expectations of the EU as a political object, and in how it may be considered to impact the Asia-Pacific countries themselves.

Europe from the Asia-Pacific: hypotheses and methods

On the basis of the theoretical elements outlined above, we can create a number of simple hypotheses about the way citizens of the Asia-Pacific region will talk about the European Union, bearing in mind that open-ended questions are particularly useful as exploratory tools and must be respected as a means of understanding what the main ideas are that come to Asia-Pacific citizens' minds when prompted to think about the European Union without *a priori* triggers.

The first hypothesis is that, based on the European identity findings of the existing literature, a number of conceptions of the European Union can be defined that will crystallize various images that may spontaneously occur to citizens from the Asia-Pacific region. Globally, they will come under the two general headings of civic and cultural images.

Civic conceptions will recover all the general perceptions of the European Union as a global actor and a political system. The first types of perceptions associated with this are positive and consistent with references to the European Union as *a model*. The reasons why one might want to emulate the European Union are numerous. It is first and foremost an economic – and to a certain extent, political and diplomatic – superpower, so the first concept attached to the European Union as a civic model may be that of *strength*. Second, European integration remains a unique attempt to unify a number of countries which history had opposed and divided. Thus, the second civic model concept that may be associated with the European Union is that of *unity* in a part of the world which perceives itself as suffering from a number of internal conflicts.

Directly related to this is the perception of the European Union as a negative civic power, that is, as a *threat*. Here, we distinguish between two important elements. Referring to Europe as an enemy or imperialist force is directly embedded in its cultural definition rather than its civic one if it does not specifically include unification as a partial source of the threat. As such, we found that the negative notion of civic threat is largely paired with either a positive desire to emulate the EU in citizens' discourse, or with a will to react to the new reality derived from European unification for Asian–Pacific countries themselves, in which case the notion of civic threat is only part of a more global trend to try to conceive the European Union as a *partner*, be it economic and commercial or political. Both notions are different from a strictly 'accounted' weighting of the combined threat of individual countries which we will include in the cultural dimension.

The third type of perception associated with the European Union as a civic object is neutral and includes all references to the Union as a *political system*; that is, without any particular connotation, references to the institutions of the European Union, to its main integrative policies (Schengen, the euro, etc.), and references to the European Union as a super-state, a quasi-state or any other consecration of its political nature.

In addition to the three main civic categories of association are two likely ways of insisting on the cultural identity of Europe and the European Union and denying its civic reality and nature. The first has to do with openly treating Europe as a *negative reference*. This is different from the partnerization outlined earlier and consists of predominantly seeing Europe as a geographical area against which a citizen's country needs to compete. These perceptions may include any ethnocentred reference to the European competition on key economic markets (agriculture, etc.), varying but equally strict immigration standards, unwelcoming culture and attitudes. The second reference may include a negation of the very concept of European Union, that is, a series of answers whereby the European Union is said to only refer to the individual countries that are part of it. As such, this is a very strong statement about the doubted civic nature of the European Union.

Finally, the second series of references to the cultural aspects of the European Union will refer to the cultural aspects of Europe as such (as opposed to its economic, political and diplomatic aspects) emphasizing the nature of Europe as an object of culture and entertainment. In other words, primary references will be made to the European Union as a mere approximation of Europe as a civilization, which may refer to the continent's specificity as a tourist destination, a set of cultural practices (from old museums and classical music to football championships), or specific religions, values, ethnicities.

All in all, applying the civic/cultural model to perceptions of Europe in the Asia-Pacific region and taking into account the background findings of previous studies, we can establish the following grid of analysis of citizens' answers to the open-ended questions posed to them about their perceptions of Europe.[12] To what extent do they perceive the European Union as:

(1)   a civic object, including references to the European Union:
  •   as a model;
  •   as a political system;
  •   as a partner or a threat
(2)   a cultural object, including references to the European Union:
  •   as a negative reference or a mere set of countries;
  •   as a source of mere entertainment

This is the model that will be tested in this chapter.

Methods

In order to test this model, we used a series of answers given by respondents from four countries which, in part, represent the great variety of the Asia-Pacific region: Australia, New Zealand, South Korea, and Thailand.

In Oceania, Australia and New Zealand remain overwhelming superpowers compared to the rest of the region, which is primarily made of small island states. Australia has (legitimate) claims to be the superpower of the region on the basis of its human, geographical and economic weight. Despite being a relatively small country on a world scale from both an economic and a population point of view, its arch-dominance over a geographical area of influence that is arguably larger than those of Europe or the United States gives Australians a different perspective on regional integration and the competition between large regional blocs in the world. By contrast, New Zealand is both much smaller than its Australian neighbour and in constant need of regional integration and dialogue as a traditionally trade-oriented economy that is open to the rest of the region and to the rest of the world. In particular, some of the primary New Zealand economic sectors (such as the meat industry) place it in direct competition with the European Union on a regular basis.

In Asia, South Korea and Thailand are partly symptomatic of a very diverse continent. First of all, they represent two of the main geographical sub-ensembles of Asia: the south-eastern and eastern parts of the continent. Secondly, South Korea is one of the original four 'dragons' which followed the Japanese example on the road to rapid economic growth and slow democratization, while Thailand belongs to a more recent wave of industrialization and economic development, which also implies extensive contrast between its fast-moving cities and a rather traditional countryside. At the same time, while South Korea has been in direct competition with the likes of the European Union for longer, nations like Thailand are more directly targeted by the European Union as prime competitors. Indeed, the extremely rapid development of its economic powers and its cheaper labour and production costs make Thailand and similar economies appear to the European Union as countries against which the most vulnerable sectors of the European economy simply cannot compete.

The survey used in the analysis asked respondents to answer the following question. 'When thinking about the term "the European Union", what *three* thoughts come to your mind?' In order to analyse their answers, we first counted individual comments, and then considered a recoding of the spontaneous answers provided using the general and more specific categories proposed in our hypotheses.

The analysis follows these two levels of generalization as well. The first part of the analysis is quantitative, using the spontaneous wordings and the recoding of the answers provided by respondents. In that section, when respondents provided several answers, they were not differentiated between as there was no indication in the question that the respondents should hierarchize their three responses. The second part of the analysis is qualitative and relies on some of the specific answers provided by the various respondents in the four countries, trying to understand what they imply and involve.

Findings

Spontaneous categories

We first looked at the spontaneous answers that respondents gave to the open ended question on meanings of the European Union. The results are reported in Table 5.1. It can be seen that a range of images and references tended to come to mind for Asia-Pacific respondents. References to unity, solidarity and identity were very regular and topped the list in Australia and South Korea (about one respondent in four). They were, however, scarce in Thailand. Similarly, the euro remained an important point of reference and, indeed, was the most common answer provided by New Zealanders (one respondent in five). However, once again, it did not tend to come to the minds of the Thai respondents very often. Again, the same contrast can be observed with regards to the European Union appearing as primarily strong for about one respondent in six in Australia, New Zealand and South Korea, but almost none in Thailand.

Altogether, Thai respondents seemed to have a completely different perception of the European Union as compared to the other three countries. Primary references were to the EU as a trade partner (for three respondents in ten), and also as a travel destination (one in four). Even the third most common answer to the question is symptomatic of the gap between Thai and other Asia-Pacific responses: in the eyes of our Thai sample, after being a trade partner and a travel destination, the European Union was represented by its individual countries, and then … football! The only country to share some of the Thai perceptions such as the emphasis on trade and on individual Member States was New Zealand, albeit, in both cases, to a lesser extent. The chapter will now consider the way in which these answers fit into the model discussed earlier.

Table 5.1 References most frequently associated with the European Union – spontaneous open-ended questions

	AUS	NZL	THA	KOR
Euro	14.4	19.2	3.5	18.1
Strength	17.0	14.3	0.7	16.7
Unity, identity, solidarity	22.3	13.6	0.7	26.0
Divisions, confusion, diversity, loss	2.9	3.3	0	0.4
Tourism, culture, history	4.1	5.8	25.3	6.9
Single market	5.7	2.7	0.7	1.9
Exports, trade, business, economy	9.7	16.5	29.1	3.7
Friends, pro	4.6	2.9	1.8	2.6
Enemies, competition, subsidies, interfering, close off, arrogant	5.1	8.7	3.2	6.3
Peace	2.6	2.7	0	1.9
EU citizenship, borderlessness	5.5	4.8	2.1	3.8
Politics, policies, diplomacy	2.0	3.7	6.3	3.3
Against, failure, difficulties, ridiculous	3.6	2.5	0	
Countries, nations	4.1	9.5	19.3	3.3
UK, monarchy, queen	1.8	2.7	**	**
Enlargement	0.2	0.8	0	
New, project, hope	1.2	0.6	0	
Bureaucracy, cumbersome	0.6	0.2	0	
Institutions (EP, EC, etc.)	0.2	0.8	2.8	
Model for region	0	0.2	0	8.3
Remote, irrelevant	1.0	0.6	0	2.1
Football	0	0	6.0	0.8
Questions? Unsure	1.6	0.2	1.1	9.6
Other	4.2	2.9	1.1	2.3
Total	506	484	285	520

Europe as a model

The first type – and most numerous series – of references presented the European Union as a model. These admiring references were surprisingly varied, and contrasted, to a certain extent, with the frequent criticisms of the European media towards the European Union political system.

The first such reference was to the European Union as a successful model of unity, identity and solidarity. At a time when Europeans seem to perpetually doubt the solidity of their union and each other's sense of solidarity, it is rather interesting to see that a distant part of the world, which could have been expected to be rather critical, perceives the EU as a model of the successful fostering of solidarity between twenty-seven nations. Respondents took various views of this perceived success in creating a bloc of internal friendship and mutual support. The unity theme was ranked first in Australia and rephrased in a multiplicity of ways. One Australian respondent seemed to summarize the overall feeling of almost 20 per cent of total respondents by explaining that 'they are just going to be one big country'. Along the same lines, another respondent openly chose to equate the EU with the US success story, by saying that the European Union is 'sort of like United States of Europe', while a third way of comparing the European unification process to that of nation-building was explained by another respondent as 'countries becoming one'. Similarly, unity references also came at the top of the spontaneous answers of the Korean respondents, but in this case, the integration process was sometimes described in an almost fantastical manner, as for one respondent who thought that the EU made him think of 'language: there is a unified language in Europe'.

Another one of the underlying approaches was that of solidarity 'against'. In this case, the USA appeared to be the most likely target of European solidarity. One respondent described the EU as countries 'united against USA' and another thought that with European unification came the 'expectation of stopping the unilateral policy of the USA and preventing the supremacy of the USA by uniting'. However, respondents in Korea also mentioned a number of other 'outgroups' against which European solidarity had been reinforced, sometimes paradoxically, as with one respondent who thought of the EU as a 'union against Christianity'. Throughout the four countries, other respondents also developed this theme by referring to the friendship between European peoples, and what they perceived to be the emergence of a single European people.

The second mode of perceptions of European unification was in reference to its strength. Once again, this description would be quite likely to surprise a number of citizens of the European Union, who do not seem to realize themselves how strong and powerful the EU is perceived to be from the outside. In this case, some Australian respondents strongly emphasized this perception, suggesting for example that the EU is the 'most powerful nation in the world', while a Korean respondent described the same European Union – rather more poetically – as 'a large dragon'. The reference to an implied competition was again rather prominent across the four countries with regards to the strength of the European Union. 'Really they have put their heads together – they could get rid of the USA' was the description of one Australian respondent. Another explained that this strength is 'positive: it's a good balance, America on one side and collective good countries on another'. The reference to strength as a factor of competition was, however, also seen as a threat at times; another Australian respondent explained that 'I don't like the idea of the whole lot going together'. Overall, references to the strength of the European Union came in second place of all the spontaneous references in Australia, and in third place in New Zealand and South Korea.

The model theme also appeared on numerous occasions in the form of references to the hope, peace, and dynamic project created by European integration, but its ultimate expression came in the form of a model that was intended to be copied by the respondents' countries themselves. Strangely perhaps, some of the strongest references of this nature came from the relatively negative New Zealand. Rather prosaically, one of the New Zealand respondents simply reckoned that 'we will end up doing the same in this corner in the world'. One of his Australian neighbours agreed with the prospect rather more emphatically, seeing European integration as a 'marvelous advance. The unity theme, certainly approve of bringing down borders, making it easier to travel and trade.' It was, however, in South Korea that the notion of the European Union as a model that would travel well was most prominent, with 8.3 per cent of respondents mentioning such a prospect (in a positive way) in some form.

Europe as a political system

The second type of references which mirrored Europeans' own growing sense of EU identity emphasized the importance of the European Union as a fully fledged political system. These references took a number of different forms. In some cases, for example, respondents associated the EU with some of its institutions, particularly the European Parliament and the European Commission. Strangely enough, this was most often the case in Thailand (2.8 per cent) where, as will be seen, references to the European Union as such were the least frequent. Other references to the European Union as a political system focused on specific policies of the EU, such as the Common Agricultural Policy, or the Common Foreign and Security Policy, or spoke of various aspects of European diplomacy and its significance. Further respondents went so far as to concentrate on specific aspects of European Union politics, such as European Parliament elections, the 2004 enlargement of the European Union to ten new Southern and Eastern European states, actual European leaders such as the President of the Commission, and the question of Turkey, among others.

A particularly important reference, however, was to the euro, which was the most frequent point of reference of New Zealanders, and the second and third most important ones of South Koreans and Australians respectively. One Australian respondent thus explained that the term European Union makes him think of 'currency, the fact they have an easily understood currency system. And there is not the necessity to equate it with the Australian dollar', thus combining the central role of the single currency and the strength theme mentioned earlier.

The most important references in this category, however, were to the elements of sovereignty of the European Union and of the right and duties of its citizens, that is, in actuality, references to the emergence of a European citizenship, which seemed to impress many of the respondents. For one of the New Zealand respondents, the European Union evoked the image of its flag: 'stars and blue background'. Far more often, however, were references to the rights of European Union citizens, particularly with regards to the highly evocative European borderlessness of the Schengen agreement and the free movement of people. This is particularly interesting to the extent that, as explained earlier, previous studies have found that borderlessness and the Europe of Schengen is also the first spontaneous reference of EU citizens when asked what this citizenship means to them.[13] In the same way, an Australian respondent thus noted that 'if you're a member of the EU you are able to travel easily'. Another one phrased it even more clearly by stating that, for him, the European Union was first and foremost 'a place with no borders'. Still in Australia, one respondent insisted on another fundamental aspect of EU citizenship by stressing that 'you can work anywhere within the Union'. Numerous other aspects of EU citizenship were mentioned by respondents throughout all four countries; one example in Thailand was where a respondent predominantly equated the European Union with a 'student exchange program'.

This theme shows that the daily reality of the European Union, that which really makes an impression on European citizens themselves, has not gone unnoticed on the other side of the planet. Beside this sympathetic Eurocentric perspective, however, citizens of the Asia-Pacific region also focused very significantly on the European Union from a more ethnocentric perspective, evaluating its positive position as a partner, or its negative one as a reference of competition and conflict.

Europe as a partner

In many ways, perceptions of Europe as a partner of the countries in the Asia-Pacific were relatively absent in the open-ended part of the survey. The main exception was Thailand, where references to the EU as a trade partner topped the list of references (Table 5.2). References to trade also came second in New Zealand but they were not often as positive as in Thailand, and similar references only came fourth in Australia and ninth in South Korea.

Occasionally, these references were positive, as for one South Korean respondent who noted that 'there are a lot of Daewoo cars in Europe'. However, in many cases, these references to the European Union as a partner were cautious if not skeptical, as the European Union was often accused of selfishness or protectionism, particularly by New Zealanders. One New Zealander summarized his perception of the European Union as a trade partner in the following way: 'I think they are trying to rule the world.' Another respondent, this time from Australia, reiterated this sentiment: '[the EU is] just for themselves and no one else', while two of his compatriots also emphasized the protectionist side of the perception by claiming respectively that 'they're shutting themselves off from other countries', and that the EU 'was set to exclude the rest of the world, really want to become a major world power and influence the rest of the world'. On the other hand, another respondent focused primarily on the more diplomatic and political aspects of what was perceived to be nothing less than European imperialism, where the goal of Europeans was perceived to be 'imposing their political doctrine on everyone around them'. Finally, one of the Thai respondents

Table 5.2 Classification of main references – aggregate

	Australia	New Zealand	Thailand	Korea
1	Unity	Euro	Trade	Unity
2	Strength	Trade	Tourism	Euro
3	Euro	Strength	Countries	Strength
4	Trade	Unity	Politics	Model
5	Single Market	Countries	Football	Tourism
6	Citizenship	Enemies	Euro	Enemies

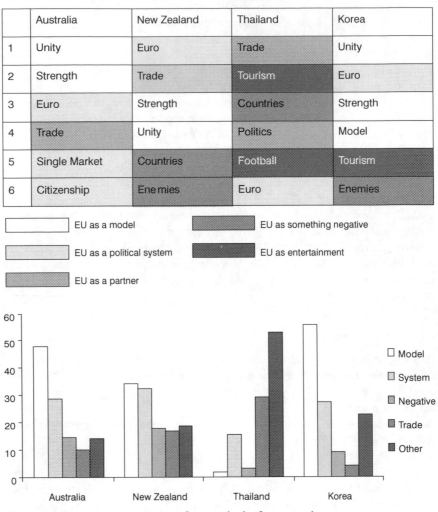

Figure legend:
- EU as a model
- EU as a political system
- EU as a partner
- EU as something negative
- EU as entertainment

Bar chart legend:
- Model
- System
- Negative
- Trade
- Other

Figure 5.1 Dominant spontaneous references in the four countries

focused more predominantly on the immigration side of the 'fortress Europe', mentioning 'strict checks on Asians' immigration'.

Europe as a negative reference

Another set of negative references concerned the European Union itself. It must be noted that references to the possible internal failure of the European Union – a sort of external euroscepticism – were overall far rarer than the parallel positive references. These references, as illustrated by Table 5.2, took three main forms. The first type was constructed through explicit references to individual

EU countries, implicitly negating the political existence of the European Union. The second type was made through overt references to the European Union as an enemy, or, in the third and rarest cases, as an internal failure.

The first type of references was particularly important in Thailand where it came fourth of all categories with 19.3 per cent of the total (Table 5.1). It was also present to a lesser extent in New Zealand where it concerned 9.5 per cent of all answers. In New Zealand and Australia, a very small minority also chose to refer to the UK, the monarchy, or the Commonwealth when asked to think about the EU, which has some obviously different implications than references to France or Germany. An example of the first type of reference can be found in Thailand where one of the respondents highlighted the presence of 'plenty of German tourists in Thailand. Prostitutes in Pattaya.' Similarly, when asked what the European Union evoked to him, one New Zealand respondent proceeded to list the names of the Member States that he knew.

The second type of references were mostly found in New Zealand and South Korea, where they came sixth with 8.7 and 6.3 per cent of all mentions respectively. With regards to the enemy/external aspects of the criticism, one New Zealander explained: 'I do not want New Zealand to be involved in the EU.' Another New Zealander took a rather particular perspective on what he perceived to be the European Union alienation by saying: 'Britain is not part of the EU – we are challenging European wines and cheeses.' With regards to the criticism directed at the success of European integration as such, one respondent for example said of the European Union that 'it's like a baby that hasn't grown up yet'. Another, taking a somewhat unusual historical perspective, explained that 'it's not going to work!' and another one, in Australia, that 'it's ridiculous!' This previous sentiment was articulated even more strongly by another New Zealand respondent who noted, somewhat scathingly, 'a European Union? It's a long way off happening.' Another Australian expressed dismay at the whole project when he asked 'why did they join?' The gloomiest comment found was that of a South Korean respondent who predicted, about the European Union, that 'people could suffer from it'.

Europe as entertainment

Finally, the last segment of the spontaneous references associated with the European Union presented Europe as a symbol of entertainment, from tourism to football. Almost all of these references which, largely reduced the European Union to just a European continent and/or civilization, were found in Asia. They were usually very positive, but clearly not centred on the European Union as a political system. One respondent thought of the European Union as 'clean and neat', while another was more impressed by its 'laid back, romantic, passionate' character. More pragmatically, another South Korean respondent associated the European Union with 'a high-speed railroad', while a Thai participant thought of the EU as more touristically evocative of 'snow, [and the] Eiffel tower'.

When it came to the EU as a civilization reference, another Thai respondent associated the Union with 'clothes, fashion', while a number of others connected the EU with football, often including specific football clubs and even occasionally David Beckham! Outside of the two Asian participant countries, however, these touristic and civilizational references were almost non-existent.

Conclusions

As has been seen, the types of references evoked by the European Union in participants from the two Asian and two Pacific countries included in the study varied quite extensively and differed comparatively. A few interesting patterns can be underlined.

The first point to be made is that, overall, particularly in Australia and South Korea, the European Union, as an entity, was spontaneously conceived and acknowledged. References to individual countries remained very scarce, except to a limited extent in Thailand and New Zealand. For the most part, when asked what they associate with the European Union, a very large majority of respondents did react to the EU as such.

The second point is that, in global terms, positive references largely outweighed negative ones, with once again a less enthusiastic attitude to be found amongst the New Zealand sample than amongst the rest. Elsewhere, the dominant perceptions of the European Union were, first and foremost, of a strong and successful model of unity, which may or may not have to be emulated by other regions but has globally participated positively in the contemporary transformation of the international scene.

The third and final point is that, from the outside as from the inside, the European Union is primarily visible from and through its symbols. Globally, the euro and the Schengen system of borderlessness remain, outside of the EU as from within (albeit in apparently opposite orders), the two main spontaneous images of what the EU means and is. If, progressively, the European flag, anthem and possibly constitution achieve similar visibility, the European Union will have achieved its most incredible challenge: to appear as a true, significant political system to the other side of the world.

Notes

1   M. Wintle (ed.), *Culture and Identity in Europe*, London, Avebury, 1996; M. Bruter, *Citizens of Europe? The Emergence of a Mass European Identity*, Basingstoke, Palgrave Macmillan, 2005; M. Bruter, 'Diplomacy without a State: The External Delegations of the European Commission', *Journal of European Public Policy* 6 (2005), 183–205.
2   *Ibid.*
3   *Ibid.*
4   T. Risse, R. Herrmann and M. Brewer, *Europeanization and Multiple Identities*, New York, Rowman & Littlefield, 2004; Bruter, *Citizens of Europe?*; Bruter, 'Diplomacy without a State'.
5   Bruter, *Citizens of Europe?*
6   M. Bruter, 'Winning Hearts and Minds for Europe', *Comparative Political Studies* 36 (2003), 1148–79; Bruter, *Citizens of Europe?*; Bruter, 'Diplomacy without a State'.

7   Risse *et al.*, *Europeanization*; U. Meinhof, *'Bordering European Identities', special issue, Journal of Ethnic and Migration Studies* 29 (2003).
8   Bruter, *Citizens of Europe?*.
9   *Ibid.*
10 *Ibid.*
11 See e.g. Bruter, *Citizens of Europe?*; M. Holland and N. Chaban, *The EU through the Eyes of the Asia-Pacific: Public Perceptions and Media Representations*, Christchurch, NCRE Research Series, 4, National Centre for Research on Europe, University of Canterbury, 2005. See also Chaban and Holland, 'Introduction', above.
12 Bruter, 'Winning Hearts'; Bruter, 'Diplomacy Without a State'; Bruter, *Citizens of Europe?*; Meinhof, *'Bordering European Identities'*; Risse *et al.*, *Europeanization*.
13 Bruter, *Citizens of Europe?*

6 What Australians think about the EU

National interests in an international setting

Philomena Murray

Today, the EU is our largest trading partner. It is our largest source of foreign direct investment and second largest investment partner overall. Alongside these strong commercial links, there is a rich network of connections throughout many sectors including the arts, in science and technology, innovation and education ... So no-one should be under any illusion about how important Europe is for Australia.[1]

Introduction

This chapter examines Australian elite perceptions of the European Union (EU), based on surveys and interviews conducted with a section of Australian political, business and media elites.[2] It is clear from these assessments that Europe's geographical remoteness, the influence of the United Kingdom (UK) connection and the long-standing conflict regarding agriculture in particular still feature prominently in the current Australia–EU relationship and that the highly contested nature of Australia–EU engagement is based on a 'collective amnesia', or lack of knowledge, about the EU.

Nevertheless, while distance, myth and memory certainly are relevant, the Common Agricultural Policy (CAP) and the British link are not the only themes in elites' assessment of the EU. These interviews demonstrate that Australian elites possess more complex and nuanced understandings of the EU as an international economic actor, although they are not aware of actual policy-making in the broadening Australia–EU engagement. Advancing national interests remains a key concern for both these elites and governments. While the government advances its interests in an international setting in extensive dialogue with the EU, across a wide range of policy areas, there is limited domestic awareness of these issues. Thus, while government rhetoric is largely negative regarding the EU, for domestic reasons, behind the scenes a productive engagement is taking place. The attitudes of the elites interviewed for this project largely reflects the public policy pronouncements of the government rather than the actual extensive and multilevel activity in the relationship between Australia and the EU.

The background and context: Australia's engagement with the EU

Asia-Pacific economic and political stakeholders, such as government agencies, businesses, service providers and investors are increasingly obliged to negotiate with, and adapt to, the fact that the EU is a regionally integrated trading bloc with global impact on economic and political governance. It is progressively more evident that non-EU nations have been influenced by the EU's international weight. In the case of Australia, this became especially clear at the end of the 1990s, with the realization that there was a need to take stock of Australian perceptions of the EU and the Australia–EU relationship. Thus, in 1998–9 and 2001–2, the first surveys of elites took place in Australia. These two original surveys were responding to a perceived need to document and analyse the perceptions of government and non-government actors in Australia dealing with the EU and the surveys targeted a wide range of analysts and top decision-makers and stakeholders.[3]

The surveys constituted a first attempt to redress the lack of data on elite perceptions. Accounts of EU–Australia relations up to that point had concluded that, although Australia and the EU had much in common, the relationship was not accorded significant public debate.[4] These surveys were designed to complement studies that had enumerated a number of factors in the relationship: the official Australian emphasis on bilateral relationships with individual Member States; the focus on the CAP and the UK connection; the lack of adequate management by Australian governments of the opportunities in the EU and problems of adaptation to the EU's complexity. There was also the claim that Australia had 'missed opportunities', due to incomplete knowledge of the EU, which resulted in negative outcomes for Australia.[5]

Given significant developments occurring in the Australia–EU relationship and the growth of the EU's international role, these surveys played a part in filling a gap in Australia's understanding of the EU, and it was suggested that this might find resonance in other parts of the Asia-Pacific.[6] Consequently, in 2005, within the context of the Asia-Pacific Perceptions (APP) project, a further set of surveys and interviews was conducted to complement these previous two surveys, addressing the 2004 EU enlargement and problems relating to the EU Constitutional Treaty and other contemporary developments.

All three surveys classified respondents by type, according to their profession, and required respondents to assess the importance, state and significance of the overall trading relationship between Australia and the EU. The 2001–2 and 2005 surveys included a further set of questions regarding the implications of the EU enlargement and the euro, as well as questions dealing with assessments of the Single Market and the EU as an economic entity. The respondents were then asked to consider whether it was necessary to promote closer links between Australia and the EU and in which areas they might support closer cooperation. There was provision for open answers, including the final question, which asked: 'In your opinion, what issues should be kept in mind when formulating Australian policy towards the EU?' Some continuity of understanding of elite perceptions was thus provided.[7]

The survey results and scholarly analysis suggest that the EU–Australia relationship has required an increased change of focus from state-to-state relations (traditional bilateralism) to new regional bilateralism and multilateralism. Australia and other Asia-Pacific countries deal with the EU at three major levels of policy-making: traditional bilateral relations, relations with the EU as an actor (new regional bilateralism) and a broader, multilateral engagement, which can be called global societal bilateralism.[8]

Traditional bilateralism and the British connection

Engagement between Australia and the EU has long been characterized by state-to-state links and a marked preference for using traditional bilateralism to further national interests, the most important example of this being the long-standing Australian–British relationship. This preference was exemplified in the 1997 White Paper on foreign policy as formulated by the Coalition government which stated that Australia's national interests are best served by 'sound and comprehensive' bilateral relations with European nation-states – especially the UK, France, Germany, Italy and Russia.[9] It is stated that strong bilateral links with EU Member States complement Australia's 'direct dealings' with the EU institutions.

In line with this long-standing government policy, survey results indicate that there is insistence by a significant number of respondents that individual Member States remain the primary focus of Australian interest in the EU[10] and it can be argued persuasively that, consistent with this, there has been an overall Australian reticence in dealing with the EU as a whole rather than traditional individual partners. For example, a 2005 APP project respondent stated that, 'The current government ... they put a lower emphasis on multi-lateral engagement, they're more into bilateral agreements with certain countries.'[11]

It is noteworthy in the recent survey that the business elites in particular think in terms of trading with individual states, and not with the EU as a whole. There was considerable ignorance among the elites regarding trade with the EU and whether or not there are different sets of regulations in different Member States. It was commented by both business and media elites that 'We don't trade with the EU, we trade with Britain, France, Germany ... ',[12] and 'I think Australian companies tend to trade with individual trading partners, not the EU as a bloc ... I think it's just ... it's bilateral.'[13] Another member of the elite group felt that 'we probably talk to people about doing business in Germany, doing business in Poland, doing business in Spain, doing business in Italy. We don't talk, you know, so much about the European Union.'[14] Yet another respondent noted:

> I was just looking back through some statistics in one of those little brochures that the EU puts out that I see from time to time, about the impact of the EU if you conglomerate it for the Australian economy. Now that's pretty significant but we probably still don't see it in those terms. We pretty much see it as the individual countries.[15]

The previous surveys of Australian elite perceptions had some respondents suggesting that the UK, of all the EU states, understands Australia best, with comments such as, 'The UK remains the major EU member which understands Australia best and has the most regard for Australia',[16] and 'The continuing relationship with Britain ... remains significant in terms of institutions, travel, migration and cultural exchange.'[17]

Australian journalist Geoff Kitney has also argued that:

> The historic ties, the language, the business connections and the deep penetration of British ideas and thinking into Australian society mean that Australia still sees much through the prism of its Britishness ... The strength of the British connection is understandable. But it may be time for it to be reviewed and recast.[18]

This attachment to the UK has been a key factor that has long influenced the Australia–EU relationship. In both government pronouncements and current elite perceptions, it is clear that old loyalties remain important.[19] However, having said this, there is evidence that a shift in Australian government understandings may be under way, as seen in former Foreign Minister Alexander Downer's recognition of the value of a new type of relationship between Australia and the EU by the early 2000s. He commented that Australia needed to 'work hard on building our links not only with the individual Member States of the EU, but also with the European institutions. We need to see Europe through a new prism, not just through the UK and traditional relationships.'[20]

Thus two quite different perspectives are apparent amongst the interviewed elites – that the EU, on the one hand, and the Member States on the other, are important partners for Australia. Both perspectives were evident in the 2001–2 survey, as seen in the comment made by one respondent that, 'By identifying closely with the US and the UK in our business and political approaches, we tend to distance ourselves from continental Europe.'[21] Alternately, another another felt that 'There is the need to cultivate cultural awareness with the countries of the EU which have contributed to Australian cultural heritage – not only the UK, but Ireland, Greece, France, Italy, Spain *et al.*',[22] while yet another believed that 'Australia has to make a bigger effort on trade and investment relationships with the EU Member States other than the UK.'[23] This sentiment was also voiced by another respondent who claimed rather strongly that 'We must overcome our Anglo centric approach to the EU!'[24]

A duality of perspectives has also been evident in the views of two leaders of government in Australia. Paul Keating, former Prime Minister, lamented that the 'image of Australia as a branch office of Britain is tenacious',[25] whereas more recent Prime Minister John Howard suggested that 'No two countries in our respective regions know each other better, trust each other more and have closer relationships than Australia and Britain.'[26] The current Prime Minister, Kevin Rudd, elected in November 2007, has yet to express clear views on the subject.

The role of trade, including agriculture

The trading relationship is the most successful part of the Australia–EU engagement, as the EU has long been Australia's largest trading partner. Yet there has been little public acknowledgement of this by government in public pronouncements. Neither the importance of the EU as a trading bloc and partner for Australia, nor the impressive trade statistics, are reflected in speeches, or, correspondingly, in elite perceptions.

Despite the very healthy trade and investment flows between the EU and Australia there was less than comprehensive understanding of the opportunities for Australian business from many elite respondents. Traders and investors have certainly recognized the value of doing business with Europe, however successive Australian governments have not conceded the value of engaging with the EU. Few respondents seemed to understand that the EU is Australia's largest trading partner – bigger than Japan or the US, in trade in goods, services and investment. On the contrary, one respondent stated, regarding Australia–EU engagement, that 'in trade terms I think the relationship is doomed to withering, but slowly'.[27]

Further, China and the US were accorded greater priority by the elites surveyed. The focus of many respondents on Asia and the US reveals, once again, considerable ignorance regarding the volume of Australia–EU trade. The findings illustrate that there is an overwhelming perception that Asia is far more important to Australia, and growing in importance, than is the EU, especially where trade is concerned. The bilateral relationships with the US and China have high priority, followed by Japan, Indonesia and Korea. This was also evident in 2001–2: when asked with whom Australia should do business, survey respondents replied, 'We're a part-Asian society with European values but the EU doesn't need us';[28] 'Developing relations with Europe and Asia are NOT mutually exclusive';[29] 'Ensuring mutually supportive and beneficial relations with the EU, Asia and North America should be given an equally high priority.'[30]

An additional challenge facing the Australia–EU trade relationship is the problem of imbalance and asymmetry – the fact that the EU is more important to Australia than vice versa.[31] Given that it is difficult for a smaller country such as Australia to get on the EU radar screen under most circumstances, the fact that the EU is not well understood by Australian elites and that it is viewed as a complex body and difficult to deal with, makes it harder for Australia to get the EU's attention and to advance its own trade agenda. The situation is rendered more difficult by the fact that trade with the EU has long been associated, in the Australian psyche, with conflicts regarding agriculture. Richardson has acutely observed that 'it has been Australia's misfortune ... that its interests have collided with those of the EC precisely where it is most protectionist'.[32]

Australia is a small economic player relative to the European giant and this has perhaps shaped Australia's rather negative outlook towards engagement with the EU, which has often focused on trade disputes and perceptions of the EU opposing Australia's interests. These perceptions are evident in the elite surveys. In many responses, the EU is often seen as obstructionist in trade talks and protectionist, especially concerning agriculture. This focus on the most negative and protectionist aspects of the EU, especially the CAP, has meant that opportunities for a broader relationship were not been fully explored until early this decade. In the case of Australia, there remains considerable ignorance regarding the broader scope and extent of the relationship.

Broader EU–Australia engagement

As is evident from the discussion above, the broad-ranging nature of Australia's relationship with the EU is not commonly well understood. Groom, for example, has recommended that the intellectual baggage of past conceptions of the Australian relationship with Europe must be cast aside.[33] The new relationship with the EU can best be understood in the context of the EU's regionalism in the global economy and its assertive role in global governances.

The Australian government is increasingly cognizant of the EU's clout, although this is a relatively recent recognition. Cooperation and mutual understanding are growing. Further, the relationship is multidimensional encompassing trade, investment, science and technology, wine market access, immigration, security and various aspects of foreign policy. This shift is seen in an increased policy community adaptation to the EU, as reflected in, for example, the Department of Foreign Affairs and Trade (DFAT) and other ministries. There is an increased willingness to engage with the EU and some evidence of a renewed interest by ministers in travelling to Brussels. While World Trade Organization (WTO) issues remain firmly on the agenda, CAP reform since the Uruguay and 2003 reforms mean that agriculture is no longer the principal focus of dialogues. This is symptomatic of the recent shift in orientation by the Australian policy community.[34] However, very little of this activity was identified in the 2005 interviews, including amongst the group of parliamentarians. This is likely because it is not publicly known. Among the elites interviewed in 2005, there was little comprehension of Australia–EU broad engagement, nor of the implications for Australia of the expansion of the EU's scope, range and influence. This engagement is set out in the Agenda for Cooperation determined by the Australian government and the European Commission, summarized in Table 6.1. Rather than an understanding of this broad relationship, there was instead a message from these elite interviews that the EU is less, not more, relevant to Australia than in the past.

Recognition of the EU as a global player

The contemporary EU of twenty-seven Member States has significant reach and influence in the world and is undoubtedly a global player of increasing weight. This is due not only to its economic clout and status as the largest single trading bloc in the world, but also to its successful exertion of soft power (notably through the projection of norms) in many domains, its civilian power instruments such as sanctions and incentives, and its continuing efforts to strengthen its Common Foreign and Security Policy (CFSP). In Australia, however, the results of the surveys and interviews to date reveal a marked tendency on the part of the Australian elite to underestimate the EU and the full extent of its global influence.

It is in the economic realm that the Australian government and elites recognize the EU as most powerful. Although we have seen that a number of respondents still view the UK as the primary focus of Australia's economic activity with Europe, and that there is little familiarity with EU trade policy international agreements, there is nevertheless an enduring perception of the EU among elites who 'see [the EU] certainly as an economic entity and as an economic power'.[35] The euro, for example, is frequently well-recognized as a global currency; several respondents were aware that the EU possesses the world's second largest currency and that some 45 per cent of the international reserves of the Reserve Bank of Australia are currently held in euros. Even if there is no full comprehension of the EU as a single trading bloc by Australian elites, there is some recognition of its economic might.

Where political power and influence are concerned, however, Australian elites appear to be much more dismissive of the EU and sceptical of its power potential. Interview responses clearly indicated that there is a perception of the EU as internally torn by crisis and dissent; that the EU lacks the internal unity required for it to become a great power. Moreover, European divisions regarding the Iraq war have served to reinforce the perception among Australian elites that the EU is not an international political leader.

As for 'hard power', here the EU did not fare much better in the Australian elite opinion. The few respondents who referred to the CFSP pointed to its weaknesses, rather than its potential; a negative focus which echoes a comment by Australian Foreign Minister Downer that the EU punches below its weight.[36] The European Security and Defence Policy (ESDP), growing military coordination and EU military operations were accorded scant attention by the interviewees.

Perhaps due to shared agendas (such as the Pacific), there was some awareness that the EU is involved in development aid, although this tended not to extend to a deeper understanding of the role of the EU in humanitarian assistance, and instead reinforces the overall impression that the EU is perceived as an international actor largely in the trade domain.

The above dimensions of global influence are what could be called the traditional constituents of power. What is distinctive about the EU and its role as a global player is that normative power, a somewhat non-traditional from of power that involves the EU promoting its conception of democracy, human rights, good governance and multilateralism, plays a large part in its international role. This image of the EU does not feature clearly on the Australian radar screen, as Australian elites show little understanding of how the EU projects a view of itself as a guardian of global governance and trade norms. Its role as a type of norms-enforcer based on civilian power instruments of sanctions, incentives, influence on global governance norms and world trade was not given much attention. Nor was the human rights clause in all trade and cooperation agreements signed by the EU with its interlocutors since May 1995, a means by which the EU explicitly links trade and norms regarding civil society and governance in a way that can adversely affect countries such as Australia on world markets.

It would be in Australia's interests to develop a better understanding of, and devote more attention to, this European global agenda and the reach of its normative power, which is evident in a number of policy areas, such as trade, human rights, and development and democratization – dominating agendas which are not traditional foreign policy or hard power. These agendas are gathering momentum and are of real concern to governments such as that of Australia, which has engaged in active dialogue on these issues, although this is not commonly acknowledged. These concerns are not reflected in the interview responses.

Of course, Australia and the EU have much in common and thus it can be argued convincingly that the EU, in its growing role as a global player, is promoting a global order that is largely favorable to Australia. For instance, there are shared values in the promotion of common political ideals such as peace, liberty and democracy; and shared economic ideologies, based on the promotion of economic liberalism, free trade and WTO rules. Both interlocutors are committed to strengthening the multilateral world order. Further, this decade has seen the development of many areas for cooperation, mutual benefit and understanding, such as security cooperation (including counter-terrorism); immigration and refugees, and enhanced cooperation on science and technology.[37] In the APP project interviews, however, there was comparatively little understanding of this. The EU's new global context and its relevance for Australia are not properly understood by Australian elites. Overall, the EU's ever-increasing influence in shaping global agendas has only recently been understood by parts of the Australian policy community and this new coming to terms with the EU as an international actor and interlocutor has not been evident in the business, policy-making or media communities as represented by the respondents to this survey.[38]

Assessments and critiques of the EU

The far-away fortress: internally focused yet irreparably divided

Critiques of the EU take a number of forms in the interviews and surveys. Three aspects stand out – first, that the EU is a fortress; secondly, that it is divided; and, thirdly, that it is internally focused. The perception of the EU as a fortress is largely a result of the widespread impression of substantial difficulties of access to the European market for Australian goods. Interviewees pointed to the problems of limited access to agricultural markets in particular and to the CAP's world market distortions, which have negative results for Australia. This view is by no means a recent development – there has long been an Australian government perception of the EU as a 'Fortress Europe' or an 'Unbound Leviathan',[39] and successive Australian governments have, to a greater or lesser degree, attacked the EU as manipulative mandarins, who are obsessed with bureaucracy, protectionism and obstructionism. This has been compounded by a focus on agriculture.

Having said this, it is important to note that there is now also a competing, albeit minority, perspective amongst Australian elites that Europe represents a massive opportunity for Australian business. Whilst many still regard the UK as the safest and most appropriate location for Australian investment and business ventures in Europe, there are others who recognize a need to move more into other European markets.

The second recurrent theme that is clear from the interviews and surveys is that the EU is a deeply divided entity. It is regarded as having too many internal disputes. This was sometimes proffered as a reason why the EU is not a leader in international politics – 'I don't think they've got adequate cohesion to operate … it hasn't got the internal cohesion to operate as a single entity in power politics'[40] – with some respondents envisaging that the EU's international influence is likely to further decrease due to future enlargements which will bring with them more potential for internal disputes. This internal friction is largely seen as being the result of the EU's history. In addition, survey respondents from all groups regarded recent EU enlargements, with the accession of more diverse Member States, as an explanation for the EU's internal diversity of objectives, with the perception that the interests of the new Member States stand in considerable contrast with those of the established Member States.

Eurocentrism, or the EU's overwhelmingly internal focus, is the other main critique levelled at the EU by Australian elites. The EU was perceived to be predominantly absorbed in issues relating to its own members, with a secondary focus on its immediate neighbourhood and its relationship with the US. It has been argued for some time that Australia has not featured on the EU radar, and this perception is also felt by the elites.[41] Even businesses have not been immune from the perception of the EU as both predatory and self-engrossed, as seen in survey replies and Downer's comment that 'Australia is deeply troubled by the EU's narrow and minimalist approach to global agricultural trade. The EU's failure to move forward on reform of the Common Agricultural Policy is a lose-lose policy for Europeans and non-Europeans alike.'[42]

Since the EU enlargement in 2004, this view of an inward-looking Union has strengthened, and this is considered to affect negatively the EU's ability to engage in foreign policy beyond its boundaries. For example one business respondent commented that '[the EU's] influence isn't going beyond its borders at the moment. Once it becomes more outward looking, then we'll see a significant change',[43] while another saw the EU 'certainly as an economic entity and as an economic power … And the political power – it's too busy and focused on the internal tensions for that.'[44]

Finally, a comment on the EU's general presence and accessibility to Australia is the question of distance. The issue of geographical distance was frequently raised in the elite interviews, the respondents' perception being that distance and remoteness render the EU inaccessible and hard to understand, as, from afar, it appears to be distinctive, unfamiliar and too complex.[45] This perception is important and anecdotal evidence suggests that it is widespread.

Bureaucratic, elitist and undemocratic

Another frequent assessment made of the EU by Australian elites (and this is a clear perception that was repeated across the interviews) is that the EU is very bureaucratic, elitist and even undemocratic. For example, when elites were asked what images the EU brings to mind, responses included 'bureaucracy out of control' and 'relentless and fairly mindless bureaucracy' – a perception that was strongly evident in comments made by former Prime Minister (1996–2007) John Howard over many years. Linked to this image of an overarching administrative apparatus is that of the EU as an elite construction, with the French influence in particular being perceived as overwhelmingly negative, 'The whole concept of the EU sort of still has a sort of overlay of stuffy old world superiority and cultural arrogance ... the EU is still associated with the French more than any other country.'[46] This sentiment was also voiced by a member of the political elite grouping:

> The one thing which I think stands out ... which is where I have my sort of primary criticism of the EU and the people who run it effectively at the moment, is the sort of dominant French influence in the institutional behavior in the EU which is highly elitist, technocratic and non-inclusive and ultimately subtly undemocratic.[47]

The idea that the French have had a greater hand in shaping the EU was expanded on by some respondents, who suggested that the EU's system of governance is undemocratic, with some Member States having considerably more power than others and dominating European integration. One such comment indicating this was that, 'There seems to be too few in Europe speaking for a much greater number in Europe under the guise of the EU, and countries within the Union who don't have a lot of influence often get taken for a ride.'[48]

The view of ruthless officials in the EU bureaucracy is linked with a certain anti-French bias, which also regards some countries as more powerful than others. This does not, however, amount to a comprehensive perception of the EU as a whole. It does contribute to a sense of unease about how the EU is structured and how it makes decisions. Results of elite surveys indicate that the EU's policy-making environment is overwhelmingly regarded as opaque, complex, hard to understand and even alienating. Not only does it appear to constitute a Byzantine network which is not readily accessible, but it is also regarded as a set of institutions governed by distant hardnosed mandarins who are not democratically accountable. This has led to media views of the EU as a ruthless bureaucracy:

> If Europe becomes integrated it becomes centralized, and in that case the central bureaucracy takes ever more power. This is bad for Australia in several ways. First, it is inherently undemocratic and may eventually compromise some of the democratic gains that joining the EU has brought in the past. However, it is especially undemocratic for nations outside the EU because it

aggregates power to a ruthless bureaucracy that will want to impose its power on other international institutions.[49]

Sheridan's comment expresses a certain media view that Brussels is in love with regulation and that this notion must be resisted by Australia, as Brussels 'badly wants to impose common regulations' with negative repercussions for Australia.[50] The Howard government expressed the view that the EU was an excessively complex body, with negative implications for Australia's interests:

> EU decision-making is complex and difficult for others to influence. And the combination of enlargement and deeper integration has created a 'crowding out' effect, whereby third countries like Australia find it increasingly difficult to win the attention of EU decision-makers. Decisions reached after intensive processes of consultation among Member States are difficult to reverse.[51]

The perception of the EU as overly bureaucratic and technocratic was repeated to a worrying degree in the APP project interviews, but is not, of course, confined only to these interviews. An article by Australian journalist Janet Albrechtsen regarded the 'grand utopian experiment' of the EU as a stealthy attempt to 'dump the nation-state'.[52] Albrechtsen described the European Commission as a 'mammoth centralised bureaucracy'.[53] It is noteworthy that in Australia there is a temptation for politicians and the media to rely on state-to-state contacts that have the merit of being familiar and comprehensible.

This view of the EU's internal machinery as complex, incomprehensible and impenetrable is not simply an Australian experience: within the EU itself there is a 'Yes Prime Minister' style of anti-Europe rhetoric in the UK and British scepticism in tabloid journalism, and there are French, Dutch and Danish fears of loss of sovereignty. Internationally as well, Australia and its elites are not alone in attempting to come to grips with the EU as a relatively new political entity. Moravcsik and Nicolaidis have noted that Americans have similar problems in understanding the EU:

> Europe is widely viewed in the United States as impotent, obstructionist, and – simultaneously – utopian and cynical. Americans instinctively understand military alliances and simple free trade agreements, such as NATO [the North Atlantic Treaty Organization] and NAFTA [the North American Free Trade Agreement]. They have no experience with Europe's complex governance system.[54]

Aside from the complexity of the Union, there are several other reasons why Australia and other countries have difficulties in dealing with the emerging European entity. For one thing, the EU has, on occasion, appeared to be advancing its own agendas, undermining national identity and sovereignty and determining international trade patterns. In doing so, it has challenged accepted notions of the nation-state, diplomacy and international negotiations and presented a challenge to notions of bordered polity within the EU, in Australia and internationally. The contested nature of the EU and its agenda are reflected in opposition to the idea of it as an emerging 'civilian power Europe'.[55]

This challenge, or sense of threat, felt by Australian (and other international) elites has perhaps led to a certain reticence to engage with the EU, and consequently to a relative lack of understanding of the EU as an influential interlocutor and of its embedded governance structure. Although the recent cohort of interviewees has demonstrated that there is more understanding of the EU as an influential body than hitherto, there are nonetheless very few among the sample of Australian elites who might agree with more objective scholarly appraisals of the EU as an entity with distinct structures of governance at a supranational level, with policy networks and political, legal and social institutions which participate in political problem-solving.[56] While the EU is commonly characterized by scholars as an example of cross-border cooperation resulting from historical experience and geographical linkages, cooperation that is systematic to the extent that a European dimension has become an embedded feature which frames politics and policy within the European states,[57] this is a feature of the Union that is not fully recognized amongst Australian elites. This has meant that the traditional bilateral relationship with the Member States and especially the UK has remained a cornerstone of Australian policy towards the EU.

Collective amnesia or the Rip Van Winkle effect?

Some two decades ago, it was claimed that a 'debilitating disease', a collective amnesia,[58] was evident in Australia concerning Europe. This disease in otherwise well-informed circles was, it was argued, creating lethargy where there was opportunity, leading to a squandering of goodwill.[59] Since Groom's provocative article was published, has the EU–Australia relationship continued to suffer from this amnesia?

Australia–EU relations have certainly been marked by controversy and marred by tensions regarding agriculture; however they have also been underpinned by some agreements that have facilitated cooperation. This combination of both controversy and interaction would indicate that Europe has *not* in fact been forgotten by Australia, that it is not a debilitating case of amnesia that has affected the relationship, but rather something quite different. Rather than *forgetting* about Europe, it appears that Australia has suffered from a *lack of knowledge* about Europe: it is ignorance and not amnesia that has prevented EU–Australia relations from reaching their full potential. As the EU grew and evolved, Australia failed to take notice, and the fact that the EU has not been very interested in Australia made this lack of attention easier to justify. In effect, Australia had something of a Rip Van Winkle experience – while it was 'sleeping' the EU wrought massive transformations and become a more distinctive type of influential international actor, and when Australia 'woke up' it was as if there were a *tabula rasa* (or lack of knowledge) in many elite perceptions of the EU.

For example, among Australian elites there is little understanding of the EU's considerable soft power in global politics. Instead, what the elites seem to understand best are the more conventional markers of power, specifically in this case, the EU's economic power and the significance of the Single Market. Even so, it could be argued that these Australian elites do not yet recognize fully the importance of the EU as a trading bloc.

This suggests a lack of understanding of the EU integration process, its external relations agenda and the importance of extensive formalized linkages with the institutions of the EU. Australia has only recently taken stock of the fact that an incomplete knowledge of the EU can have serious negative outcomes for Australia,[60] and this has resulted in a marked shift among some officials and ministers in recent times. While the message from these elite surveys is that negative perceptions of the EU have not altered, in actual government public policy practice and dialogue there has been considerable change and dynamism in the form of increased dialogue and agreement between the EU and the Australian government.

Advancing Australian interests

Australia has much to gain from a constructive partnership with the EU, but there are also significant difficulties to be faced in the relationship, such as its asymmetry and the problem of distance. Engagement is broad and deep: multidimensional, multi-policy, multi-actor and multi-sector. It increasingly encompasses issues of governance, EU norms and attributes, and not simply politics, diplomacy and economics. Australia has developed negotiating skills and strategies with the EU as an international actor.

Yet there is a reticence on the part of some elites in dealing with the EU, and while this may be understandable in the short term due to the problems of the CAP and perceptions of a special relationship with the UK, it is not beneficial for Australia in the long term. Recent developments such as the rapid expansion of the EU policy sphere and policy remit, and its recent territorial enlargements have global consequences as the EU appears to act as a type of superpower. These developments then, are of crucial contemporary relevance to Australia, and yet they do not feature throughout the elite interviews in any comprehensive or systematic manner.

The Australian government has recognized that the enlarged EU's strategic weight is likely to increase steadily and that 'a more unified Europe is already having a noticeable impact on the processes and agenda of international diplomacy'.[61] The EU's relatively complex nature is a major challenge, and the importance for Australia to keep abreast of developments in the EU's external capacity is self-evident. The study of these elite perceptions may well contribute to strategic choices for both EU and Australian policy-makers, when taking into account policies relating to future foreign policy, trade and diplomatic strategies. Having only a partial understanding of EU policies, institutions, market structures and regulatory mechanisms can be detrimental to Australia's interests. The point that it is in Australia's long-term interest to ensure that Australia maintains and improves knowledge of the EU has been keenly understood by the Australian government recently, and the DFAT has engaged the Contemporary Europe Research Centre at the University of Melbourne to run a series of training courses for officials who deal with the EU in a number of government departments, entitled 'Utilising the EU Institutions in Pursuit of Australian Interests'.

Australian engagement with the EU is multidimensional. However, there is little recognition of this in the interviews to date, with Australian elite perceptions of the EU as a multidimensional entity being largely restricted to its economic persona (although the experience of travel and working in the EU has contributed to some respondents having a more nuanced understanding of the EU's political agenda). Essentially, the 2001–2 and the 2005 elite interview responses indicate that the broader EU–Australia relationship is not well understood. While there is significant elite understanding of *aspects* of the EU, elite perceptions currently do not reflect the many important initiatives by the government and its policy community.

There is scope for the EU–Australia relationship to expand and to build on perceptions of common values and convergence of interests such as trade, security, immigration, refugees and peacekeeping. The relationship is building on perceptions of mutual benefit; on recognition of the limits of the relationship and of differences regarding the role of regional integration and global agendas. Australian elites thus far have limited understanding of this. There is scope for the EU to seek recognition from its interlocutors in a proactive manner, and there is scope too for the EU to recognize the concerns of its interlocutors in a more overt manner, such as those of Australia. More understanding of the EU and less propaganda-style brochures may help to bring about a greater understanding of the value of the EU and of the Australia–EU relationship. What then is the message for the EU and Australia? To not only negotiate in the many forums where they currently engage, but to be seen to do so and for this to be seen as productive dialogue, even when marred by tensions and conflicts.

Official Australian government attitudes reveal increased engagement with the EU as a single entity.[62] Overall, however, Australian elite and media perceptions of the Union continue largely to reflect traditional notions of state-to-state relationships, especially the enduring link with the UK, rather than viewing the EU as an important partner in its own right. It is interesting that, in the most recent analysis, the APP project interviews revealed a consistent view that the EU's importance to Australia is declining. Regardless of this view though, there are shared values between the two partners, as was reiterated by form Foreign Minister Downer: 'As friends and partners, Europe and Australia have the chance to make a real difference to each other's future, to ensure that our common values and commitment are fostered – to ensure a better future for our children.'[63]

However, while there is common ground, Australia and the EU were until early 2008 also worlds apart on some key policy stances, such as the Kyoto Protocol, which was signed by the Rudd government in early 2008.[64] While shared values are alluded to on occasion, they do not constitute a major part of the interview responses. Finally, the relationship between Australia and the EU has been dominated by a single-issue focus on the CAP and the single-prism focus on the United Kingdom, both evident in the responses under analysis.

Among elite respondents in the three surveys, there was certainly some ignorance about the EU. Nevertheless, there was also sophisticated knowledge of the EU, especially regarding the euro, individual EU–Australia agreements (especially the Wine Agreement) and economic aspects in general. There were also trenchant critiques of the EU. There were measures of both approval and disapproval of the Howard government's close relationship with the UK. More than in the 2001–2 surveys, there was sharp condemnation of the CAP in 2005, notwithstanding the 2003 CAP reforms.

In all three surveys, there was considerable criticism of the EU, as seen in condemnation of CAP protectionism and problems of market access. There continued over all three surveys, and particularly in the 2005 APP project interviews, a perception of the EU as being internally focused and divided.

Conclusions

While Australian governments increasingly engage with the EU as an international actor in trade, foreign policy, security and soft power issues, as part of a deep and broad relationship, there has been little public prime ministerial acknowledgement of this reality. The recognition that a solely realist view of the EU is not beneficial to Australia's interests has been evident particularly from the late 1990s until 2007. This recognition is not evident in most elite responses, which instead reveal a clear realist streak. Notable exceptions are not necessarily found with the government. Rather, they tend to be in non-government parties. The elites interviewed continue an enduring trend by regarding the EU as less important to Australia than the US or Asia. A recognition of the EU as a trade actor does not automatically bestow upon it the role of most important economic actor for Australia – although the facts bear out that Australia's major trade partner has long been the EU. A realist approach is evident in the view that national interests are most often served through what is termed by this author as traditional bilateralism. In certain cases, government engagement with the EU as a single entity, in new regional bilateralism, is acknowledged but rarely comprehensively understood. The idea of the EU as an interlocutor in what can be termed global societal bilateralism, that is, EU–Australia relations in multilateral forums, for example, is not in step with the current government engagement in development aid, security, immigration dialogue and cooperation in the UN.

It is clear that public policy pronouncements regarding the EU are not based on the perceptions that have emerged from these surveys. It is equally clear that the Howard government was guided by its own principles of national interest which gave more credence to speeches attacking the EU, for a national audience, than to the established, quiet habit of cooperation that developed concurrently over a number of years, in an international context. This is not completely surprising, as all Australian governments play to their domestic constituencies, just as much as European governments do to theirs. Howard's attacks on, and apparent lack of interest in, the EU, was not entirely different from national leaders in Europe taking credit for policies at the EU level that serve the national interest and blaming Brussels for those that do not augur well for that nation's welfare. The Rudd government view is still to be clearly enunicated What is perhaps distinctive about the Australian elite case is the lack of understanding of the EU across so many policy areas and levels. This can be attributed to two main factors: the influence of the British connection and the fact that the most difficult negotiations take place on the precise area of conflict of interests that lead to extremes of language and problems in achieving compromise, such as the CAP. The confluence of national interest and a past dependence on a relationship with the British great and powerful friend can be seen in the context of the more recent friend, the US, in terms of security and a free trade agreement for the Howard government up until the end of 2007..

It has been suggested that Australia regards the US as big brother,[65] yet it appears to regard the EU as a distant and recalcitrant cousin. That perception of the EU is based on national interests. Yet, equally importantly, quiet negotiations with EU behind the public glare continue apace – and the elites are not catching up with these. There is little evidence that those interviewed guide Australian policy towards the EU. There is evidence that these elites are somewhat out of step with government practice – because they are simply not aware of it and, further, are not made aware of it in any public manner nor in any briefings, as there are none currently initiated by government. Interestingly, there is little evidence that the EU is making substantial inroads in the mindsets of the elites interviewed and there is a remarkable lack of awareness of the EU delegation and scant regard for its role.

So neither the EU nor the Australian government provides a window into current developments, at least according to the elites surveyed. The interviews have served a useful role in shedding light on the way the EU is understood by those associated with interaction with the EU and influencing those in the business of serving or framing national interests.

While official Australian engagement with the EU is multidimensional, elite recognition of the EU is largely restricted to its economic persona. There is scope for the relationship to expand and to build on perceptions of common values and convergence of interests such as trade, security, immigration, refugees and peacekeeping. There is scope for the EU to seek recognition from its interlocutors in a proactive manner. There is scope too for the EU to recognize the concerns of its partners, such as Australia, in a more overt manner. What then is the message for the EU and Australia? One is that they should continue to negotiate in the many forums where they currently engage, but also to be seen to do so – and this needs to be regarded as productive dialogue, even when marred by tensions and conflicts. There is value in continuing dialogue and agreements. Yet, outside of government circles, the EU remains largely invisible on the radar screens of Australian elites, as suggested by these surveys.

Acknowledgement

My thanks to Belinda Cleeland for research assistance.

Notes

1   A. Downer, 'Australia and Europe: Sharing Global Responsibilities', The Schuman Lecture, Canberra, 11 May 2006.
2   Nine parliamentarians, ten business people and eight journalists constituted the Australian elite cohort that was interviewed in Canberra, Sydney and Melbourne in the latter half of 2005 during the APP project. In the project, 'policy-makers' were identified as current members of national parliaments representing different parties. 'Media elites' were identified as editors/news directors and lead reporters of the media outlets that were established as the national leaders in the EU coverage. 'Business elites' were identified as members of national business round tables, and other official business networks, and leading exporters to the EU. The study used two types of questionnaires – the first one was developed for business and political elites and the second one for media. The questionnaire to the media elites incorporated questions related to the EU news production as well as questions regarding personal perceptions of the EU. Each interview lasted 40 minutes on average.
3   In 2001–2, over 650 surveys were sent out for written response and 133 received, providing a response rate of 21 per cent. The survey method adopted involved written replies to a standard questionnaire. The data were entered into a Statistical Packages for the Social Sciences (SPSS) file and analysed using descriptive statistical techniques. The respondent group could be broken out into eight broad groups: academic; business; trade/investment promotion; government advisor; parliamentary delegation; diplomat; media and other. These were further aggregated into three or four groupings, as appropriate, in order to distinguish differences and variations across responses to different items. All subsequent references and quotes from these interviews are listed only with the year from which they were conducted, owing to the need for anonymity. For more information about these interviews see P. Murray, 'An Asia Pacific Response to the European Union: Australian Elite Perceptions', *Asia Europe Journal* 1 (2003), 103–19. The list of recipients for the 2001 survey was drawn up from a smaller survey carried out by the author in 1998–9; companies profiled in the DFAT 2001 publication ExportEU; all contactable Australian members of the European Commission's EU Visitors Program, members of Australian parliamentary delegations to the EU; officials in government departments; government ministers; banks; insurance companies; all major exporters; alcohol exporters; mining companies; meat and cattle exporters; members of the Global Foundation; law firms dealing with Europe; members of Australian Business in Europe; Austrade, DFAT; Department of Education, Science and Technology; Australian Bureau of Agricultural Resource Economics; Chambers of Commerce; consultancy firms; the media; academics involved in research on Australian trade, investment, economics, politics and law and European studies and some members of the Contemporary European Studies Associations of Australia.
4   A. Benvenuti, 'Australia's Battle against the Common Agricultural Policy', *Australian Journal of Politics and History* 45 (1999), 181–96; A. Benvenuti, 'Australian Responses to the Common Agricultural Policy, 1973–1993', *Australasian Journal of European Integration* 1 (1998–9), 58–78; A. Benvenuti, 'The Howard Government's Diplomacy toward the European Union on Agriculture: An Early Assessment', *Political Expressions* 2 (1998), 103–19; A. Burnett, *Australia and the European Communities in the 1980s*, Canberra, Australian National University, 1983; P. Murray, 'Australia and the European Union', in J. Cotton and J. Ravenhill (eds), *Seeking Asian Engagement*, Melbourne, Oxford University Press with Australian Institute

for International Affairs, 1997, pp. 230–47; J. Richardson, 'Australia and Western Europe', in P. Boyce and J. Angel (eds), *Diplomacy in the Market Place: Australia in World Affairs 1981–90*, Melbourne, Longman, 1992, pp. 208–24.

5 See P. Murray, A. Elijah and C. O'Brien, 'Common Ground, Worlds Apart: The Development of Australia's Relationship with the European Union', *Australian Journal of International Affairs* 56 (2002), 395–416; P. Murray, 'Australian Views on Europe and the EU–Australia Relationship: An Assessment', paper to European Union–Australia Relations Workshop, Contemporary Europe Research Centre/National Europe Centre, University of Melbourne, 2002; P. Murray, 'Australian Perspectives on the European Union', *European Information,* 8 (1999), 2–5; A. Groom, 'Europe: A Case of Collective Amnesia', *Australian Outlook* 42 (1989), 1–15; E. Papadakis, 'Australia and Europe', in J. Cotton and J. Ravenhill (eds), *The National Interest in a Global Era: Australia in World Affairs 1996–2000*, Melbourne, Oxford University Press with Australian Institute for International Affairs, 2002.

6 Murray, 'An Asia Pacific Response'.

7 It is noteworthy that the earlier surveys carried out had written responses, while the elite surveys as part of the APP had face-to-face interviews with 27 people representing business, media and political elites.

8 P. Murray, *Australia and the European Superpower: Engaging with the European Union*, Melbourne, Melbourne University Press, 2005.

9 Department of Foreign Affairs and Trade, *Advancing the National Interest: Australia's Foreign and Trade Policy White Paper*, Canberra, Department of Foreign Affairs and Trade, 2003. Available <http://www.dfat.gov.au/ani/index.html> (Accessed 25 August 2005).

10 See also P. Murray, 'Australian Voices: Some Elite Reflections on the European Union', *CESAA Review* 29 (2002), 5–18, available <http://www.cesaa.org.au/publications.htm>; P. Murray, 'Australian Views on Europe and the EU-Australia Relationship: an Assessment', paper presented to the European Union-Australia Relations Workshop, Contemporary Europe Research Centre/National Europe Centre, University of Melbourne, July 2002; P. Murray, 'What Australians Think About the EU: Elite Perceptions and the Current Context', paper presented at Conference on the EU in International Affairs, National Europe Centre, Canberra, 3–4 July 2002, available <http://www.anu.edu.au/NEC/MURRAY-updated1July.pdf>; Murray, 'An Asia Pacific Response'.

11 Political elite respondent, interviewed 21 June 2005.

12 Media elite respondent, interviewed 7 June 2005.

13 Business elite respondent, interviewed 15 June 2005.

14 Business elite respondent interviewed 16 June 2005

15 Media elite respondent, interviewed 10 June 2005.

16 2001 Respondent, see n. 3 above.

17 2001 Respondent, see n. 3 above.

18 G. Kitney, 'Britain a Side Street on Road to Brussels', *Australian Financial Review* (21 April 2005), 14.

19 Murray, *Australia and the European Superpower*.

20 A. Downer, cited in *EU News* 20, p. 2.

21 2001–2 respondent, see n. 3 above.

22 2001–2 respondent, see n. 3 above.

23 2001–2 respondent, see n. 3 above.

24 2001–2 respondent, see n. 3 above.

25 P. Keating, 'A Prospect of Europe', Speech at University of New South Wales, Sydney, 9 May 1997.

26 J. Howard, 'Address to the Confederation of British Industry', Landmark Hotel, London, 24 June 1997, available <http://www.pm.gov.au/news/media_releases/1997/cbi.html1997> (Accessed 12 April 2004).

27 Media elite respondent, interviewed June 2005.
28 2001–2 respondent, see n. 3 above.
29 2001–2 respondent, see n. 3 above.
30 2001–2 respondent, see n. 3 above.
31 P. Murray, 'Problems of Summitry and Symmetry in the EU–Australia Relationship', in S. Lawson (ed.), *Europe and the Asia Pacific: Culture, Identity and Representations of Region*, London, Curzon Routledge, 2003, pp. 66–85.
32 Richardson, 'Australia and Western Europe', p. 212
33 A. Groom, *The European Community in Context*, Canberra, ANU, Australian Foreign Policy Publications Programme, 1992.
34 See Murray, *Australia and the European Superpower*.
35 Business elite respondent interviewed June 2005.
36 A. Downer, 'Australia and the EU into the New Millennium', speech in Adelaide, 12 May 2000, available <http://www.dfat.gov.au/media/speeches/foreign/2000/000512_aust_eu_millenium.html>; see also Kitney, 'Britain a Side Street'.
37 Murray, *Australia and the European Superpower*.
38 It is worth noting here, however, that there are a few exceptions, and that perhaps an understanding of the EU's global role is just beginning to emerge: for one thing, the fact that the EU is promoting a global order that is favouable to Australia was a theme of the most recent speech by the Foreign Minister regarding the EU (Downer, 'Australia and Europe'). Also, one politician interviewed did clearly regard the EU as a 'great moral power' and a force for good and for peace in the future.
39 Murray, *Australia and the European Superpower*.
40 Business elite respondent, interviewed 2005.
41 Murray, 'Problems of Summitry and Symmetry'.
42 A. Downer, 'EU Enlargement: Meeting the Challenges of the Global Security and Trade Environment', speech at the National Europe Centre Conference on EU Enlargement, Canberra, 16 April 2003, available <http://www.foreignminister.gov.au/speeches/2003/030416_eu.html>.
43 Business elite respondent, interviewed June 2005.
44 Business elite respondent, interviewed 2005.
45 Murray, 'An Asia Pacific Response'.
46 Business elite respondent, interviewed 2005.
47 Business elite respondent, interviewed 23 June 2005.
48 Political elite respondent, interviewed 21 June 2005.
49 G. Sheridan, 'Bigger the Better – Europe – A Worldwide Special Report – Australia and the EU', *The Australian* (3 May 2004), T08.
50 *Ibid.*
51 Department of Foreign Affairs and Trade, *Advancing the National Interest: Australia's Foreign and Trade Policy White Paper*, Canberra, DFAT, 2003. Available <http://www.dfat.gov.au/ani/index.html> (Accessed 11 April 2005).
52 J. Albrechtsen, 'Risks in the EU's Pursuit of Happiness', *The Australian* (11 May 2005).
53 *Ibid.*
54 A. Moravcsik and K. Nicolaidis, 'How to Fix Europe's Image Problem', *Foreign Policy* (2005), available <http://www.foreignpolicy.com/story/files/story2837.php>.
55 F. Duchêne, 'Europe's Role in World Peace', in R. Mayne (ed.), *Europe Tomorrow: Sixteen Europeans Look Ahead*, London, Fontana, 1972; H. Bull, 'Civilian Power Europe: A Contradiction in Terms?', *Journal of Common Market Studies* 21 (1983), 149–70; M. Leonard, *Why Europe will Run the 21st Century*, London and New York, Fourth Estate, 2005.

56 M. Green Cowles and T. Risse, 'Transforming Europe: Conclusions', in M. Green Cowles, J. Caporaso and T. Risse (eds), *Transforming Europe*, Ithaca, NY, and London: Cornell University Press, 2001, p. 217.
57 H. Wallace, 'Europeanisation and Globalisation: Complementary or Contradictory Trends?', *New Political Economy* 5 (2000), 370.
58 Groom, 'Europe'; See also A. Ward, '"Collective Amnesia" of Europe v. Engagement with Asia: Forging a Middle Path for Australia in the Age of Regionalism', in C. Saunders and G. Triggs (eds), *Trade and Cooperation with the European Union in the New Millennium*, Amsterdam, Kluwer, 2002.
59 *Ibid.*
60 Murray *et al.*, 'Common Ground, Worlds Apart'; Groom, 'Europe'; Ward, 'Collective Amnesia'.
61 Department of Foreign Affairs and Trade, European Union Brief, 3 Feb. 2005, available <http://www.dfat.gov.au/geo/european_union/eu_brief.html>.
62 See e.g. A. Downer, 'Advancing the National Interest: Australia's Foreign Policy Challenge', speech at the National Press Club, Canberra, Australia, 7 May 2002; Downer, 'Australia and Europe'.
63 Downer, 'Australia and Europe'.
64 Murray *et al.*, 'Common Ground, Worlds Apart'; Murray, *Australia and the European Superpower*.
65 M. Fraser, 'Just a Vassal of the US', *The Age* (26 July 2006).

7   The Asia-Pacific power elite and the soft superpower

Elite perceptions of the EU in the Asia-Pacific

Jessica Bain, Katrina Stats, Sung-Hoon Park and Heungchong Kim

The power elite is composed of [people] whose positions enable them to transcend the ordinary environments of ordinary men and women; they are in positions to make decisions having major consequences ... they are in command of the major hierarchies and organizations of modern society. They rule the big corporations. They run the machinery of the state and claim its prerogatives. They direct the military establishment. They occupy the strategic command posts of the social structure, in which are now centered the effective means of the power and the wealth and the celebrity which they enjoy.[1]

Introduction

So far this book has examined mass media representations and public perceptions of the EU in the Asia-Pacific and has sought to explain the relationship between the two. This chapter now turns to another important variable in this relationship – the impressions and influence of the national elite in each of the four Asia-Pacific countries. According to William Zimmerman, '[e]lites, attentive publics, [and] mass publics ... are the conventional actors in the drama of foreign policy making in open political systems everywhere'.[2] However, since 'power and competence are asymmetrically distributed in all political systems',[3] elites assume a leading role in this drama. The influence of elites is considered greater in the case of foreign as opposed to domestic affairs since the mass public typically lacks extensive knowledge about and interest in matters of foreign policy and is thus 'viewed as teachable in foreign policy matters'.[4]

It is something of an etymological irony that the term 'elite' comes from the Latin word *eligere*, meaning 'to elect'. The 'power elite' (to employ the term famously coined by Charles Wright Mills in his book of that name) of any given society certainly possess the resources to shape that society, however, with the exception of incumbent political elites, their ability to do so comes not from democratic mandate but rather from the commercial and/or cultural power they possess. Observing the American example, Chittick and Billingsley argue that elite power operates to 'both structure public debate on foreign policy and influence the decisions of top foreign policy officials'.[5] That is to say, elites influence foreign policy in two main ways: by generating public support for elite concerns, or by bypassing the public altogether.[6]

The former occurs since public support for executive action on foreign policy issues, as Oldendick and Bardes note, 'is difficult to gain because the mass public is generally regarded as less informed and unconcerned about foreign policy problems than about domestic issues'.[7] In this context, elites – typically more highly educated and informed about political affairs than the general public, and generally possessing a stronger investment in foreign policy outcomes than the so-called 'attentive public' – play a crucial role in the democratic process by amassing public support for foreign policy initiatives.[8] Here, those in control of the production and dissemination of images of political and economic counterparts, namely, the media elite, play a significant role in shaping the public agenda, a role that Edward Herman and Noam Chomsky famously critiqued in their book (and documentary of the same name), *Manufacturing Consent*. Essentially, Herman and Chomsky argue that all (US) 'news' is propagandistic. They maintain that the US media act,

> to inculcate and defend the economic, social, and political agenda of privileged groups that dominate the domestic society and the state ... through selection of topics, distribution of concerns, framing of issues, filtering of information, emphasis and tone, and by keeping debate within the bounds of acceptable premises.[9]

In contrast to Herman and Chomsky's view that the media are a propagandistic tool controlled by elites to serve their ends, another school of literature argues that the media create the 'reality' in which elite decision-making takes place. That is to say, rather than simply a 'channel for delivering messages ... the media are a crucial part of the foreign policy decision-making environment'.[10] This alternative conception of the relationship between foreign policy and the media is often referred to as the 'CNN effect'.[11] Livingstone identifies three ways in which the CNN effect might operate; first, by setting the policy agenda; secondly, by acting as an impediment to achieving policy goals; and finally, as an accelerant to policy decision-making.[12] But in any case, the widely debated techniques of 'manufacturing' consent are not the only means of influencing the political agenda since, as noted, the exercise of elite power does not always depend upon gathering public support. As Wright Mills observed, because the power elite occupy privileged positions, 'the strategic command posts of the social structure',[13] they have greater access to, and influence over, the democratically elected elite and political processes and are consequently able to bypass the ordinary chains of democratic influence.

The disproportionate amount of influence national elites are thus able to wield over the direction of foreign policy is particularly disturbing in light of the frequently observed instances where substantial disjuncture exists between elite and public opinion.[14] It is for this reason that studies looking at elite opinion and influence over the conduct of foreign (and indeed, domestic) policy have attracted a significant amount of attention since the latter half of the last century, notably in the aftermath of the Vietnam War, a war which many considered to be funded by elite support and fought in defiance of powerful public objections.[15] Continuing this tradition, the APP project sought to reveal and examine the perceptions of the EU held not only by the public, but also by those 'in positions to make decisions having major consequences'[16] in the Asia-Pacific. This was considered vital in terms of understanding the relationships between the four Asia-Pacific countries and the EU since, as Michael Brecher notes, decision-makers, like the rest of us, 'act in accordance with their perception of reality, not in response to reality itself'.[17] Motivated by the conviction that 'elite images are no less "real" than the reality of their environment and are much more relevant to an analysis of the foreign policy flow',[18] this survey was designed to assess elite *perceptions* of the EU's importance as a national partner and as an international actor in each of the four participating countries. The final stage of the APP project, the elite survey, was conducted in order to contrast and complement the data collected on public perceptions and media representations of the EU which was reported in Chapters 1–5. In order to complete the picture of Asia-Pacific perceptions of the EU, this chapter addresses the following primary research question: 'What type of actor do the Asia-Pacific elite consider the EU to be, and how effective is it perceived to be in this role?'

Methodology

The data for this chapter come from a series of in-depth, face-to-face interviews with Australian, New Zealand and Thai elites, conducted between June and September 2005 under the auspices of the APP project, and from a set of email interviews with elites undertaken in South Korea between 30 May and 2 June 2006.[19]

The term 'elite' can be applied in many different contexts to describe a particular subset within a given cohort, for example, the intellectual elite, cultural elite, sporting elite, etc. For the purposes of this study, three elite cohorts were selected for investigation; to paraphrase Wright Mills, those who rule the big corporations, those who run the machinery of the state and those who control images and help shape the public agenda. Seen as possessing an actual or potential investment in the EU, the first cohort of elites was composed of business elites and included members of national business round tables, other official business networks and leading exporters. True to the etymological roots of the term, the second elite cohort comprised political elites who were selected because of their perceived potential to influence the shape and direction of the home country–EU relationship. This included key parliamentarians from all major parties, particularly those occupying positions of leadership or having responsibility for key portfolios such as foreign affairs and trade. Finally, the third cohort, media elites, were included in the study because of their responsibility, as already outlined, for the production and dissemination of public images of the EU and included international, political and business editors, television news broadcast producers and both key locally and Europe-based correspondents from each of the outlets monitored in the media analysis phase of the APP project (see Chapter 1). It is important to note that the results of the Korean survey were not separated into these elite categories and that the sample included an additional elite cohort – academics. For this reason, the Korean results are presented separately.

The face-to-face interviews, averaging approximately 45 minutes in length, were conducted in the political and economic centres of the three countries: in the federal capital of Australia, Canberra, as well as three of its state capitals, Sydney, Melbourne, and Adelaide, where much of the nation's media and finance is concentrated; in the political capital of New Zealand, Wellington, its financial capital, Auckland, and a third important metropolis, Christchurch; and in Thailand's capital, Bangkok. In total, 70 Asia-Pacific business, political and media elite members were interviewed by researchers in Australia, New Zealand and Thailand, with an additional 20 respondents to the Korean email questionnaire.[20]

Participants were informed about the purpose and aims of the survey and asked for their permission to use their names in publications resulting from the research (anonymity was given if a participant preferred) and, in the case of the face-to-face interviews, to audio-record the interviews. These interviews were transcribed verbatim and made available to interviewees if requested. A standard semi-structured questionnaire was used and was made available in advance only upon request. The questionnaire was not tailored for the different national contexts, but rather was designed to translate identically across the three countries (Australia, New Zealand and Thailand) to ensure comparable cross-national data. Although it differed slightly, the Korean email survey was modelled very closely on its APP counterpart, so as to be broadly comparable with the APP results. Questions posed to our elite respondents were similar to those asked of respondents in the public survey but allowed for greater elaboration. Full copies of the questionnaires can be found in Appendix IV. This chapter, however, focuses on the following three questions asked of all three cohorts in all four countries in order to address the primary research question:

1   What are the dominant spontaneous images that Asia-Pacific elites have of the EU and what inferences and implications can be drawn from these images?
2   How important is the EU perceived to be for each of the four Asia-Pacific countries by their national elites, both at present and in the future?
3   Is the EU considered by Asia-Pacific elites to be a leader in international politics?

The remainder of this chapter will address the responses to these questions from each elite cohort in Australia, New Zealand and Thailand, and will then examine the Korean elite responses, before turning to a discussion and comparison of Asia-Pacific elite perceptions of the EU.

Results

Spontaneous images

One of the first questions asked of the participating Asia-Pacific elites during the interviews was designed to prompt their immediate perceptions of the EU. Our researchers asked respondents what the first three thoughts or images were that came to mind when they heard the words, the European Union. The responses provided some interesting images and a number of shared images were identified between elite cohorts and across national borders.

Business elites: Australia, New Zealand and Thailand

Amongst the interviewed business elites, two broad groups of spontaneous images were noted. The first group comprised responses related to the various institutional and operational structures of the EU while the second group of responses were more concerned with symbols and ideas considered to represent the EU. Within the former, trade restrictions and bureaucracy were commonly cited by interviewees across all three countries. Images of the EU's bureaucracy were often discussed, beginning with the image of 'Brussels', which did not generally refer to the city itself but to the EU institutions with which it arguably has become synonymous. For example, one New Zealand businessman simply said 'Brussels'.[21] Another noted that, 'Brussels is the first thing that comes to mind', and rather colourfully described Brussels as being 'a whole naked bureaucracy',[22] while an Australian counterpart described what he saw as an 'over-regulated bureaucratic maze'.[23] Whereas bureaucracy and the EU as an 'old boys club for aging and marginalized national politicians'[24] were frequent images in the minds of Australian and New Zealand business elites, the idea of trade barriers and restrictions was particularly prominent in each of the three countries. High tariff regimes in the EU, particularly for Australian beef exports, for example, were cited as a spontaneous EU image by one Australian respondent, who reported that 'at the forefront of our minds is trying to get those trade barriers down … it's number one'.[25] A New Zealand businessman also involved in the export of meat products to the EU described the Union as being 'a pantomime in regard to the legislative compliance or compliance issues for our industry',[26] while 'trade barriers'[27] and EU trade bargaining power were also referenced amongst Thai business elites. One Thai business elite even felt that EU 'integration [exists] for the purposes of trade bargaining power,'[8] and another felt that, as a consequence of the EU's power and influence in trade negotiations, 'it's hard to get in there [to the EU]'.[29]

Other images of the EU that were common amongst both Australian and Thai business elites included environmental protection and animal welfare. One Australian business elite believed that '[t]he EU sees agriculture as a way of looking after the environment',[30] while a Thai counterpart noted that '[t]hey are … the leader in environmental protection'.[31] Such images seem to suggest a perception of the EU as a normative model, at least in these areas.

In addition to these somewhat 'pragmatic' perceptions of the EU, a number of more symbolic images were also identified. The association of the EU with continental Europe was particularly evident among Australian and New Zealand business people, one of whom noted: 'I guess I still see ... most of Europe as being continental. And ... I don't know why I think that ... [b]ut I very much see it as the makeup of the original Member States of France, Germany so and so forth, as the kind of [centre] or the core if you like.'[32] This 'picture of a map'[33] was sometimes connected with more cultural understandings of the EU, as in the case of one New Zealand respondent who stated that 'I think about culture, history and I guess ... people and food! And lifestyle – I think they've really sorted out how to live over there.'[34] Thai business people also picked up on the lifestyle 'image' when thinking about the EU, as noted by one who thought of 'the living standard of the Europeans. They have a very good standard [of living].'[35]

Finally, and perhaps predictably for this particular elite cohort, the symbol and image of the euro, both the euro zone and the actual currency itself, were often cited by respondents in all three countries.

Political elites: Australia, New Zealand and Thailand

While the business elites in the Asia-Pacific countries shared a number of perceptions, interestingly, perhaps, the responses of the three countries' political elites were all quite different, with few collective images across the region. One image though, that of unity, was identified to some extent in all three countries, although the specific focus given to this notion varied across national borders. In Australia, for example, this 'much greater unity across [Europe]',[36] was seen to meet the 'need for Europe to countermeasure the United States in international affairs'.[37] In contrast to this political association, the unity of the EU was connected more with economics in Thailand; as one respondent described, 'although we thought that European unification was impossible, Europe is now an economic unit'.[38] Finally, in New Zealand, the unity achieved by the EU was viewed predominantly as a highly positive consequence of end of the two world wars. As one New Zealand politician noted, for him, 'the image of European unity is about not losing another generation of young New Zealanders in a European war ... a really good reason for supporting European unity'.[39] Another of his New Zealand counterparts rather fervently emphasized this point. He thought of 'the amazing ability of leaders in the rubble of war in 1946 ... to look literally beyond the horizon ... But from that rubble and the Coal-Steel community [there is] ... an amazing legacy ... The EU is the triumph for history, [a] triumph of courage.'[40]

The importance of the EU bringing peace to Europe was by far the most prominent image of the EU amongst New Zealand political elites, with only a couple of references to the more contentious issues in the EU–New Zealand relationship like the Common Agricultural Policy (CAP). In Australia, however, there was less cohesion in the responses of political elites. Some respondents were quite critical of the EU's current integration process, with one interviewee in particular describing it as being 'probably one of the most remarkable Trojan horses that I've ever seen in my public life where there seems to be too few in Europe speaking for a much greater number ... under the guise of the EU'.[41] However, not all of this respondent's colleagues were so sceptical in their perceptions of the EU, with one in particular seeing it as a 'force for good'[42] in the world.

In contrast to their Pacific neighbours who appeared more inclined to view the EU in terms of its political achievements, many of the Thai political elites noted economic images when thinking about the EU. One connected the EU directly to the image of 'the currency – the euro [and] integration for economic protectionism',[43] while another Thai political respondent associated the EU with EU–Thai trading relations specifically.[44]

Media elites: Australia, New Zealand and Thailand

In the spontaneous images of Asia-Pacific media elites there was a distinct similarity in the two Pacific nations' newsmaker perceptions, and a very different set of images in the Thai case.

In the two Pacific countries, images that came to the minds of newsmakers when thinking about the EU tended to be very dull and ordinary – arguably ones that by usual standards would not be dramatic or sensational enough to make the news headlines themselves![45] The association of the EU with bureaucracy again was particularly common, with one Australian newsmaker describing the EU as a 'relentless and fairly mindless bureaucracy',[46] while another of his counterparts saw it as 'bureaucracy out of control'.[47] This notion of unchecked bureaucracy was also found in the perceptions of New Zealand newsmakers, and was seen in the descriptions many newsmakers had to hand of what were seen as some of the stranger EU regulations. One New Zealand news editor, for example, spoke of having heard 'things like all those stories about people who have not been able to make their moldy cheese because they go against the ... stupid kind of rulings from the European Community [regarding] food hygiene ... You read lots of those, and they tend to make you go, "how incredibly stupid".'[48] Another of his New Zealand colleagues also noted this, saying that, '[w]e've all got this stereotype of Brussels [with] all sort of loony stories [like how] the carrot must be 2.63mm long or whatever'.[49] The perceived stupidity of EU bureaucracy was a trend noted in Australia too, with one respondent referring to it as '[t]he state of the European sausage and all that sort of thing'.[50]

In contrast to the fixation of Pacific newsmakers on the perceived omnipresence of the EU's bureaucracy, the interviewed Thai newsmakers tended to think of more culturally inspired images when considering the European Union. The association of the EU with the former European colonial powers was an often discussed image amongst Thai newsmakers, with one noting that 'the first thing [I think about] is old powers in Europe ... we all have learnt that these countries were colonial power in our region ... We saw a lot of films about European countries as colonial powers. That's what I mean about "old powers" [who are now] trying to find a way back to the greatness.'[51] Associations of the EU with culture and education were connected to this historical notion. One foreign news reporter thought of the EU 'as a region where there are so many things to learn. Personally I'm interested in history, science and technology, lifestyles and local cultures ... I think Europe has a lot of things like this.'[52] Additionally, several Thai media elites regarded the EU as a potential model for the future of international interactions, with one describing it as 'one of the potential pillars in the future multi-polar world',[53] while another saw it 'as a model of integration', although this latter respondent tempered their response by saying, 'I can't say it's a successful model [just yet].'[54]

Korean elites

Because the Korean elites interviewed were not categorized according to the same elite cohort groups as those in Australia, New Zealand and Thailand, it was more useful to examine the unified results of the Korean elite survey.[55] When asked about the three images that reminded them of the EU, most of the interviewed members of Korean elites singled out the EU's economic integration as their most salient image. In particular, the EU was considered by many to be a model of economic integration. Additionally, and connected to this, was the commonly discussed image of the euro currency, which many Korean elites felt was a 'symbol' of the EU. A commonly held 'European identity' developed through such policy initiatives as the Schengen agreement and the common European passport was also a spontaneous image generated in the minds of a number of Korean elites. In addition, and echoing the responses of some Thai media elites, a number of the Korean respondents immediately associated the European Union with images such as 'history and culture', or an advanced civilization. While most Korean spontaneous references to the EU were connected to an idea of EU unity and cohesion, a few respondents did associate the EU with images of its individual Member States.

Importance of the EU to the Asia-Pacific region

While a variety of spontaneous images of the EU were identified in the above section, there were few responses which indicated a particular connection between the home country of the respondents and the EU. To further investigate these connections and links, this study wanted to establish how important Asia-Pacific elites considered the EU to be for their countries.

Business elites: Australia, New Zealand and Thailand

A variety of questions were posed to the interviewees to assess their perceptions of the EU's importance for their country, both now and in the future. Respondents in Australia, New Zealand and Thailand were asked to rate the importance of the EU to their country at present and in the future, according to a scale from 1 to 5, where 1 was not important at all, and 5 was very important. In both questions, the New Zealand business elites rated the EU most highly, according it an average rating of 4 out of 5 in both instances.[56] Australian and Thai business people, by comparison, felt the EU was of little more than average importance to the domestic interest now; both groups of national business elites rating the EU on average as 2.8 out of 5 in the present. Australian elites did anticipate this importance increasing slightly however, rating the EU's likely future importance to their country as 3 out of 5, while their Thai counterparts felt that the EU's importance was likely to decrease by this same margin, ranking the future importance of the EU to Thailand at 2.6 out of 5.

Respondents were also asked to compare the importance of the EU to other international counterparts, and a range of verbal perceptions were gathered. While in their numeric ranking of the EU's importance there were greater parallels between the Australian and Thai respondents, in the comparison of the EU to other regions, stronger similarities were identified between the New Zealand and Australian perceptions. The importance that then current administrations in the two Australasian countries placed on the relationship with the EU was seen to be a key factor shaping that relationship in both Pacific countries. Many Australian respondents, for example, felt that the EU was undervalued in Australia, and this, as well as a perceived lack of potential to grow in importance, was connected to the focus of the Howard government at that time.[57] Several interviewees identified a problematic deficit between the reality of the EU's importance to Australia (in their perception) and the government's assessment of its importance and suggested that the future importance of the EU–Australia relationship thus depends very much on the direction of the government and the resolution of certain 'difficult' trading issues: '[i]t depends how the government steers the ship in terms of trade policy and particularly bilateral trade agreements'.[58] According to this interviewee, the Australian government's focus was on Asia and the US to the detriment of its relationship with Europe. Other Australian interviewees also lamented this current trend: '[i]t's frightening to face that fact, … that assessment, I know. For me it's disappointing but that's how it is.'[59]

Like their Australian counterparts, New Zealand business interviewees also felt that the position of the current government shaped the importance of the EU for their national interest, as did the historical connections between New Zealand and the countries of the EU. One respondent in particular felt that the importance of the EU to New Zealand in the future was directly related to the type of government in New Zealand's capital; ranking the likely importance of the EU in the future, this respondent felt that it would be '2 if centre right government [comes to power], and 4 if there's a centre-left government in Wellington'.[60] However, it was also noted by many New Zealand respondents that, while the EU and Europe had been of the utmost importance to New Zealand in the past, this was not necessarily the case now. One respondent felt that 'Europe used to be where NZ sought … [and] that mindset has changed enormously',[61] while another felt that 'New Zealand's roots are with Europe', and that, he argued, was 'the important bit about Europe'.[62]

Both New Zealand and Australian business respondents also felt that the EU, regardless of the possible advantages to the relationship, was often a difficult or 'challenging'[63] partner to interact with. This largely stemmed, in both countries, from the perceived difficulties of overcoming what were seen as restrictive trade regulations on the part of the EU. As one respondent noted, '[t]here are issues with EU that aren't experienced in [our] relations with other countries – in terms of access, for example – restrictions on access to markets in EU aren't found in the US, for example'.[64] An Australian interviewee supported this notion, claiming that, because of these restrictions on access in the EU, Australian business had focused a lot more attention on alternative markets recently.[65] This perception was considered one that could easily be changed, however, with the same Australian respondent believing that 'it could become more important if they allowed more product in'.[66] Thai business people concurred with their Australian and New Zealand counterparts in this regard, and one even felt that the EU was able to impose harsh new restrictions at will, which Thailand had no choice but to adhere to, if they wished to continue their trade with Europe.[67]

Because of the restrictions on the European market, both Australian and New Zealand business people had tended to focus on other regions, and in particular the Asian markets were noted. One Australian interviewee felt that the future importance of Europe 'depends on what happens in Asia', with China particularly possessing the potential to 'replace Europe and the European Union as a significant power base'.[68] While New Zealand and Australian business people were in agreement about the role of Asian markets in displacing some of the EU's importance for their countries, Australian and Thai business respondents tended to both compare the EU to the US; a comparison that often resulted in a poor outcome for the EU. In the opinion of one Australian respondent, 'I think more recently the United States and Asia have become more significant to Australia in a lot of senses, in trade terms [and] in political terms',[69] while one Thai business person claimed: 'I think there are still too many internal disputes within the EU. It hasn't achieved internal unity yet',[70] although it was felt that the EU could yet become a 'match' for the US in terms of global politics and trade.[71]

Despite these often negative perceptions and comparisons of the EU's importance for their domestic interest, business people in all three countries tended to feel that, in the future, the EU's importance would at least remain at the status quo, with some respondents feeling that it may increase slightly, although one Thai interviewee warned, the EU was unlikely ever to be considered 'something flashy'[72] and exciting to deal with.

Political elites: Australia, New Zealand and Thailand

In the political elites' perceptions of the EU's importance, there were greater differences between the countries than there were similarities. In the numerical rankings, both Australian and Thai political elites ranked the EU's importance for their countries as a little over 3 (an average of 3.2 in the case of Australian political elites, and 3.3 in the Thai case), with marginal increases perceived in both cases for the future. In the case of the New Zealand political elites, however, the perceived picture of EU importance was significantly rosier. New Zealand political leaders ranked the EU on average as 4.25 out of 5 in the present, with a slight increase to 4.42 in the future.[73] In their verbal responses, there was a higher correspondence between the Australian and Thai interviewees again, although, in general, the Australian verbal responses indicated a slightly more positive tone than did the Thai ones. Australian politicians tended to view the EU as being of relative importance to their country, however it was certainly not the most, nor even often the second most important partner. One Australian felt that

> we don't undervalue [the EU] in any sense of the word, but it doesn't trump the crucial importance of our relationship with our neighbours in our region. It doesn't trump our crucial relationship with the United States. It doesn't trump our role as major economy in this particular Pacific area and the responsibility, especially [the] responsibility we have [with] the Pacific island countries.[74]

Another claimed that 'at this stage economically [the EU] is probably not as important as say Japan, China and even the US',[75] while yet another Australian political elite felt that 'China, Japan, Korea, Indonesia, and increasingly India' were all of greater importance to Australia than was the EU currently. However, while for most Australian politicians the EU was not yet the most important partner for Australia, as one warned, 'Europe should not be forgotten.'[76]

Thai political elites felt broadly similarly to their Australian counterparts, in that while the EU was seldom considered the most important partner for their country, it was still generally regarded as somewhat important. One member of the Thai political elite felt that, as a partner for Thailand, the EU was 'number three. They come after the US. Number one is Japan, then the US, the EU, South Korea, Taiwan and China.' Thai political elites tended to emphasize what they saw as a lack of unity within the EU as the primary reason for it not being of greater importance for Thailand and for other countries. One Thai interviewee felt that 'at the moment, the EU Member States are splitting up. If they can achieve closer integration, their importance will definitely increase. If they become further disunited, the EU will become a weak organization. Now they are fighting one another badly.'[77] However, one member of the Thai elite in particular was less than enthusiastic about the EU's significance for his country:

> Europe is irrelevant to us. If we can strategically align ourselves with the US, China, Japan and South Korea, we can survive without Europe. There's nothing from Europe that is vital to us, nothing at all. Let's say if tomorrow we cut ties with Europe, everything in Thailand will still be able to go on.[78]

In contrast to the negatively tinged Australian and Thai responses, the New Zealand political elites seemingly had only good things to say about the EU and its importance both globally and regionally. Europe was regarded by New Zealand politicians as being of particular historical significance: 'it provides a focal point for what's been [a] very important historical relationship, not just with the UK, but also with the other countries of Europe'.[79] This had increased since the entrance of the UK to the EU in 1973, an event which was emphasized by one

New Zealand political respondent: 'I can think of nothing in recent decades of New Zealand history [that] had such a profound effect on our country as Britain's decision to join the European Common Market; that had [a] huge impact on New Zealand which still reverberates to this day.'[80] As in the case of Australia and Thailand, though, some New Zealand respondents also felt that, while the EU was important, it was only one of several significant international regions, the US and Asia being the most common comparisons.[81] One trend that was notable only amongst New Zealand respondents with regards to the EU's importance for New Zealand was the notion of the EU as a key normative influence in the world. Respondents referred to the EU's standards of living, its influence in international peace and stability as well as the EU's 'belief systems' as key features of the EU's importance, not just for New Zealand but, according to one interviewee, 'hopefully ... for the rest of the planet'.[82]

Media elites: Australia, New Zealand and Thailand

When asked to consider the importance of the EU for their countries, Asia-Pacific media elites expressed a range of perceptions. Generally, amongst all three countries' media elites, the EU's current importance for their countries was ranked relatively highly: averaging 3.5 out of 5 in Thailand, 3.6 in Australia and 3.8 in New Zealand. However, in the verbal responses of the media respondents, the attitudes tended to vary. Responses from the Thai media elites tended to be the least positive towards the EU, compared to their Australian and New Zealand counterparts, although most New Zealand respondents were also fairly subdued in their comments. One Thai media editor interviewed ranked the EU highly because of its potential to act as a model for Thailand, the Asia-Pacific region and ASEAN, however, this was considered to be a largely limited potential since '[Thailand] and the EU speak absolutely different languages',[83] on many crucial issues such as human rights. This notion of difference and distance was also noted by another Thai media respondent who felt that the EU 'hardly matters to us at all'.[84]

Although New Zealand and Australian media elites were not generally as negative as their Thai counterparts, there were perceptions in their responses which indicated a somewhat confused understanding of the EU. Interviewees in both Pacific countries felt that it was difficult for them and their audiences to separate the idea of the EU from its constituent member countries.[85] One New Zealand respondent felt that '[p]eople still think about Europe as a group of nations and I don't think people think of Europe as *Europe*',[86] however, this interviewee did also see that this perception was beginning to change.[87]

When comparing the importance of the EU to their countries to that of other international actors and regions, media elites in all three countries tended to rate the EU as being of secondary – or lower – importance. Particularly in Australia and Thailand, the US and Asia were seen to be more important domestic counterparts than the EU, although in many cases the EU's importance was seen as rising. One Australian respondent, for example, noted that 'it's really early days for the EU, I mean it could take decades for them to find their feet',[88] and felt that over time, the EU's currently 'latent'[89] power would manifest, not only for Australia but for the world more widely. This idea was supported by a Thai colleague who felt that '[the EU] will be increasingly important ... on every issue'.[90]

Korean elites

In general, the South Korean elites regarded the European Union an important partner for their country. The great majority (eighteen out of twenty respondents) considered the EU to be either 'very important' or 'important' for South Korea at the present time. One particularly noteworthy aspect of these responses was the prominence once again of inherent comparisons of the EU and the US: five out of the eighteen positive Korean elite responses to this question focused on the notion of the EU as an important counterbalance to the current global 'superpower', the United States. This was particularly emphasized in connection to the EU's stance on North Korea which, unlike that of the United States, was viewed by Korean elites as a 'softer' approach and ultimately preferable.

In addition to being an important partner for Korea, the EU–Korean relationship was described by respondents as being a mutually respectful and conciliatory one. The relationship was commonly viewed by Korean elites as being shaped by issues of economics – although unlike the elites in the remaining three countries, these economic relations were not viewed by Korean elites as being problematic – as well as a strengthened cultural interaction between the two parties. Following from this primarily positive assessment of the EU's importance in the present, all Korean respondents felt that the EU would be an important or very important partner for Korea in the future.

The EU as an international political leader

Business elites: Australia, New Zealand and Thailand

Although the EU's position as a global economic power is firmly established, the EU is also increasingly seen as playing a growing role in international politics. This study was interested in assessing whether elites in the Asia-Pacific recognized this role, and in which areas they considered it to be important. It was broadly anticipated that the business elites would stress the economic importance of the EU and that its political role may be diminished in their minds, owing to the specific nature of their involvement with the Union.

A number of business respondents in each of the three countries did see the EU's international power and influence stemming from its economic capacity. One New Zealand respondent, for example, felt that 'it's still got a really important part to play in a whole range of areas – trade is the key one in that',[91] and a Thai respondent felt that it was the sheer size of the EU economy which made it a powerful force.[92] Additionally, one Australian business person noted that the EU's power and influence globally is strongest in areas like international trade negotiation and rules, because 'in those areas it does speak with one voice for the whole 25 ... so yes it's very important in that area'.[93]

The above quote highlights another key trend in the business responses to the EU's international political leadership; it was discussed by the majority of respondents that global power and influence necessarily relies on a great level of cohesion in decision-making and that, in the fields of foreign affairs and defence particularly, the EU's many constituent parts had resulted in fragmentation and a lack of unity which were seen to significantly nullify its capacity as an international leader. One Thai respondent, for example, felt very strongly that 'the EU cannot become a leader unless it achieves internal unity',[94] while another felt that while 'they try to achieve a common stance ... there are still frictions between Member States'.[95] Australian and New Zealand business elites shared these sentiments. One New Zealand respondent was quite pragmatic about this perceived problem, however, noting that 'I guess when you put nations together, you always have the various baggage, I suppose, that people have to overcome, and sometimes that can take considerable time',[96] and an Australian interviewee felt that the EU 'is still sorting itself out'.[97] The feeling did appear to be, among many of the business elites interviewed, that while these problems of Member State fragmentation, and the constant 'frictions'[98] between EU Member States were holding the EU back in terms of its international power, there was a sense that it had the capacity to move past these problems and become a more influential global player in the future.

Political elites: Australia, New Zealand and Thailand

When asked whether they felt that the EU was a leader in international politics, political elites across the three countries were divided in their opinions. A split was notable between those who did feel that the EU was clearly an international political leader, and those who felt that the EU fell short of such a description. Additionally, there were a number of common themes between the three nationalities, in their descriptions of the EU's capacity in this field. Australian and Thai politicians particularly perceived the EU to be beset by a lack of unity, and that these various divisions between its Member States were a leading cause of its limitations as an international leader. One Thai politician felt that '[t]here is a deep and real rift within Europe', which stemmed from the fact that 'they can't even agree among themselves'.[99] Another Thai political elite thought that the EU's solidarity at present was 'questionable',[100] while an Australian political leader wondered if 'maybe it's still struggling to make its mark in the world'.[101] One New Zealand respondent supported these claims, and felt that the EU's multilateral structure necessarily meant that it would be challenged to have a unified stance internationally.[102]

There was also a sense, from a number of the respondents, that while the EU was one of a group of international leaders, it tended to suffer from what is described in EU studies literature as a 'capabilities-expectations gap'.[103] New Zealand politicians indicated that, while they felt the EU had potential for international influence, it was not 'there yet'.[104] One New Zealand politician felt that '[s]adly, the EU, while it is undoubtedly a political leader in terms of strength and power and influence, at times does not exercise the leadership in a way that I would call a real leadership'.[105]

Although it was generally agreed that '[t]he EU still has got a lot of problems', most political respondents indicated that there were a number of areas in which the EU was certainly an international leader. These included matters of international trade and economy, and 'soft' issues, like development and humanitarian aid, culture and lifestyle. One Australian politician considered the EU 'as a bit of a litmus test'[106] in most of these areas, although he also remarked that the EU was not above 'ignoring' some of its standards on matters like human rights, if they had key trade interests involved.[107] However, this respondent also noted that 'no one's perfect … [and] in general I think they're very positive on those fronts'.[108] Another Australian interviewee felt that the EU 'set many [aspects] of the international agenda',[109] and as such, was a substantial source of global influence. This international 'clout' was considered by a member of the New Zealand political elite to derive from its ability to connect culturally with so many countries around the world: 'I think in Europe you have the EU as more of an opportunity than anyone else to bridge cultural barriers … Europe is the only part of the world that has been able to reach the whole world.'[110]

Media elites: Australia, New Zealand and Thailand

The sentiments of the three countries' media elites with respect to the EU's leadership in international politics were similar to those of the political and business elites. A number of trends in the other two cohorts were also evident amongst the media interviewees. As with the political elites, many of the media respondents felt that the EU's capacity as an international political power was limited because of the diversity of 'voices' that were present amongst EU leaders. One New Zealand news editor, for example, felt that 'it's a place of many voices'[111] and that this was why it was often limited in its global political power. One Australian respondent also felt that one of the causes of this lack of unity stemmed from the individual Member States wanting to maintain their own bilateral relationships, and being reluctant to relinquish these to the European Community institutions.[112] Additionally, Asia-Pacific media elites were generally in agreement with their political counterparts in their evaluation that the EU had the potential to act as an international leader, but that, until now, it had not managed to achieve that potential. One member of the Thai media elite, for example, noted that the EU was beginning to take a role in the international arena, but also felt that 'we can't really call them … leaders yet'.[113] This was reiterated by an Australian media respondent who felt that 'no they haven't got their act together quite frankly, just yet'.[114] Many of the media responses of this kind were qualified with this type of 'not yet' comment, indicating that the media elites of the Asia-Pacific region do perhaps perceive that the EU will grow to assume a much stronger leadership role in international politics in the future. This notion was rather frankly summarized by an Australian respondent who indicated what he felt was the necessary path for the EU's future:

> I just don't see how it can be [an international leader] until they can actually solve their internal problems and work out where they want to speak with one voice and where they want to devolve sovereignty to their Member States, and then get on with embracing the world.[115]

In the meantime, however, Thai media elites in particular perceived that the EU showed most of its international leadership capacity in the realm of economics. As one Thai interviewee stated, 'I think they are powerful economically. They are vocal in the economic area only',[116] while another of his counterparts felt that '[i]t's their economy that matters to us'.[117] Some New Zealand respondents agreed with these descriptions, with one noting that the EU would only be an international leader 'on trade issues of course ... unanimity on that',[118] thus bringing the discussion of international leadership once again back to the notion of unity amongst the Union Member States.

One trend that was observed in all three countries' media was that of the EU displaying what was perceived as international 'influence' rather than true 'leadership'. One New Zealand editor, for example, noted of the EU that 'it stands up for some really important things, and it's ... had some fantastic influence on the world', while an Australian counterpart felt that 'it's certainly having a greater influence [now] than it has had',[119] indicating perhaps a perception that the EU had 'improved' in its international competence. Many of the Thai media elite shared these sentiments, although one in particular demonstrated a reluctance to describe the EU as an international power, preferring instead to note that 'I see them as being influential. I don't want to call them a great power. It's better to call them [influential]. They are influential in a lot of countries in many areas.'[120]

The other trend that was evident amongst some of the media elites was that of a comparison of the EU's international leadership abilities with those of the United States. While the question posed to interviewees did not contain a comparative component, this was almost inherently assumed by many respondents. One Thai respondent was rather grim in his comparison of the EU's capabilities, stating that 'they are [an international political leader], but they are not as dominant as the US. Their influence in the world is less than the US. They are even less influential to Asia than Japan and China.'[121] Another Thai respondent also ranked the EU behind the US, stating that he felt 'the EU's still playing the secondary role, behind the US',[122] while yet another Thai media respondent felt that, 'speaking about leadership, there are many degrees ... the EU can be a leader, but only of the second or third degree'.[123] While this perception was most prominent amongst the Thai media elites, it was echoed by some of the Pacific media respondents also, like one Australian reporter who made an inherent comparison of the EU to the US when she noted that 'it would be good if they could challenge the US but I don't see them in the same league yet'.[124]

Korean elites

Amongst the interviewed South Korean elites, the EU was broadly regarded as being an international leader, although this leadership was perceived to be limited to a range of areas, and performing better in some than others. Perhaps predictably, the EU as an international economic leader was noted by Korean elites, and this was considered a particularly outstanding feature of its international persona. In international political relations, many Korean elites, arguably in contrast to their Asia-Pacific counterparts, considered the EU, to some extent, to be a 'superpower', and its strength as a normative global influence and its increasing capabilities in the military sphere were seen to contribute to this perception. However, South Korean elites were not all as enthusiastic about the EU's international leadership. Some agreed with their Australian, New Zealand and Thai equivalents when they stated that the EU could not yet be described as an international 'superpower'. These elites felt that, at the current time, the EU was more suited to acting as a regional leader, and was better focusing its attentions on its own regional agenda.

Discussion

General trends

Overall, a number of general trends were observed across all cohorts and in all countries. First, although its significance was often considered subordinate to that of other international partners, namely Asia and the US, there was a general consensus amongst all of the interviewed elites that the EU is nevertheless an important domestic partner for each of their respective countries. It was also considered to be a player of some sort on the international scene, however, outside of the economic sphere, it was most commonly viewed as a superpower-in-waiting; that is, on the whole, possessing potential rather than exercising actualized global political power.

Importantly, while Asia-Pacific elites were not particularly impressed by the EU's performance at present, nor were they intimidated by its latent potential. In fact, many of the interviewed elites expressed a desire to see the EU's global influence increase, primarily to counter the perceived US hegemony. It is, of course, possible that the former is merely a function of the latter; that is, precisely because the EU's potential is not currently actualized, Asia-Pacific elites do not fear it. However, this might also reflect a preference for the 'soft' style approach to international governance promoted by the EU and characterized by the employment of economic sanctions and incentives to drive political change and exchange as opposed to military intervention, in contrast to the US's 'hard' approach; certainly this was explicitly articulated by the Korean elites. Indeed, recent polls around the world have reported a growing dissatisfaction with the US's dominant role in and self-assumed responsibility for international politics.[125] Accompanying this mounting discontent with the incumbent superpower, there has been growing interest in the EU as an alternative political model and source of international leadership. Reflecting this, occasional references to the EU's normative influence were made by elites from each of the four countries. Thai and Australian elites acknowledged the EU's importance as an environmental champion, while New Zealand and Korean elites spoke of the EU's international normative influence more generally.

The one area in which the EU was almost unanimously perceived to be performing well, predictably, was the economic sphere. Although only an aspirant political actor, and an occasional normative influence, the EU was widely perceived by the interviewed elites to be a trade success and, indeed, its limited political and normative power was often considered to stem from its economic might. Undermining this largely positive image, however, was the perception of divisions between, and the dominance of, the Member States in the minds of the Asia-Pacific elites. This was a frequently discussed notion amongst all elite cohorts and in all four countries, and is one which warrants further investigation.

There may be a number of factors contributing to this perception. First, the year this survey took place should be considered as an influencing factor; 2005 saw the failure of the French and Dutch referenda on the draft EU constitutional treaty, the fallout from which may have fostered the perception of fragmentation between EU Member States. Secondly, it might be a function of the fact that many the elites interviewed as part of this survey – particularly in the case of the business elites – have extensive contacts with individual countries in Europe, rather than with the institutions of the EU. Although EU initiatives such as the Single European Market have simplified the process of gaining access to the many diverse European economies, business people, as noted by our interviewees, still largely conduct their business in and with various European countries. Similarly, political representatives of the Asia-Pacific countries still meet more frequently with their Member State counterparts than they do with EU officials.[126] And media producers still tend to rely on a traditional map of the world, rather than the new one the EU is promoting, in the way they cover events in Europe.

Certainly, if we assume that a country's elite act according to their perception of reality, as Brecher has argued they do, and if the news media are seen to play a role in shaping this image of 'reality' for elites, then it is possible that the news media framings of the EU have contributed to this particular elite perception. As was discussed in Chapter 1, Member State actors – in terms of the actual countries and their individual leaders – were referenced far more prominently in the news coverage of the EU than their Community counterparts. This continued emphasis in the media on the intergovernmental components of the EU, instead of the unified supranational ones, might have contributed to this common perception of EU fragmentation amongst the interviewed elites. This hypothesis would support the CNN effect, namely, that elites react to the reality created by the news media.

Alternatively, and in line with Herman and Chomsky's thesis on manufacturing consent, the focus on the EU's parts rather than the whole might well be driven by elite preferences. It could be argued, for example, that each of the three elite groups has an interest in perceiving and perpetuating the perception of the EU in this manner. Certainly for media elites, one way of meeting the challenge of presenting this 'unprecedented, complicated and evolving international entity to their targeted audiences', is to employ 'comprehensible concepts'.[127] For this reason, Manners and Whitman observe, the EU is generally addressed and understood by its external partners in terms of the traditional nation-state.[128] The representation of the EU in terms of a nation-state or as a collection of nation-states also arguably serves the interests of the other two investigated elite cohorts. Business elites, for example, may consider trading and negotiating with the individual Member States, in addition to being a more traditional method of international trade, to be a simpler way of operating. This argument was in fact identified in the interviews with a number of business elites, like one Australian who claimed that 'we are looking at specific countries because ... even though it's trying to be one [entity], the perception is that they are all individual countries ... so you have to approach each one of them differently'.[129] Likewise, political elites may also prefer to interact with the individual Member States of the EU because of a perception that there is more power and influence to be gained from bilateral relationships than from dealing with the large Community institutions. Indeed, one New Zealand political elite felt that, not only was this how others often approached the EU, but currently, this bilateral approach was how the EU Member States operated within their external partner countries: 'we don't really get the sense that the French office, or the British office, or the German office, or the Italian office actually go around promoting *Europe*, they are promoting their own narrow interests'.[130] Certainly, this was the previous Australian government's preferred approach as well. Its foreign policy White Paper, *Advancing the National Interest*, for example, emphasizes the importance of the 'countries of Europe' and of Australia's individual bilateral relations with each of them, described as 'the bedrock of Australia's European engagement'.[131]

Country comparisons: no such thing as a regional picture?

In addition to these common trends, there were some noticeable differences between elite cohorts and between the four countries and these were not explained by regional factors; that is to say, they did not fall neatly into the categories of 'Pacific' and 'Asian'. In terms of the current and projected state of the EU–home relationship, for example, New Zealand and Korean elites were far more positive than their Australian and Thai colleagues. This could be attributed to a hypothesized link between the state of the relationship and the attitude of government of the day, as was suggested by elites in the two Pacific countries.

In Australia, business elites attributed a predicted decline in the EU's importance for Australia to the then conservative coalition government – under the leadership of Prime Minister John Howard – maintaining a narrow focus on the US and Asia to the exclusion of Europe. The Australian government's relationship with the EU has historically been tempered by strong disagreement on agricultural issues, particularly the EU's programme of agricultural subsidies, the CAP. The then Australian government had been particularly vocal in the Cairns Group of agricultural exporting countries in calling for an end to the market-distorting practices undertaken by the EU and US, and pushed for the reform of protectionist policies, in particular, the CAP.[132] In addition, it found itself in conflict with the EU on a number of other key issues including climate change and human rights.[133] These factors might explain Australian business elites' pessimism and the lower overall rating of the EU–home country relationship.

Also a member of the Cairns, the CAP has been a sticking point in the EU–NZ relationship as well, however, arguably to a lesser degree; when the UK – Australia and New Zealand's colonial 'parent' – joined the EU in 1973, New Zealand was able to negotiate more favourable access conditions than Australia, for example.[134] More broadly speaking, under the supervision of centre-left Prime Minister Helen Clark, New Zealand's relations with the EU have been less troubled than those of its Pacific neighbour. Additionally, it might be argued that, at least until very recently, New Zealand has been more closely aligned with the EU on issues such as climate change and social welfare than is Australia. Thus, the largely positive relations between New Zealand and the EU might well explain the apparent optimism amongst the country's elites; on average, New Zealand elites rated the present relationship higher than their Asia-Pacific counterparts and anticipated an augmentation in the importance of the EU–New Zealand relationship in the future. Indeed, it was suggested that the maintenance of this positive relationship was contingent upon the current government, who maintained that the EU 'has always been of great importance to New Zealand, and always will be',[135] remaining in office.

A similar dichotomy is evident in the case of the two Asian countries. Along with its two Pacific 'neighbours', Thailand is a fellow member of the Cairns Group. The Thai–EU relationship has been described as 'passive, rather than passionate'[136] and the two actors have been in conflict over issues such as non-tariff barriers and Myanmar. Relations between the Korean government and the EU tend to be less vexed than in Thailand and Australia (and arguably, also New Zealand) since they do not centre on the problematic issue of agriculture. Indeed, the EU's stance on North Korea in particular, and the importance of EU investment in the Korean market have enabled relations between the two partners to be relatively unproblematic in recent years.[137] Again, these key temperamental differences might explain the variation in the perceived relevance of the EU for the two Asian countries.

Nevertheless, some regional patterns (that is, similarities between the two Asian counties and similarities between the two Pacific countries) did emerge. While Australian and New Zealand elites tended to focus on the EU bureaucracy, which they considered to be a messy attempt at *political* integration, the Thai and South Korean elites more commonly emphasized the *economic* aspects of European integration. Here, historical circumstances may play a part in accounting for the regional differences; the political culture of both Australia and New Zealand is based upon European models, both having adopted the UK Westminster system of government, for example. This, as well as the Pacific countries' colonial past, might engender a stronger interest in the EU's political developments as opposed to the two Asian counterparts whose greatest interest in European integration is related to trade. Similarly, it is possible that, because the European way of life is less familiar, and thus appears more exotic, to the two Asian countries than the two former dominions of the British Empire, the Asian elites also tended to refer to European culture and lifestyle more than their Pacific counterparts, for whom it is arguably similar to their own societies and cultures.

Cohort comparisons: points of contention or cohesion?

As well as differences between the four countries, there were also noticeable points of difference amongst the three cohorts in Australia, New Zealand and Thailand.[138] Business elites in each of these three countries were, on average, less optimistic about the EU–home country relationship than their respective political elites, rating both its current and projected importance for their country lower than their political counterparts. In the Australian case, this might be explained by the disappointment expressed in the way the government was currently 'steering the ship', a plausible explanation in the Thai case also. It does not adequately explain the New Zealand case, however, where there was less of a gap between the perceived and the desired state of the EU–domestic relationship expressed by local business elites. Although New Zealand business elites did not give the relationship as high a rating as their political counterparts, they did rate it considerably higher than the Thai and Australian business elites; in fact, they rated it higher than any of the Thai or Australian elite cohorts. Thus, the higher rating by political than business elites in New Zealand might simply be explained by the ostensibly stronger, more positive relationship between the New Zealand government and the EU than in the other two countries.

It is interesting to note that the euro was one of the few images that was considered to be a symbol of European integration by all cohorts and in all four countries, arguably supporting the earlier observation of the common and dominant perception of the EU as a successful economic experiment.

Conclusion

The APP project aimed not only to expose and explore perceptions of the EU in the Asia-Pacific region, but also to enhance the profile and increase public awareness of the EU in the Asia-Pacific, and to establish avenues of action that could be of use in doing so. In light of this goal, it is pertinent to ask what the elite perceptions uncovered in this particular study mean in terms of their practical implications for the EU–Asia-Pacific relationship.

The elite perceptions discussed in this chapter paint a rather ambiguous picture of the EU in its dealings, not only with the countries involved in this study, but also with the world more broadly. The EU was seldom seen by any of the elite groups in any of the four countries to be an international leader as such, however it was generally regarded to be a key source of global influence, and a source which is likely to increase in importance and effectiveness in the future. While the EU's economic prowess was widely acknowledged by Asia-Pacific elites, so too were its bureaucratic convolutions, which were perceived to be limiting its efficacy as an international actor. The continued preference of the Asia-Pacific countries to trade and negotiate with the Member States of the EU, and to portray it in this fragmented manner, combined with the frequent perception of disunity within the EU also arguably contribute to the ambiguous perception of the EU among Asia-Pacific elites.

Such ambiguity, it is argued, has important consequences for the four countries of this study in terms of their interactions with the EU. The continued insistence on dealing primarily with the Member States may prove detrimental to the Asia-Pacific countries in the future. As the integration process continues, it is likely that the importance of the Community structures of the Union will augment in importance in order to manage and contain the growing breadth and diversity of its membership. If its partners abroad are unable (or unwilling) to accept these changes to traditional forms of international interaction, then they risk being left behind and dropping off the radar of the ever-shifting EU as it looks more and more towards inter*regional* rather than international engagement with global partners.

For business elites in the four countries, failing to stay abreast of the EU's developments, and confusion and misapprehensions about their nature, can translate to the loss of significant trade and business opportunities presented by the world's largest single market. As one business interviewee pointed out, it was not necessarily barriers themselves but the *perception* of barriers that was limiting, and would continue to limit, the success of local businesses in the European market.[139] Politically speaking, greater understanding of the current and future nature of the EU is demanded by the fact that it provides the most advanced model of regional engagement in a world, according to Chris Patten, 'that desperately needs new paradigms for the management of its affairs'.[140] European integration is understood by many as a pragmatic response to the increasingly global nature of the world, from which the Asia-Pacific is neither isolated from nor immune to, as the Bali bombings and the Asian bird flu, for example, clearly illustrated. The EU offers a model of a new type of global engagement which, despite its shortcomings, should not – indeed, on account of the EU's considerable size and growing weight, cannot – be ignored.

If the common impression of the EU as largely an intergovernmental trading organization is of concern in the case of business and political elites who might thus overlook its growing political role and increasing supranational weight, it is no less troubling in the case of the media elites. As has been discussed previously in this chapter, and extensively in earlier chapters in this volume (see e.g. the Introduction and Chapters 1 and 2), the media play a key role in influencing not only the public's perceptions but also, it is argued, the perceptions of key national decision-makers. Thus if, as this survey suggests, newsmakers themselves have a limited and arguably outdated image of the EU, it is unlikely that their audiences are going to grasp a fuller picture of the EU. In order to counter some of these possible implications, the following recommendations are therefore proposed, and are addressed not only to Asia-Pacific elites, but also to the representatives of the EU in the Asia-Pacific region.[141]

From a business perspective, the European Commission delegations in each of our four countries may prove useful in ensuring an effective EU–Asia-Pacific dialogue in the future. Increasing the operational budgets of the delegations abroad would allow these EU representatives to extend the reach of their efforts, and allow them to engage in more effective outreach activities within the business, political and media communities of the Asia-Pacific countries. The sponsoring or co-sponsoring of trade fairs, for example, would be one means of raising the profile of the EU within the business communities of its external partners, as would the establishment of an efficient and comprehensive EU information bureau alongside the delegation offices.

Politically, the approach of a nation-state towards a partner like the EU is inevitably, as noted by some of our respondents, dependent on the stance of the government in power. However, there are courses of action which may be adopted at a parliamentary level to help to counter these administrative shifts, and to ensure that, regardless of the government's position, the EU stays on the country's 'radar'. For example, establishing parliamentary 'Friends of Europe' groups where they do not already exist, and increasing the support and profile for such groups where they do, is one means of ensuring EU awareness at a national political level, irrespective of the preferences of the government of the day. Additionally, developing greater and more regular dialogue between centres for research on Europe at universities in the region and members of Parliament with interests or portfolios that may warrant a 'European perspective' may also be of benefit.

As noted in the Introduction to this volume, the EU is not less but more important, economically speaking, to the two Pacific countries than the US or other partners in Asia. It is also South Korea's second largest export destination and its largest investor[142] and Thailand's third most important economic partner, accounting for approximately 15 per cent of the country's international trade.[143] Moreover, the EU is an important aid donor, provider of peacekeeping and democratic accountability in the Asia-Pacific region. Globally, it has assumed a leading role in terms of environmental issues, most notably, climate change. In the context of these facts, the media findings reported in Chapter 1 and the perspectives of interviewed media elites reported in this chapter suggest that a reprioritizing of the EU–home country relationship in the local media of each of the four Asia-Pacific countries needs to occur so as to more accurately reflect the reality of the EU's importance for the Asia-Pacific region in general, and the four countries involved in this study in particular. In order for this to occur, local media producers must allocate the resources and news space necessary for covering the EU and its developments as appropriate to its current and growing importance for each of the four countries. They may also need to adopt deliberate methods of ensuring that the developments of the peaceful European integration project are newsworthy in the absence of controversy, by including a 'national hook' for example, to designate domestic relevance for local audiences as discussed in Chapter 1.

There are lessons here too for the EU. As Lynch wrote, the EU runs the risk of becoming '[a] global player with increasing responsibilities and capabilities that focuses on telling the world what it should think about it, but [is] quite deaf to what the world actually thinks'.[144] It has been suggested – indeed, it is one of the key motivations behind the APP project and this book – that the EU's internal identity and its role as an international actor is in part informed and formed by the expectations and perceptions of its external counterparts.[145] Consequently, the perceptions reported here, held by the key decision-makers, stakeholders and image-formers in one of the EU's important regional partners, the Asia-Pacific, however erroneous or static, should not be disregarded. The fact remains that, despite its own efforts to act and be recognized as a polished political performer, and indeed, in spite of the interesting observation reported in Chapter 1 that the EU was most frequently framed as a political actor in the Asia-Pacific media, it is still regarded by both the public and elites of the region as a largely economic entity. Despite its ambitions for 'an ever closer union amongst the people of Europe',[146] the EU is still viewed from the outside as a collection of nation-states rather than a cohesive entity. Ultimately, the success of the unique, ambitious and important European integration project will depend not only on how it views its own achievements but on how the world views them. But regardless of the outcome, it seems clear that the countries of the Asia-Pacific would benefit from greater understanding and more accurate perceptions amongst their respective power elites of the so-called soft superpower.

Notes

1 C. Mills, *The Power Elite*, New York, Oxford University Press, 1956. Available <http://www.thirdworldtraveler.com/Book_Excerpts/HigherCircles_PE.html>   (Accessed 2 May 2007).

2 W. Zimmerman, *The Russian People and Foreign Policy: Russian Elite and Mass Perspectives, 1993–2000*, Princeton, NJ, Princeton University Press, 2002, p. 42.

3 G. Almond, *The American People*, cited *ibid.*, p. 89.

4 R. Oldendick and B. Bardes, 'Mass and Elite Foreign Policy Opinions', *Public Opinion Quarterly* 46 (1982), 368–9.

5 W. Chittick and K. Billingsley, 'The Structure of Elite Foreign Policy Beliefs', *Western Political Quarterly* 42 (1989), 201–24.

6 See G. Almond, *The American People and Foreign Policy*, New York, Praeger, 1950; W. Lippman, *Essays in the Public Philosophy*, Boston, MA, Little, Brown, 1955.

7 Oldendick and Bardes, 'Mass and Elite Foreign Policy Opinions', p. 368.

8 *Ibid.*, p. 369. Oldendick and Bardes cite the following: R. Dahl, *Congress and Foreign Policy*, New York, Harcourt Brace, 1950; J. Rosenau, *Public Opinion and Foreign Policy: An Operational Formulation*, New York, Random House, 1961.

9 E. Herman and N. Chomsky, *Manufacturing Consent*, New York, Pantheon Books, 1988, p. 298.

10 See C. Naveh, 'The Role of the Media in Foreign Policy Decision-Making', *Conflict and Communication Online* 1 (2002), 2, available <http://www.cco.regener-online.de/2002_2/pdf_2002_2/naveh.pdf> (Accessed 21 February 2007).

11 See e.g. P. Jacobsen, 'National Interest, Humanitarianism or CNN: What Triggers UN Peace Enforcement After the Cold War?', *Journal of Peace Research* 33 (1996), 205–15; N. Gowing, 'Real-time TV Coverage from War: Does it Make or Break

Government Policy?', in J. Gow, R. Paterson and A. Preston (eds), *Bosnia by Television*, London, British Film Institute, 1996; S. Livingston, 'Clarifying the CNN Effect: An Examination of Media Effects According to Type of Military Intervention', *Research Paper R-18*, Joan Shorenstein Center on the Press, Politics and Public Policy, John F. Kennedy School of Government, Harvard University, June 1997, available <http://www.ksg.harvard.edu/presspol/research_publications/papers/research_papers/R18.pdf> (Accessed 13 June 2007).

12 *Ibid.*, p. 2.

13 Mills, *Power Elite*.

14 See e.g. D. Flint, 'Heaven Forbid that the Endless Chatter of Elite Opinion should Get its Way', *The Australian* (25 August 2003), available <http://www.onlineopinion.com.au/view.asp?article=677> (Accessed 13 March 2007).

15 See e.g. N. Chomsky, 'The Responsibility of Intellectuals', *New York Review of Books* (23 February 1963), available <http://www.chomsky.info/articles/19670223.htm> (Accessed 3 May 2007).

16 Mills, *Power Elite*.

17 M. Brecher, *India and World Politics: Krishna Menon's View of the World*, New York, Frederick A. Praeger, 1968.

18 *Ibid.*

19 The Korean elite survey was part of a follow-up study of Asian perceptions of the EU involving South Korea, Thailand, Singapore, Hong Kong, China, Mainland China and Japan, also coordinated by the National Centre for Research on Europe at the University of Canterbury and supported by Asia-Europe Foundation (ASEF).

20 The response rates to the request for interview or the questionnaire in the case of South Korea were not high. In Australia, of approximately 105 people who were contacted, 27 agreed to and participated in interviews. In South Korea, the survey questionnaire was emailed to over 500 identified experts; just 20 were returned. The respondents in South Korea were eleven university professors, five researchers in economic research institutes, three businessmen and one journalist.

21 Charles Finney, Head of Wellington Regional Chamber of Commerce, interviewed in Wellington, June 2005.

22 Charlie Pedersen, National President, Federated Farmers, interviewed in Wellington, July 2005.

23 Egon Vetter, Director of EWV Management, interviewed in Melbourne, 28 July 2005.

24 John Walley, CEO of the Canterbury Manufacturers' Association, interviewed in Christchurch, July 2005.

25 David Inall, Executive Director of the Cattle Council of Australia, interviewed in Canberra, 15 August 2005.

26 John Upton, Marketing Manager for Horizon Meats, interviewed in Auckland, 20 June 2005.

27 Anonymous Thai business respondent representing the tapioca products industry.

28 Orapin Banjerdrongkajorn, woodcraft industry, interviewed in Bangkok, 19 August 2005.

29 Jen Namchaisiri, garment and textile industry, interviewed in Bangkok, 8 August 2005.

30 David Inall, Executive Director of the Cattle Council of Australia, interviewed in Canberra, 15 August 2005.

31 Jen Namchaisiri, garment and textile industry, interviewed in Bangkok, 8 August 2005.

32 Anonymous Australian respondent, member of the European Australian Business Council, interviewed in Melbourne, 29 July 2005.

33 Christine Gibbs Stewart, General Manager of International Trade, Australian Business Limited, interviewed in Sydney, 16 June 2005.

34 Anne Berryman, General Manager, Meat and Wool NZ, interviewed in Wellington, July 2005.

35 Prasert Jensiriwanich, garment industry, interviewed in Bangkok, 24 August 2005.

36 Anthony Albanese MP (ALP), Shadow Minister for Environment, interviewed in Canberra, 16 August 2005.

37 Laurie Ferguson MP (ALP), Shadow Minister for Immigration, interviewed in Canberra, 21 June 2005.

38 Prof. Dr Likhit Dhiravegin, Thai Rak Thai Party, Vice Chairman of the Parliamentary Foreign Committee, interviewed in Bangkok, 18 June 2005.

39 Jim Sutton, Minister for Agriculture and Fisheries, New Zealand Labour Party, interviewed in Wellington, July 2005.

40 Martin Galagher, Member of Parliament, New Zealand Labour Party, interviewed in Wellington, July 2005.

41 Bruce Billson MP (Lib.), Parliamentary Secretary for Foreign Affairs and Trade, interviewed in Canberra, 21 June 2005.

42 Senator Lyn Allison (DEM), Leader of the Democrats, interviewed in Melbourne, 21 July 2005.

43 Korn Chatikavanij, Thai Democrats, interviewed 20 June 2005.

44 Krisak Chunhawan, Senator and Committee of Foreign Affairs, interviewed in Bangkok, 13 July 2005.

45 News values, according to Shoemaker and Reese, 'help [media] gatekeepers select content for its appeal'. (See P. Shoemaker and S. Reese, *Mediating the Message: Theories of Influences on Mass Media Content*, White Plains, NY, Longman Publishers, 1996, p. 112.) The most commonly identified news values include: prominence/ importance, human interest, conflict/controversy, the unusual, timeliness and cultural proximity. See M. Stephens, *Broadcast News*, New York, Holt, Rinehart & Winston, 1980.

46 Jack Waterford, Editor in Chief, *Canberra Times*, interviewed in Canberra, 18 August 2005.

47 Rowan Callick, Asia Pacific Editor, *Australian Financial Review*, interviewed in Melbourne, 7 June 2005.

48 D. Hill Cone, New Zealand media respondent, interviewed in Wellington, 18 March 2004.

49 J. Gardener, Editor, *The New Zealand Herald*, interviewed in Auckland, 2004.

50 Jack Waterford, Editor in Chief, *Canberra Times*, interviewed in Canberra, 18 August 2005.

51 Bavorn Tosrigaew, *Thai Rath* Foreign Editor, interviewed in Bangkok, 9 June 2005.

52 Pairat Pongpanit, *Matichon* Foreign Editor, interviewed in Bangkok, 8 June 2005.

53 Saguan Pisalrasmee, *Manager* Foreign Editor, interviewed in Bangkok, 7 June 2005.

54 Pairat Pongpanit, *Matichon* Foreign Editor, interviewed in Bangkok, 8 June 2005.

55 The questions posed to the Korean elites, while conducted during a different time period than the Australia, New Zealand and Thai elite interviews, were translated so as to be identical (and thus comparable) to the first group of elite interviews.

56 However, it should be noted here that while the average ranked importance of the EU to New Zealand in the future remained the same, there were some variations to this in the individual rankings of some participants, and some other respondents also indicated a perceived decline or increase but did so verbally and did not attribute a number to this perception.

57 For example: Anthony Albanese, Shadow Minister for Environment, House of Representatives (ALP), interviewed in Canberra, 16 August 2005; Senator Lyn Allison (DEM), Leader of the Democrats, interviewed in Melbourne, 21 July 2005.

58 Christine Gibbs Stewart, General Manager of International Trade, Australian Business Limited, interviewed in Sydney, 16 June 2005.

59 John Tinney, former Head of Austrade, interviewed in Melbourne, 5 September 2005.
60 John Walley, CEO of the Canterbury Manufacturers' Association, interviewed in Christchurch, July 2005.
61 Charles Finney, Head of Wellington Regional Chamber of Commerce, interviewed in Wellington, July 2005.
62 Charlie Pedersen, National President, Federated Farmers, interviewed in Wellington 2005.
63 Jim Grennell, Export Development Manager, Wrightson Seeds, interviewed in Christchurch, 20 June 2005.
64 *Ibid.*
65 David Inall, Executive Director of the Cattle Council of Australia, interviewed in Canberra, 15 August 2005.
66 *Ibid.*
67 Anonymous Thai business respondent, representing the tapioca industry.
68 Kevin McDonald, General Manger of Operations and Acting CEO of Australian Business Limited, interviewed in Sydney, 15 June 2005.
69 *Ibid.*
70 M. L. Ladadip Devakul, Director, Orientours Ltd., interviewed in Bangkok, 19 August 2005.
71 Jen Namchaisiri, garment and textile industry, interviewed in Bangkok, 8 August 2005; Prasert Jensiriwanich, garment industry, interviewed in Bangkok, 24 August 2005.
72 Jen Namchaisiri, interviewed in Bangkok, 8 August 2005
73 However, this is clearly skewed by the lack of numerical responses to this second question since most argued it would stay the same and equal numbers of respondents saw it increasing or decreasing.
74 Bruce Billson MP (Lib.), Parliamentary Secretary for Foreign Affairs and Trade, interviewed in Canberra, 21 June 2005.
75 Senator Grant Chapman (Lib.), Head of the EU–Australia Parliamentary Friendship Group.
76 Anthony Albanese MP (ALP), Shadow Minister for Environment, interviewed in Canberra, 16 August 2005.
77 Jon Ungpakorn, Senator (Committee on Social Development and Human Stability), interviewed in Bangkok, 20 June 2005.
78 Japabob Penkhae, Thai Rak Thai Party, interviewed in Bangkok, 18 June 2005.
79 Peter Dunn, MP, United Future Party Leader, interviewed in Wellington, June 2005.
80 Lockwood Smith, MP, New Zealand National Party, interviewed in Wellington, June 2005.
81 For example: Tim Barnett, Labour MP, Member of the Parliamentary Select Committee on Foreign Affairs interviewed in Christchurch, 18 June 2005; Harry Dunhoyven, Minister of Transport, Member of 'Friends of Europe' Parliamentary group, Labour Party, interviewed in Wellington, June 2005; John Carter, Member of Parliament, New Zealand National Party, interviewed in Wellington June 2005.
82 Martin Galagher, Member of Parliament, New Zealand Labour Party, interviewed in Wellington, July 2005.
83 Pairat Pongpanit, *Matichon* Foreign Editor, interviewed in Bangkok, 8 June 2005.
84 Saowaros Ronakit, *Matichon* Business Editor, interviewed in Bangkok, 8 June 2005.
85 Rowan Callick, Asia Pacific Editor, *Australian Financial Review*, interviewed in Melbourne, 7 June 2005.
86 J. Gardener, Editor, *The New Zealand Herald*, interviewed in Auckland, 2004. Emphasis added.
87 *Ibid.*

88 Emma McDonald, Political Reporter, *Canberra Times*, interviewed in Canberra, 15 August 2005.
89 *Ibid.*
90 Kavi Chongkittavorn, *The Nation* Foreign Editor, interviewed in Bangkok, 3 June 2005.
91 Anne Berryman, General Manager, Meat and Wool NZ, interviewed in Wellington, June 2005.
92 Prasert Jensiriwanich, garment industry, interviewed in Bangkok, 24 August 2005.
93 John Tinney, former Head of Austrade, interviewed in Melbourne, 5 September 2005.
94 M. L. Ladadip Devakul, Director, Orientours Ltd., interviewed in Bangkok, 19 August 2005.
95 Orapin Banjerdrongkajorn, Woodcraft Industry, interviewed in Bangkok, 19 August 2005.
96 Jim Grennell, Export Development Manager, Wrightson Seeds, interviewed in Christchurch, 20 June 2005.
97 Vincent Price, Government Strategy and Market Development, Kronos, interviewed in Melbourne, 18 July 2005.
98 Orapin Banjerdrongkajorn, Woodcraft Industry, interviewed in Bangkok, 19 August 2005.
99 Korn Chatikavanij, Thai Democrats, interviewed 20 June 2005.
100 Jon Ungpakorn, Senator (Committee on Social Development and Human Stability), interviewed in Bangkok, 20 June 2005.
101 Anne McEwen (ALP), Senator for South Australia, interviewed in Adelaide, 2 August 2005.
102 Tim Barnett, Labour MP, Member of the Parliamentary Select Committee on Foreign Affairs, interviewed in Christchurch, 18 June 2005.
103 See C. Hill, 'The Capability-Expectations Gap, or Conceptualising Europe's International Role', *Journal of Common Market Studies* 31 (1993), 305–28.
104 Tim Barnett, Labour MP, Member of the Parliamentary Select Committee on Foreign Affairs interviewed in Christchurch, 18 June 2005.
105 Lockwood Smith, MP, New Zealand National Party, interviewed in Wellington, June 2005.
106 Laurie Ferguson MP (ALP), Shadow Minister for Immigration, interviewed in Canberra, 21 June 2005.
107 *Ibid.*
108 *Ibid.*
109 Bruce Billson MP (Lib.), Parliamentary Secretary for Foreign Affairs and Trade, interviewed in Canberra, 21 June 2005.
110 Harry Dunhoyven, Minister of Transport, Member of 'Friends of Europe' Parliamentary group, Labour Party, interviewed in Wellington, June 2005.
111 Paul Thompson, Editor of *The Press*, interviewed in Christchurch, 5 July 2005.
112 Tony Hill, Head of International Coverage, ABC News, interviewed in Sydney, 17 June 2005.
113 Saguan Pisalrasmee, *Manager* Foreign Editor, interviewed in Bangkok, 7 June 2005.
114 Emma McDonald, Political Reporter, *Canberra Times*, interviewed in Canberra, 15 August 2005.
115 Ben Potter, Melbourne Bureau Chief, *Australian Financial Review*, interviewed in Melbourne, 14 June 2005.
116 Tanita Saenkhum, *The Nation* Social Editor, interviewed in Bangkok, 17 June 2005.
117 Chib Jitniyom, *ITV* Foreign News Editor, interviewed in Bangkok, 15 July 2005.
118 Simon Kilroy, Editor, *The Dominion Post*, interviewed in Wellington, June 2005.
119 Tony Hill, Head of International Coverage, ABC News, interviewed in Sydney, 17 June 2005.

120 Tanita Saenkhum, *The Nation* Social Editor, interviewed in Bangkok, 17 June 2005.
121 Pairat Pongpanit, *Matichon* Foreign Editor, interviewed in Bangkok, 8 June 2005.
122 Saguan Pisalrasmee, *Manager* Foreign Editor, interviewed in Bangkok, 7 June 2005.
123 Bavorn Tosrigaew, *Thai Rath* Foreign Editor, interviewed in Bangkok, 9 June 2005.
124 Emma McDonald, Political Reporter, *Canberra Times*, interviewed in Canberra, 15 August 2005.
125 See e.g. Chicago Council on Global Affairs in Partnership with the Asia Society and in Association with the East Asia Institute and Lowy Institute for International Policy, *Global Views 2006: The United States and the Rise of China and India. Results of a 2006 Multination Survey of Public Opinion*, Chicago, 2006. According to the survey, a great majority of Australian respondents agreed with the statement that 'the US does not have the responsibility to play the role of world policeman' (69 per cent) and 79 per cent felt that it 'is playing the role of world policeman more than it should be' (p. 51).
126 In Australia e.g. between 1999 and 2000, visits by the Prime Minister, John Howard, and his government ministers to London outnumbered visits to Brussels by a ratio of four to one. See P. Murray, 'Australia's Relations with the European Union: Branch Office or Independent Actor?', in C. Saunders and G. Triggs (eds), *Trade and Cooperation with the European Union in the New Millennium*, The Hague, Kluwer Law International, 2002, p. 163.
127 N. Chaban, K. Stats and J. Bain, 'Under Construction: Images of the Enlarging EU in the Australasian News Media', *Critical Approaches to Discourse Analysis across Disciplines* 1 (2007), 79–95.
128 I. Manners and R. Whitman, 'Towards Identifying the International Identity of the European Union: A Framework for Analysis of the EU's Network of Relationships', *European Integration* 21 (1998), 237.
129 Christine Gibbs Stewart, General Manager of International Trade, Australian Business Limited, interviewed in Sydney, 16 June 2005.
130 Charles Finney, Head of Wellington Regional Chamber of Commerce, interviewed in Wellington, June 2005. Emphasis added.
131 Department of Foreign Affairs and Trade (DFAT), Australian Government, *Advancing the National Interest: Australia's Foreign and Trade Policy White Paper*, Canberra, 2003, p. 98.
132 See T. Fischer, 'Speech to Cairns Group Opening Session', Sydney, 2 April 1998, available   <http://www.dfat.gov.au/media/speeches/trade/1998/cairns_opening_010498.html> (Accessed 14 May 2006).
133 The human rights issue was most visibly played out in the failure of the negotiations for a Framework Agreement between Australia and the EU in 1997. Despite reiterating a strong commitment to human rights, the newly elected Howard government vehemently opposed the inclusion of a human rights clause, standard in all the EU's international trade agreements. The Framework Agreement was subsequently abandoned and a weaker Joint Declaration, containing reference to human rights but with no legal obligations for breaches, was adopted. See F. Brenchley, 'Canberra, EU Dodge Human Rights Stand-off', *Australian Financial Review* (18 April 1997), p. 7; G. Barker, 'Stretching a Friendship', *Australian Financial Review* (31 January 2004), p. 20. Additionally, under the Howard government, Australia refused to sign the Kyoto Proocol, however on 3 December 2007, the newly elected Labor Government led by Kevin Rudd kept an election promise and signed the agreement.
134 See D. McDougall, *Australian Foreign Relations: Contemporary Perspectives*, Longman, South Melbourne, 1998, p. 82.
135 H. Clark, 'New Zealand's Relationship with Europe', Annual Europa Lecture, National Centre for Research on Europe, 22 November 2002, p. 9.
136 Chris Patten quoted in Goh Chok Tong, 'Making Passion Last in the EU–SEAsia Ties', *The Nation* (30 June 2004).

137 HE Ban Ki-moon, 'Korea's Major Security Issues and Korea-EU Cooperation', luncheon speech by the Minister of Foreign Affairs and Trade of the Republic of Korea at the European Union Chamber of Commerce in Korea, 19 March 2004, available <http://www.mofat.go.kr/me/me_a002/me_b006/1158488_980.html> (Accessed 31 March 2007).
138 As noted earlier, the South Korean survey did not distinguish between types of elites.
139 Member of the European Australian Business Council, interviewed in Melbourne, 29 July 2005 (name withheld).
140 C. Patten, 'How National is the National Interest?', paper presented at the seminar External Dimensions of the European Union, Miami European Union Centre, FL, 1 October 2002.
141 The following recommendations were generated at the final APP workshop, 'EU and Dialogue between Peoples and Cultures: Seeing the EU through the Eyes of Others', at Te Papa in Wellington in November 2005 by the APP research team in collaboration with representatives of each of the three elite cohorts who were invited to participate. See <http://www.europe.canterbury.ac.nz/appp/recommendations/>.
142 European Commission, 'Bilateral Trade Relations – Korea', *Trade Issues*, last updated May 2007, available <http://ec.europa.eu/trade/issues/bilateral/countries/korea/index_en.htm> (Accessed 10 May 2006).
143 European Commission, 'The EU's Relations with Thailand, *European Union in the World*, last updated in November 2006, available <http://ec.europa.eu/external_relations/thailand/intro/index.htm> (Accessed 10 May 2007).
144 D. Lynch, *Communicating Europe to the World: What Public Diplomacy for the EU?*, European Policy Centre Working Paper 2, Brussels, 2005, p. 31.
145 See e.g. M. Holland, 'The Common Foreign and Security Policy', in L. Cram, D. Dinan and N. Nugent (eds), *Developments in the European Union*, London, Macmillan, 1999, pp. 230–46; O. Elgström, *Leader or Foot-dragger? Perceptions of the European Union in Multilateral International Negotiations*, Swedish Institute for European Policy Studies, Report 2006/1, 2006, available <www.sieps.se/publ/rapporter/bilagor/20061.pdf> (Accessed 7 May 2007); S. Lucarelli, 'EU Political Identity, Foreign Policy and External Image', *The External Image of the European Union: A Global Survey*, GARNET Working Paper Series 17, 2007, available <http://www.garnet-eu.org/fileadmin/documents/working_papers/1707/1%20Survey%20Front%20Page-Content-Authors-Acknowledgments.pdf> (Accessed 5 June 2007).
146 European Commission and Council, 'Preamble', Treaty Establishing the European Community, Rome, 25 March 1957.

Appendix I

Media environments and sample selection

Australia

Australia's federal configuration influences media content, distribution and reach; there are only two national daily newspapers and no national news broadcasts on commercial television.[1] There is much greater diversity at the state level with a total of twenty-six daily major capital city newspapers (including their weekend versions) and three commercial and two public daily news bulletins. In addition to these state and territory capital city dailies, there are at least thirty-eight regional dailies, a further 315 non-daily regional papers and 155 suburban newspapers.[2] When viewed from a media ownership perspective, however, this apparent diversity is revealed to be misleading. One of the dominant trends for the written press worldwide is the 'concentration of ownership of titles, in the same period, into the hands of a small number of powerful business groupings'.[3] Media ownership in Australia is, in fact, amongst the most highly concentrated in the world.[4] Currently, four groups account for over 80 per cent of Australian newspaper titles and 96 per cent of their readership.[5] Rupert Murdoch's News Limited has interests in more than 100 newspapers throughout Australia. It controls a staggering 67.8 per cent of the capital city and national newspaper market, 76.1 per cent of the Sunday newspaper market, 46.6 per cent of the suburban newspaper market and 23.4 per cent of the regional newspaper market.[6] At least 65 per cent of Australia's adult population read at least one metropolitan or national News Limited paper each week.[7] Fairfax controls 21.4 per cent of the capital city and national newspaper market, 22.8 per cent of the Sunday newspaper market, 18.1 per cent of the suburban newspaper market and 15.4 per cent of the regional newspaper market.[8] The broadcast media is equally monopolized by a number of major players, most notably the late Kerry Packer and now his son, James Packer, under the auspices of Publishing and Broadcasting Limited (PBL) (Channel Nine) and Kerry Stokes (Channel Seven). In spite of this tendency towards oligopoly, according to the Australian Department of Foreign Affairs and Trade (DFAT), 'Australia's news and entertainment media have a robust tradition of free expression and vigorous analysis of public policy.'[9] All of the major Australian newspapers and the television networks' news programmes regularly employ the services of local international news agencies including Australian Associated Press (AAP), Reuters, Associated Press (AP) and Agence France-Presse (AFP).

The newspapers selected for analysis from Australia included the two national dailies, *The Australian* and the *Australian Financial Review,* representing Australia's two major newspaper empires, News Limited and Fairfax respectively. While previous studies have excluded tabloid-style newspapers such as News Limited's Melbourne-based *Herald-Sun* or Sydney's *Daily Telegraph*, it was deemed important to include at least one of these on account of their popularity and broad demographic appeal.[10] Equally, it was necessary to include one of the more reputable Fairfax broadsheet papers, namely, the *Sydney Morning Herald*, routinely rated amongst the top newspapers in the world.[11] Finally, the sample included one of only two independent capital city papers, the *Canberra Times*, so that the nation's capital was included in the sample.[12]

The selection criteria for television news included the additional stipulation that the sample should include one public and one commercial broadcaster – the leading and most respected news bulletins in each case. In Australia, PBL's Channel Nine was the obvious selection from the commercial networks due to its broad demographic appeal and, in 2004, dominance of the viewing market. The publicly funded ABC (Australian Broadcasting Corporation) is the only truly independent national network in Australia. Moreover, in 2004 audience figures for the ABC evening news broadcast were second only to Nine's news broadcast.[13]

New Zealand

Despite New Zealand's diminutive population in relation to its counterparts in this study, a competitive media environment still exists. New Zealand has no national daily newspaper, but there are eleven daily regional newspapers, as well as two national Sunday newspapers. In addition, there are over sixty community newspapers operating through out the country. As with Australia, however, this robust profile is marked by a relative uniformity of media ownership. Sixty-nine New Zealand newspapers are owned by Fairfax, which is an Australian company that bought out Independent Newspapers Limited (INL) in 2003. Fairfax's newspapers include two of New Zealand's three metropolitan titles: Wellington's *Dominion Post* and Christchurch's *Press*. With the exception of its two dailies and of its two national Sunday titles (the tabloid *News* and the broadsheet *Star-Times*), all Fairfax's other newspapers were regional broadsheets serving local markets.[14]

While New Zealand does not have a national daily newspaper, the print media environment is characterized by a multitude of regional newspapers. Three of the newspapers chosen for the New Zealand analysis, the *Waikato Times*, *Dominion Post* and *Press*, all serve different regions of the country (ranging from the middle and south of the North Island to the middle of the South Island) and are all owned by the Fairfax Corporation. Though the *Dominion Post* serves the nation's capital, it is the *New Zealand Herald* that is considered to be the more popular choice among politicians and policy-makers and this is one reason why the *Herald* was included in the sample. The *Herald* also has the largest circulation of all New Zealand newspapers, and has been owned by Tony O'Reilly's Independent Newspapers and then by its APN subsidiary. While the New Zealand Fairfax newspapers have recently been known for a high emphasis on cost-cutting, reducing editorial staff and focusing on local news,[15] the *Herald* is regarded for the priority given to maintaining and improving editorial quality. The final newspaper chosen for the New Zealand sample, the *Otago Daily Times*, is owned by its New Zealand shareholders and is published out of the university city of Dunedin in the south of New Zealand. It takes an editorial approach designed to differentiate it from its Fairfax counterparts, and routinely wins national journalism awards.

There is a limited number of television networks in New Zealand and, at the time of this study, only two had full nationwide access; these being Television New Zealand (TVNZ) and CanWest's TV3/C4 network.[16] Because of this, it was necessary to select both networks for this analysis. TVNZ is a state-owned enterprise operating with a commercial charter, and broadcasting on two channels – TV1 and TV2. TV2 is known for a more popular screening selection, while TV1 screens the 'flagship' TVNZ news bulletin – *One News* – which airs at 6 p.m. nightly.[17] Canadian owned CanWest operates New Zealand's fully commercial network which broadcasts from two channels also – TV3 and C4. The latter is a music channel while TV3 airs both popular television programming and the network's primetime news bulletin – *3 News* – which airs in the same time slot as *One News*. Both *One News* and *3 News* were thus chosen for our analysis.

South Korea

In the extremely diverse background of print media in South Korea, the number of dailies reached 137 in 2004.[18] In 2004, these newspapers accounted for almost 59 per cent of the total circulation of all newspapers in the country[19] (the remaining newspapers included foreign-language, finance, youth, sports, specialized and free ones). Among the dailies, the South Korean newspaper market has been traditionally dominated by three leading newspapers of national distribution and high circulation (all three feature an impressive circulation above 2 million copies a year each),[20] namely *Chosun Ilbo*, *JoongAng Ilbo* and *Dong-A Ilbo*. These 'big three' papers are recognized as highly influential voices in the Korean pubic discourse and are known for their successful attempts to actively influence political events in the country (e.g. presidential elections) through their news coverage, columns and editorials. Logically, these three newspapers were a natural choice for the Korean media sample in this research. *Dong-A Ilbo* is a Seoul-based, family-owned quality newspaper. It is one of the leading newspaper titles in South Korea,[21] and is one of the world's ten biggest dailies by circulation. It covers major events in South Korea and around the world, maintaining around 1,500 domestic plus twenty foreign editorial offices.[22] *Joongang Daily* and *The Chosun Ilbo* – Korea's other largest newspapers included in the sample – are both leading daily newspapers providing their audiences with authoritative news coverage, in-depth reports and analysis of domestic and foreign events. All three of these chosen newspapers are generally considered to represent the conservative element of South Korean society.[23]

According to some observers, the dominance of the 'big three' in the Korean print media landscape is becoming more pronounced. In the current Korean media environment, the market for daily newspapers has been shrinking and only the strongest and the most competitive can survive.[24] Some attribute this decrease in interest in newspapers as a source of information to the expansion of internet-based news formats as well as to distribution of free morning dailies for commuters. There are eight free dailies distributed in Korea – six in Seoul and two in other localities. Among those, the *Metro* newspaper is the most well known. Metro International, founded in Sweden, is the world's largest chain of free newspapers, publishing and distributing (mostly in subways) 25 editions in 54 major cities from 16 countries in 15 languages across Europe, North and South America and Asia. Seoul's *Metro* is among these. *Metro* has a unique global reach – attracting a young, active and well-educated audience. 530,000 copies of the two *Metro* editions attract 1.2 million daily readers, making it the fourth most read newspaper in the country, and thus warranting its inclusion in the sample.[25]

In addition, there are eight foreign-language newspapers in Korea. An international English-speaking newspaper, *The Korea Times*, is the oldest independent and most influential English-language daily in Korea. It is published by one of the largest circulation newspaper companies in Korea, the Hankook Ilbo. It brings foreign and business news for Korean elite, foreign businessmen, diplomats and tourists. Currently, the newspaper circulates in more than 160 countries. It is well known for its constructive, well-balanced coverage, ranging from socio-politics and economics, to culture and sports.[26]

Two Korean television channels were chosen for news monitoring – KBS and MBC. As the nation's public broadcaster, KBS (Korean Broadcasting System) is the leading television and radio network in Korea with twenty-five local broadcasting stations. KBS is firmly committed to its self-appointed mission of providing unbiased and independent public broadcasting with the highest priority placed on the public interest.[27] The second Korean television selection for this study was MBC (Munhwa Broadcasting Corporation). With public ownership comprising the main shareholders, MBC is a public service broadcaster. But MBC is, according to relevant civil and commercial statutes, also a corporation, and consequently must balance its need to serve the public with its commercial interests. Unlike other publicly owned broadcasters, however, MBC receives no government funding, but earns its revenue similarly to private broadcasters, largely by selling commercial airtime.[28]

Thailand

According to a number of international surveys, the level of press freedom in Thailand was one of the highest in East Asia (at the time the research was conducted).[29] In 2000, Press Freedom Survey by Freedom House showed that only Japan, Taiwan and South Korea had greater press freedom than Thailand. With the

1997 Constitution,[30] Thailand had one of the strongest legal and constitutional protections for the media in Asia.[31] Despite the fact that all of the television channels were owned by the government and operated by concessionaires, freedom of speech was guaranteed. There were no special regulations controlling the press, not even a clause about national security or public morals. It was worth noting that, although there was a clause on *lese majesté*, the Thai media automatically exercised self-censorship in this matter, aware that discussing the monarchy and royal affairs in public was totally unacceptable in the Thai society.[32] Press behaviour was hence only regulated by the legal mechanism of civil and commercial code, for example, defamation, libel and invasion of privacy. The media environment in Thailand was also marked by robust competition. Media ownership in Thailand was rather diversified. There were a large number of business groups from various industries, other than news industries, such as entertainment and advertisement industries owning the media in Thailand.[33] It could be said that the complexity of relationship among media owners/patronages, overlapping between various business groups and state powers, automatically served as a 'check-and-balance' mechanism within and among media outlets, making the media in Thailand relatively freer than those in other South East Asian countries.[34]

Due to the cost of sending correspondents abroad, the Thai media regularly employed the wire services such as Reuters, AFP and AP. The world's leading media organizations were also employed. These included the BBC, CNN, ABC, Xin Hua and NHK.

To represent diversity of the Thai press, the newspapers selected for analysis were three Thai-language publications (*Thai Rath, Matichon* and *The Manager*) and two English-language ones (*The Nation* and the *Bangkok Post*).

The selection of the Thai-language press was from three main types of newspapers found in the country: mass-oriented, quality and business. *Thai Rath* is a mass-oriented newspaper with the highest circulation in Thailand of 1,000,000 copies per day, published by The Watcharapol Ltd. *Matichon* is a newspaper with the highest circulation among 'quality' newspapers (200,000–300,000 daily copies) published by The Matichon Group. With a rather progressive editorial policy, it targets the educated and middle-class readership. *The Manager* is a newspaper with the highest circulation among 'business' newspapers (approximately 100,000 copies per day). It is published by Manager Media Group, owned by Sondhi Limthongkul. The online edition of the paper has been registered among the five most visited websites in Thailand. As for the two English titles, *Bangkok Post* is the most popular English-language newspaper in Thailand with a daily circulation of approximately 75,000 copies. Its major shareholders include the Chiravivat family (owners of The Central Group, one of the Thailand's largest retailers), the South China Morning Post of Hong Kong and GMM Grammy Pcl, an influential media and entertainment firm in Thailand. *The Nation* is another Thai English-language newspaper, arguably with more local flavour and a more progressive stance than *Bangkok Post*. The newspaper is owned by the Nation Multimedia Group Public Company Limited. Its circulation was in the range of 60,000–80,000 copies per day.

Thailand has six nationwide free television channels, all of which are owned by public bodies. Channel 7 news bulletin, aired from 6.00 to 6.30 p.m. and from 7.30 to 8.30 p.m., was selected because it was the most popular primetime news programme.[35] Its popularity might be due to the fact the programme was slotted in between highly popular local dramas. Channel 7 is owned by the Royal Thai Army and operated by the concessionaire, Bangkok Entertainment. The other selection was ITV news, aired at 6.00 p.m. The news programme might not as popular as those of Channel 7 or Channel 3[36] but it was selected because ITV positioned itself as the only news-oriented channel among free television channels in Thailand.[37] In 2004 ITV was state-owned and operated by the concessionaire, Siam Infotainment Co. Ltd.[38]

Notes

1 There are two public broadcasters, the Australian Broadcasting Corporation (ABC) and the Special Broadcasting Service (SBS). The latter broadcasts foreign-language news to a national (though limited) audience.
2 These figures are taken from the *Press, Radio and TV Guide: Australia, New Zealand and Pacific Islands*, Neutral Bay Junstion, NSW, Country Press Ltd (35th edn), 1998–9.
3 P. Anderson and A. Weymouth, *Insulting the Public: The British Press and the European Union*, New York, Longman, 1999, p. 15.
4 T. Barr, *newmedia.com.au: The Changing Face of Australia's Media and Communications*, Sydney, Allen & Unwin, 2000, pp. 2–3.
5 These are News Limited, Fairfax, Australian Provincial Newspapers (APN) and the Rural Press group. For profiles of each of these groups see ketupa.net, Media Profiles, 'Australia', available <www.ketupa.net/australia.htm> (Accessed 3 March 2004).
6 See J. Schulz, 'The Press', in S. Cunningham and G. Turner (eds), *The Media and Communications in Australia*, Crows Nest, NSW, Allen & Unwin, 2002, p. 111.
7 News Limited, 'News Medianet – Contact us', available <http://newsmedianet.com.au/home/NetworkContactUs.jsp> (Accessed 15 May 2004).
8 See Schulz, 'The Press'.
9 Australian Government, Department of Foreign Affairs and Trade, 'Media', *Australia in Brief*, available <http://www.dfat.gov.au/aib/media.html> (Accessed 3 March 2004).
10 As Putnis *et al.* note, the exclusion of popular, tabloid press from their sample limits the discussion of their results to 'elite' audiences. See P. Putnis, J. Penhallurick and M. Bourk, 'The Pattern of International News in Australia's Mainstream Media', *Australian Journalism Review* 22 (2000), 3.
11 D. Lupton, *Moral Threats and Dangerous Desires: AIDS in the News Media*, London, Taylor & Francis, 1994, p. 152.
12 J. Henningham, 'Journalists' Perception of Newspaper Quality', *Australian Journalism Review* 18 (1996), 13–19.
13 See B. Peters, 'The Free-to-Air Television Industry in Australia: Trends and Issues', *Get the Picture*, Australian Film Commission, available <http://www.afc.gov.au/GTP/wftvratingstrends.html> (Accessed 7 June 2004).
14 Available <http://www.stuff.co.nz/nz_newspapers.html> (Accessed 17 March 2006).
15 J. Drinnan, 'Sundays, Bloody Sundays: Sunday Newspapers Prepare for War', *National Business Review* (6 August 2004), 22.

16   While Prime channel reached about 90 per cent of the New Zealand public in 2006, it was still not available nationwide, and it certainly was not at the time of the project (2004), which was why it was excluded from the sample.

17   TVNZ, 'TVNZ's Channels', available <http://tvnz.co.nz/view/page/816460/845005> (Accessed 22 May 2007).

18   Ministry of Culture and Tourism, 10 March 2005.

19   9,556,800 copies from the total number of 16,347,000 copies (data taken from Korean Association of Newspapers).

20   Audit Bureau of Circulation in Korea, 'Korea', available <http://ifabc.org/documents/KOREA.doc> (Accessed 11 June 2007).

21   *Dong-a Ilbo*, available <http://www.newspapercatalog.com/newspapers/dong-a+ilbo.htm> (Accessed 11 June 2007).

22   Koenig and Bauer AG, available <http://www.kba-print.de/en/news/zeitungsdruck2/2003-02-25-00.html> (Accessed 14 March 2007).

23   *Chosun Ilbo*, available <http://chosun-ilbo.wikiverse.org/> (Accessed 12 June 2007).

24   The situation surrounding newspapers consumption in Korea has been characterized by the following figures: the paid newspaper subscription figures in Korea dropped from 53 per cent in 2001 to 41 per cent in 2005, and the percentage of readers who read newspapers dropped from 59 to 43 per cent in the respective period of time (Nielson Media Research Report 2005).

25   The Metro, available <http://mtroa.client.shareholder.com/downloads/040708MetroSKorea_shareholding.pdf> (Accessed 15 November 2006).

26   Korean Media, available <http://www.asiamedia.ucla.edu/fmwebpages/kt.asp> (Accessed 15 November 2006).

27   Korean Broadcasting System, available <http://www.kbs.co.kr/> (Accessed 15 November 2006).

28   MBC Network News, available <http://www.imbc.com/> (Accessed 15 November 2006).

29   Thailand: Media Profile, available <http://www.seamedia.org/thailand.php?story_id=14#foot8> (Accessed 20 December 2006); CPJ, 'Attacks on the Press 2003', available <http://www.cpj.org/attacks03/asia03/thai.html> (Accessed 13 March 2007).

30   The 1997 Constitution expired due to the coup in Sept. 2006. At the time this section was written, Thailand was under a provisional constitution.

31   D. McCargo, *Politics and the Press in Thailand: Media Machinations*, Bangkok, Routledge, 2000.

32   *Ibid.*

33   *Ibid.*

34   *Ibid.* See also A. Vejjajiva, 'State Policies in the Thaksinomic Era and the Press Freedom', Public Seminar at Thammasat University, Bangkok, April 2004.

35   Information from AC Nielson, 2005.

36   Information from AC Nielson, 2005.

37   It was stipulated in the ITV's Term of Reference that the channel must be information/education oriented.

38   Om 2007, ITV lost its concession due to unpaid fees. That year, it was taken over by the Thai government amd renamed Thai Independent Television (TITV). In January 2008, the station was closed and its frequency re-assigned to Thai PBS.

Appendix II

Portrait of the survey respondents: Australia and New Zealand

The Australian and New Zealand samples accurately describe population characteristics of the two nations. With regard to age, gender, and income, the sample characteristics map the general population well.

In Australia, 37 per cent of respondents were between 25 and 44 years old, 49 per cent were full-time employees and self-employed, 70 per cent had a household income over AU$35,000 and 91.5 per cent voted in the previous election.

In New Zealand, 41 per cent of respondents were between 25 and 44 years old, 48.5 per cent had a university degree, 57 per cent were full-time employees and self-employed, 67 per cent had a household income over NZ$40,000, and almost 82 per cent voted in the previous election.

Population

The Population Division of the United Nations Department of Economic and Social Affairs estimated Australia's 2005 population to be about 20.2 million (10 million males, 10.2 million females).[1] The median age in Australia is 36.6 years and the life expectancy at birth is about 81 years. About 13 per cent of the population is aged 65 and older while about 37 per cent is 24 years or younger. About 93 per cent of Australians live in urban areas (18.7 million). Owing to its large size, population density in Australia is extremely low, approximately 3 people per square kilometre.

New Zealand's 2005 population is estimated to be about 4.03 million (1.98 million males, 2.05 million females). The median age in New Zealand is 35.8 years and the life expectancy at birth is about 79 years. About 12 per cent of the population is aged 65 and older while about 36 per cent of the population is 24 years or younger. About 86 per cent of New Zealanders live in urban areas (3.45 million) and the population density per square kilometre is approximately 15 people.

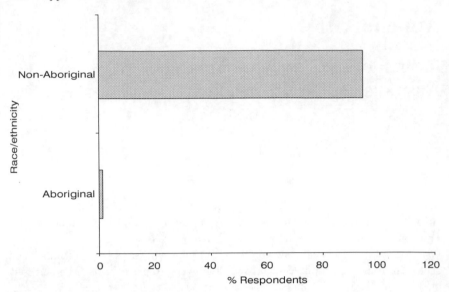

Figure AII.1 Ethnic groups (Australia)

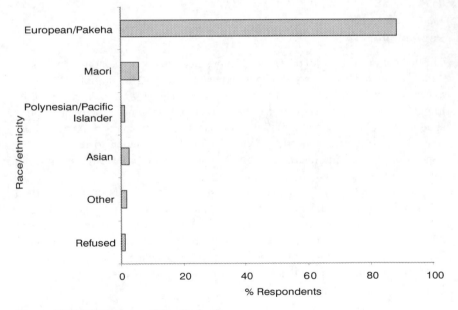

Figure AII.2 Ethnic groups (New Zealand)

Age, gender and ethnicity

In general, about 70 per cent of the Australians sampled were aged 35 or older, and about 75 per cent of the New Zealanders sampled were aged 35 or older. In terms of the distribution of males and females, more women than men are represented in the four samples (52.75 per cent in Australia; 50.25 per cent in New Zealand). Figures AII.1 and AII.2 show the ethnic make-up of the survey sample.

Employment status

About 36 per cent of the Australian respondents and 46 per cent of the New Zealand respondents reported full-time employment. In contrast, about 18 per cent of the Australian sample and 16 per cent of the New Zealand sample was categorized as retired. A small portion of the sample (4.5 for Australia and 1.75 for New Zealand) reported employment status as 'unemployed/beneficiary'.

Of those indicating employment of some sort, occupational status was ascertained. The distribution across occupational categories for the two samples is shown in Figures AII.3 and AII.4. The modal occupational category of Australian respondents is the 'teacher/nurse/police' category. About 16.5 per cent of the Australian sample falls in this category. Roughly 36 per cent of the Australian sample was in the 'business manager/executive', 'trained service worker' and 'clerical sales employee' categories.

Similar remarks apply to the New Zealand sample. The modal category is 'teacher/nurse/police' (13.2 per cent) while a little over 33 per cent of the sample was in the 'business manager/executive', 'trained service worker' and 'clerical sales employee' categories. Nearly 4 per cent of the New Zealand sample and 6.5 per cent of the Australian sample was characterized as 'labourer' while nearly 11 per cent of New Zealand respondents and 12.5 per cent of Australian respondents reported themselves as being 'self-employed' (either in a professional or trade category).

Income

According to the World Bank, gross national income per capita in Australia is estimated to be US$21,950. GNI per capita in New Zealand is estimated to be US$15,530.

The modal category for the Australian survey is $20,001–$35,000 (Australian dollars); 19.25 per cent of the sample fell into this category. There is wide variability in reported household income: 13.75 per cent of the respondents had household incomes $100,001 or greater, while 11 per cent of respondents reported household income less than $20,001.

The coding for income levels is slightly different for the New Zealand sample; however, the distribution was similar to Australia. 16.75 per cent of respondents reported household income to be $100,000 (NZ dollars) or greater while 11.25 per

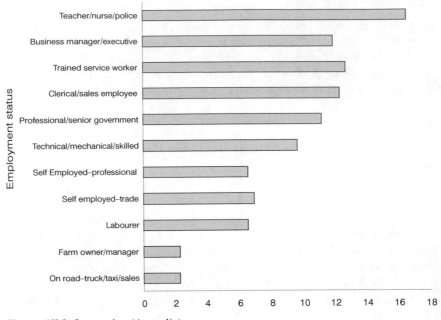

Figure AII.3 Occupation (Australia)

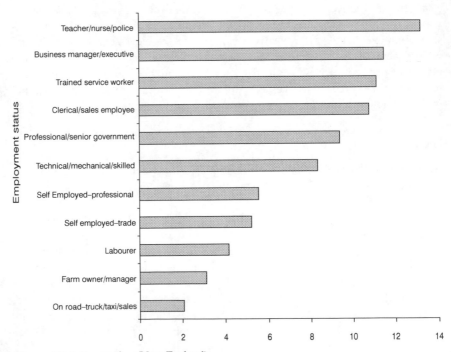

Figure AII.4 Occupation (New Zealand)

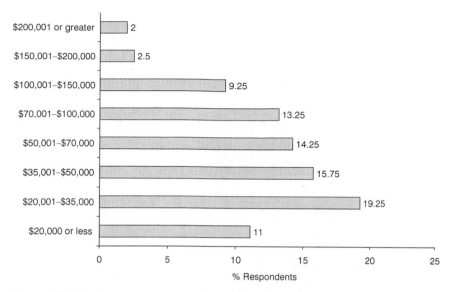

Figure AII.5 Total household income (Australia)

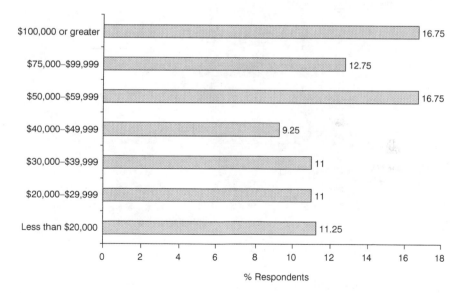

Figure AII.6 Total household income (New Zealand)

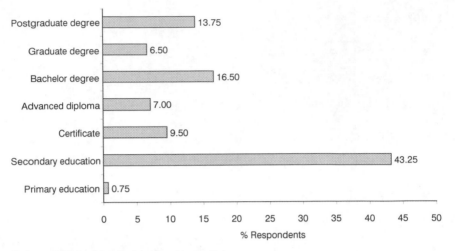

Figure AII.7 Levels of education (Australia)

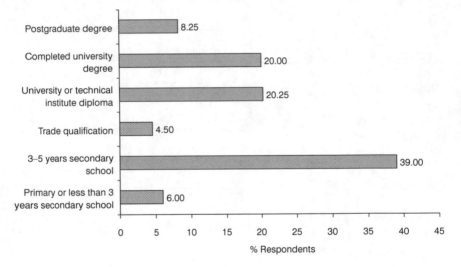

Figure AII.8 Levels of education (New Zealand)

cent reported household income to be less than $20,000. About 22 per cent reported family income between $20,000 and $39,000.

Education level

The modal category in two samples (Australian and New Zealand) was 'secondary education', while the level of tertiary education in the Australian sample is about 36 per cent; in the New Zealand sample it is about 28 per cent.

Note

1 Source: United Nations' World Population Prospects, *The 2004 Revision Population Database*, available <http://esa.un.org/unpp/> (Accessed 12 October 2006).

Appendix III

Portrait of the survey respondents:
South Korea and Thailand

Population

According to the United Nations,[1] Thailand's population was estimated to be 64.2 million in 2005. There were 96.5 males per 100 females. The median age was 30.5 years. Eight per cent of the population was aged 65 years and over. Life expectancy was 68.5 years for males and 75 years for females. Urban population accounted for 67.5 per cent of the population. The major ethnic groups were Thai (75 per cent) and Chinese (14 per cent).

South Korea's population was estimated to be 48.2 million in 2005. There were 100.5 males per 100 females. The median age was 35.1 years. Almost 11 per cent of the population was aged 65 years and over. Life expectancy was 74.5 years for males and 81.9 years for females. Urban population accounted for 81 per cent of the total population. The demographical profile of the survey respondents reflected that of the population in both countries in 2005 (Table III.1).

Employment status

In Thailand, full-time employees accounted for 42 per cent of respondents, followed by the self-employed (18 per cent), full-time parents (17 per cent), students (11 per cent), the unemployed (7 per cent), retirees (3 per cent) and part-time employees (2 per cent). Similar to the South Korean sample, the self-employed formed the biggest occupation group amongst respondents in Thailand. More respondents claimed to be professional, managers and executives (19 per cent), white-collar workers (14 per cent) and blue-collar workers (9 per cent). There were far fewer full-time parents among the Thai respondents than their South Korean counterparts.

In South Korea, the biggest group respondents were full-time parents (30 per cent). Other groups include full-time employees (21 per cent), self-employed (19 per cent), students (16 per cent), the unemployed (11 per cent), part-time employees (4 per cent) and the retired (0.7 per cent). While the self-employed form the largest occupational group in the sample, there were also professional, managers and executives (11 per cent), white-collar workers (8 per cent) and blue-collar workers (7 per cent).

Table AIII.1 Demographical profile of respondents

		Thailand %	South Korea %
Gender	Male	47.0	49.6
	Female	53.0	50.4
Age	18–24	15.3	15.2
	25–34	24.7	25.4
	35–44	26.3	22.4
	45–54	19.2	17.7
	55–64	9.9	11.5
	65 and above	4.7	7.7
Ethnic group	Thai	89.1	N/A
	Thai-Chinese	7.6	N/A
	Chinese	2.6	N/A
	Indian	0.7	N/A
	Korean	N/A	100

Levels of education and political activity

In Thailand, degree holders (37 per cent) and university or technical institute diploma holders (19 per cent) constituted the largest groups of the respondents. 19 per cent of respondents received just primary or less than three years secondary education, whereas another 16 per cent received three to five years secondary education. A small number of respondents obtained postgraduate education (5 per cent).

South Korean respondents mainly consisted of those who completed three to five years of secondary education (34 per cent) or university degree holders (32 per cent). University or technical institute diploma holders came third with 13 per cent. A small number of respondents had had postgraduate education (6.5 per cent).

Respondents showed a high degree of political awareness in their respective country, as indicated by the fact that well over 70 per cent of the South Korean and Thai respondents claimed to have voted at the previoius election.

Note

1 World Population Prospects, *The 2004 Revision Population Database*, available <http://esa.un.org/unpp/> (Accessed 17 October 2006).

Appendix IV

Questionnaires

Questionnaire for Asia-Pacific business and political elites

1. Could you describe the nature of the involvement your organization and/or you professionally have with the EU

2. When thinking about the term 'the European Union', what three images come to your mind?

3. Do you see the EU as a great power?
   a. If not, why not?
   b. If yes:
      Why?
      What type of great power?

4. How would you compare the importance of the EU to [home country] in relation to other global actors?

5. How would you characterize the state of the relationship between [home country] and Europe/the European Union?

6. In your opinion, which issues in [home country]-EU present day interactions have the most impact on [home country]?

7. What issues should be kept in mind when [home country] is developing trade or government policy relating to the EU in the future?

8. Do you see the EU as a leader in international politics?
   a. If yes: in what areas? In what ways?
   b. If not: why not?

9. What kinds of opportunities did you see for [home country] when new countries joined the EU in May 2004?

10. What kinds of risks did you see for [home country] when the new countries joined the EU in May 2004?

11. How do you see any future EU enlargements changing the relationship between [home country] and the EU?

12. How do you see the Euro as an international currency vis-à-vis the US dollar?

13. What sources (including media outlets) do you prefer to access to learn more about the EU?

14. How would you describe [monitored home country newspapers] as reliable sources of information on the EU?

15. How would you describe [monitored home country television news broadcasts] as reliable sources of information on the EU?

16. Do you have personal contacts with the EU?
    a. If yes, in which countries?

17. On a scale of 1 to 5, where 1 is not important at all, and 5 is very important, how would you rate the importance of the EU to [home country] in the present?

18. On the same scale, how would you rate the importance of the EU to [home country] in the future?

19. The EU has a Delegation in [home country capital]. What mutually beneficial ways of interaction with the Delegation could you envision?

Questionnaire for Asia-Pacific media elites

EU coverage

1. How is coverage of EU issues organized at [media outlet]?
    (Probes: Where do you get the news?
    How cost effective is having correspondents on the ground vs. purchasing
        news from the wires)

2. Are special preparations made in advance of presenting news on EU?
    (Probe/explanation: Research?)

3. Is a special budget allocated?
    (Probe/explanation: Additional funds allocated?)

4. Will staff reporting on the EU increase in the future?

Editorial approach

5. What is the officially formulated policy on covering foreign news?
   a. And the policy on news on the EU?

6. Does your media outlet assume a reactive role or proactive, initiating role?
   (Probe: Are stories initiated on their own/do you actively set the agenda)

7. Do studio headquarters and central newsroom cooperate with political units/
   Ministry of Foreign Affairs/embassies/delegation (including EU Delegation)
   /news organizations in Brussels?

8. Where do you see that the balance of foreign reporting will shift in the
   future?

News selection criteria

9. Which criteria of newsworthiness are applied when covering the EU?
   a. Are there any special criteria applied?

10. Are special news segments implemented or does news about the EU compete
    equally against the other news?
    (Probe: how difficult is it to sell an EU story?)

Personal perceptions

11. When thinking about the term 'the European Union', what three thoughts
    come to your mind?

12. Do you see the EU as a great power?
    If yes:
    >   Why?
    >   What type of great power (military – economic – diplomatic –
    >   normative?)
    If not:
    >   Why not?

13. Do you see the EU as a leader in international politics?
    If yes:
    >   What areas?
    >   In what ways?
    If not:
    >   Why not?

14. In your opinion, which issues in [home country]-EU interactions have the most impact on [home country]?

15. On a scale of 1 to 5, where 1 is not important at all and 5 is very important, how would you rate the importance of the EU to [home country] in the present?

16. On a scale of 1 to 5, where 1 is not important at all and 5 is very important, how would you rate the importance of the EU to [home country] in the future?

Index

Printed in the United States
by Baker & Taylor Publisher Services